SOCIAL MOVEMENT DYNAMICS

The Mobilization Series on Social Movements, Protest, and Culture

Series Editor

Professor Hank Johnston
San Diego State University, USA

Published in conjunction with *Mobilization: An International Quarterly*, the premier research journal in the field, this series disseminates high quality new research and scholarship in the fields of social movements, protest, and contentious politics. The series is interdisciplinary in focus and publishes monographs and collections of essays by new and established scholars.

Other titles in this series

Urban Mobilizations and New Media in Contemporary China
Edited by Lisheng Dong, Hanspeter Kriesi, Daniel Kübler

Israeli-Palestinian Activism
Shifting Paradigms
Alexander Koensler

From Silence to Protest
International Perspectives on Weakly Resourced Groups
Edited by Didier Chabanet and Frédéric Royall

The Fight for Ethical Fashion
The Origins and Interactions of the Clean Clothes Campaign
Philip Balsiger

Understanding the Tea Party Movement
Edited by Nella Van Dyke and David S. Meyer

Dynamics of Political Violence
A Process-Oriented Perspective on Radicalization and the
Escalation of Political Conflict
Edited by Lorenzo Bosi, Chares Demetriou and Stefan Malthaner

Social Movement Dynamics
New Perspectives on Theory and Research
from Latin America

Edited by

FEDERICO M. ROSSI
Tulane University, USA

MARISA VON BÜLOW
*Pontifícia Universidad Católica, Chile
and Universidade de Brasília, Brazil*

Routledge
Taylor & Francis Group

LONDON AND NEW YORK

First published 2015 by Ashgate Publishing

Published 2016 by Routledge
2 Park Square, Milton Park, Abingdon, Oxon OX14 4RN
711 Third Avenue, New York, NY 10017, USA

Routledge is an imprint of the Taylor & Francis Group, an informa business

British Library Cataloguing in Publication Data
A catalogue record for this book is available from the British Library.

The Library of Congress has cataloged the printed edition as follows:
Social movement dynamics : new perspectives on theory and research from latin america / [edited] by Federico M. Rossi and Marisa von Bülow.
    pages cm. -- (The mobilization series on social movements, protest, and culture)
Includes bibliographical references and index.
    ISBN 978-1-4724-1767-1 (hardback) -- ISBN 978-1-4724-1768-8 (pbk.) -- ISBN 978-1-4724-1769-5 (ebook) -- ISBN 978-1-4724-1770-1 (epub) 1. Social movements--Latin America. I. Rossi, Federico M. II. Von Bülow, Marisa.
    HN110.5.A8S6276 2015
    303.4098--dc23

2015004241

ISBN 13: 978-1-4724-1767-1 (hbk)
ISBN 13: 978-1-4724-1768-8 (pbk)

Contents

List of Figures and Tables

Figures

Tables

Notes on Contributors

Rebecca Neaera Abers is Professor of Political Science at the University of Brasília, Brazil, where she conducts research on state-society interactions, participatory policy-making, and the role of agency in institutional creation and change. Her current work focuses on the role of activists inside government bureaucracies in Brazil. She is the author of *Inventing Local Democracy: Grassroots Politics in Brazil* (Lynne Rienner Publishers, 2000) and *Practical Authority: Agency and Institutional Change in Brazilian Water Politics* with Margaret Keck (Oxford University Press, 2013), among other publications.

Paul D. Almeida is an Associate Professor of Sociology at the University of California, Merced, in the United States. His work analyzes civil society responses to political and economic transitions in the developing world. Almeida's research has appeared in the *American Journal of Sociology, Mobilization, Social Forces, Social Problems*, and other scholarly outlets. He is the author of *Waves of Protest: Popular Struggle in El Salvador* (University of Minnesota Press, 2008) and *Mobilizing Democracy: Globalization and Citizen Protest* (Johns Hopkins University Press, 2014).

Adrian Gurza Lavalle is an Associate Professor of Political Science at the University of São Paulo, Brazil. He is also Researcher of the National Council of Technological and Scientific Development (CNPq), and Coordinator of the Democracy and Collective Action Research Group at the Brazilian Center of Analysis and Planning (CEBRAP) and the Center for Metropolitan Studies (CEM). He is the editor of the *Brazilian Journal of Social Sciences*.

Margaret E. Keck, Professor of Political Science at Johns Hopkins University in the United States, is the author or co-author of *Practical Authority: Agency and Institutional Change in Brazilian Water Politic*s (Oxford, 2013), with Rebecca Abers; *Greening Brazil: Environmental Activism in State and Society* (Duke, 2007), with Kathryn Hochstetler; *Activists Beyond Borders: Advocacy Networks in International Politics* (Cornell, 1998), with Kathryn Sikkink; and *The Workers' Party and Democratization in Brazil* (Yale, 1992).

Ann Mische is an Associate Professor of Sociology and Peace Studies at the University of Notre Dame in the United States. Her work focuses on processes of communication, deliberation, and leadership in social movements and democratic politics. Her book, *Partisan Publics: Contention and Communication Across*

Brazilian Youth Activist Networks (Princeton, 2008), examines changes in the field of Brazilian youth politics during two decades of democratic reconstruction. She is currently studying the role of future projections in contentious public deliberations, including an analysis of future-oriented discourse during the People's Summit of the Rio+20 Conference.

Federico M. Rossi is a Research Fellow at the Center for Inter-American Policy and Research in Tulane University in the United States. His research focuses on trade unions and social movements in Argentina and Brazil, democratization and contentious politics in Latin America and Europe, and youth political participation. His work has been published in several edited volumes, *International Sociology*, *Social Movement Studies*, *Mobilization*, *Latin American Perspectives*, *Latin American Politics and Society*, *European Review of Latin American and Caribbean Studies*, and *Desarrollo Económico*, among others.

Rose J. Spalding is a Professor of Political Science at DePaul University in Chicago in the United States. She is the author of *Contesting Trade in Central America: Market Reform and Resistance* (University of Texas, 2014) and *Capitalists and Revolution in Nicaragua: Opposition and Accommodation, 1979–1993* (University of North Carolina Press, 1994).

Luciana Tatagiba is Professor of Political Science at the State University of Campinas in São Paulo, Brazil, where she conducts research on participation and social movements. Her work focuses on the relations between social movements and political institutions, and their implications for policy design processes and for the expansion of citizenship rights.

Ligia Tavera Fenollosa is Professor of Sociology at the Facultad Latinoamericana de Ciencias Sociales in Mexico City. Her areas of research include social movements and political sociology. She has published on urban social movements, student movements, and pain and loss movements. Most recently, she has co-authored with Hank Johnston "Protest Artifacts in the Mexican Social Movement Sector: Reflections on the 'Stepchild' of Cultural Analysis" in Paul Almeida and Allen Cordero (eds) *Handbook of Social Movements Across Latin America.* New York: Springer (forthcoming).

Marisa von Bülow is a Professor of Political Science at the University of Brasília, Brazil, and a researcher at the Pontifícia Universidad Católica in Chile. Her work analyzes transnational civil society networks and, more recently, the uses of digital tools for activism. Von Bülow's research has appeared in *Mobilization* and other scholarly outlets. She is the author of the award-winning book *Building Transnational Networks: Civil Society and the Politics of Trade in the Americas* (Cambridge University Press, 2010, published in Portuguese in 2014).

Chapter 1

Introduction
Theory-Building Beyond Borders

Federico M. Rossi and Marisa von Bülow[1]

The publication of this book comes at a moment of profound changes in the scholarship on social movements, characterized not only by the broadening of the empirical boundaries of the field, but also by greater methodological and theoretical pluralism. This book stretches the current horizons in social movement studies even further, by proposing new concepts and questions. Contributors have very different objects of study and theoretical backgrounds, but they all share a commitment to a dynamic and relational approach to the study of collective action. The volume is organized around three broad themes, which address key current debates in social movement theory: the interactions between routine and contentious politics, the relationship between protest and context, and the organizational configurations of social movements.

The research agenda put forward by the authors is neither defined nor restricted by geographical boundaries, even though the chapters are all based on field research undertaken in Latin America. As such, this volume contributes to what we consider a much-needed and still underdeveloped theory building dialogue in social movement studies, among scholars from the South and from the North, as well as among scholars specialized in different regions.

In the late 1980s, a group of United States and Western European scholars led an important North Atlantic debate that proposed to build common ground for social movement studies (Klandermans et al. 1988; McAdam et al. 1996). In the same spirit of this pioneering dialogue, this book contributes to current efforts to further expand the theoretical frontiers of social movement studies. More specifically, as other authors have been arguing for the past two decades (Foweraker 1995; Gohn 1997; McAdam et al. 2001), we believe that much more can be done in terms of fostering exchange among researchers that study Latin America and other social movement scholars. We propose neither the uncritical adoption of the theories developed in the Global North, nor a stark opposition between the Global South and the Global North. Instead, we hope to contribute to overcoming what Sidney Tarrow (2012, p. 8) has recently called a "tendency to

---

1   Authors' names appear in alphabetical order, having both contributed equally to this chapter. We thank comments made on a previous version by Rebecca Abers, Adrian Gurza Lavalle, Margaret Keck, and an anonymous reviewer.

closure" in the social movements literature, in reference to the lack of integration between the "growing strand of theorizing" coming from the Global South and research by other scholars.

In Latin America, research groups and publications have bourgeoned, without necessarily committing to any specific or rigid set of methods or theories. Whereas in the 1980s the focus of debates in the region was on the challenges and opportunities created by transitions to democracy (Jelin 1985; Eckstein 1989), in the 1990s this focus changed, with a more explicit recognition of the plurality of subjects, repertoires, and processes (Gohn 1997; Álvarez et al. 1998). More recently, we have witnessed an increase in the number of scholars studying Latin American social movements and protests from diverse social science traditions (Johnston and Almeida 2006).[2]

Important research agendas within social movement studies have emerged as a result of Latin American scholarship.[3] A prominent example is Keck and Sikkink's (1998) path-breaking analysis of advocacy coalitions, which kicked-off a boom in studies about the multi-scalar dimension of social movements in Latin America and all around the world.[4]

Too often, however, arguments and research agendas from various regions have developed in parallel and opportunities for collaboration have been missed. We mention only a few potential areas of dialogue in this introduction. For instance, research on Latin America pioneered studies on the relationship between democratization and contentious politics in the 1980s and 1990s,[5] but this literature is not well known among social movement theorists that study other regions (Rossi and della Porta 2009). The recent wave of studies about new participatory arenas presents other opportunities for dialogue and theory building. There is a large and fast growing literature that brings together social movement theories, democracy theories, and state theories to analyze a myriad of experiences, going from local councils to national conferences and participatory budgets.[6] Research on this topic

---

2   For an analysis of these changes in the recent literature produced by Brazilian scholars, see Abers and von Bülow 2010 and Kunrath 2011.

3   In part, of course, the visibility of important texts has been hindered by the lack of translations from Spanish and Portuguese. In the past few years, however, social movement scholars studying Latin America have sought increasingly to publish their work in English. According to Poulson et al. (2014, Figure 1), between 2002 and 2010 Latin American movements have been the focus of 16 percent of the articles published in the two main journals of the sub-discipline—Mobilization and Social Movement Studies.

4   For example, Hochstetler (2002); Bandy and Smith (2005); della Porta and Tarrow (2005); Tarrow (2005); Grimson and Pereyra (2008); Pleyers (2010); von Bülow (2010); Silva (2013).

5   For example, Mainwaring and Viola (1984); Jelin (1985); Slater (1985); Calderón (1986); Boschi (1987); Mainwaring (1987); Eckstein (1989); Corradi et al. (1992); Escobar and Álvarez (1992); Brysk (1994); Doimo (1995); Oxhorn (1995); Schneider (1995); Collier (1999).

6   For example, Abers (2000); Avritzer (2002); Baiocchi (2005).

has promoted innovative ways to analyze the intricate and changing relationships between the state and social movements. As we explain in the next section, various chapters of this volume speak to this debate.

Another area that calls for a more intensive dialogue is the integration of identity and cultural studies with social movement research. Since the 1980s, for example, scholars of Latin American movements have been making connections between the cultural and economic dimensions of collective action that non-Latin Americanists would certainly find valuable.[7] Finally, since the 2000s, another focus of debate and theory-building comes from the literature on the political economy of mobilization cycles, which integrates the economic and political dimensions of struggles.[8] In the context of the recent wave of anti-austerity protests in the United States and the European Union, this literature gains renewed relevance, in order to better understand how economic crises and grievances affect mobilization. Again, various chapters in this book address these debates in different ways.

With this concern for expanding and diversifying the conversation among scholars of social movements everywhere, this book speaks to crucial contemporary debates in the general literature. Each chapter includes a review of the international literature, and identifies gaps highlighted by empirical research.

All chapters are empirically grounded in current Latin America and shed new light on key social movements, but they do not seek to present a comprehensive overview of the social movement landscape in the region. Thus, most relevant are not the empirical findings of each author (in many cases—though not all—these have been published elsewhere), but the efforts to situate the actions and challenges faced by the social movements they study in a broader conversation, shedding light on key research problems, and allowing us to move forward in sometimes unexpected ways.

Routine and Contentious Politics

The first section of this book brings together three chapters, all of which focus on the interactions between routine and contentious politics, or what are sometimes called "conventional" and "unconventional" forms of political participation. The chapters by Rossi, Mische, and Abers and Tatagiba present a common general approach to this problem. The authors go beyond the artificial boundaries that much of the social movement literature builds between routine and contentious forms of collective action, while acknowledging the need to analyze the challenges

---

7 For example, Sader (1988); Jelin (1990); Escobar and Álvarez (1992); Dagnino (1994, 2003); Foweraker (1995); Álvarez et al. (1998); Garretón (2002); Lucero (2008); Warren (2012).

8 For example, Walton and Schefner (1994); Auyero (2003); Yashar (2005); Almeida and Johnston (2006); Rhodes (2006); Roberts and Portes (2006); Almeida (2007); Roberts (2008); Silva (2009); Rice (2012); Almeida (2014); Rossi (2015).

faced by social movements when choosing how and where to make claims. For all of these authors, this debate requires exploring the interaction between social movements, political actors, and state institutions.

The chapter by Federico M. Rossi presents an innovative conceptual framework for understanding the different strategies of social movements. By differentiating between the well-known concept of "repertoire of contention" and the new concepts of "repertoire of strategies" and "stock of legacies," readers are offered a different window into the historically rooted processes of strategy making and performing by social movements. These concepts allow us to understand what happens when movements do not deploy their repertoire of contention. This chapter is empirically grounded in a study of the Argentine *piquetero* movement—one of the most important social movements of the region in the past decade. Based on in-depth fieldwork, the author walks us through the maze of organizations, strategies, and ideologies that together make up this fragmented movement.

Ann Mische analyzes the tensions between partisan and civic modes of engagement, thus presenting an important contribution to the literature on activism, and, more specifically, the literature on the relationships between social movements and political parties. She focuses on youth activism during Brazil's period of democratic reconstruction, presenting an analysis that emphasizes the ambivalence and the tensions inherent in these relationships, which, nonetheless, do not present unsurmountable obstacles to collective action. To explore movement activities in the context of these tensions, she reformulates the concept of "publics" and proposes to go beyond the divide between instrumental and communicative forms of action, so often present—as she demonstrates—among theorists of democracy and of civil society.

Rebecca Neaera Abers and Luciana Tatagiba analyze what they call "institutional activism." Based on the interactions between social movements and government in Brazil, they present an important contribution to better understanding the porous boundaries between state and civil society. In spite of the recent upsurge in attention to this topic in the context of the rise of leftist governments in the region, the authors argue that this is not a new phenomenon. It is also not limited to a specific public policy issue, as their past research on other policy arenas unequivocally shows. Perhaps, they suggest, this kind of activism has had less visibility in the literature because it has less visibility empirically, and its impacts are unknown.

Interestingly, Abers and Tatagiba show how their analysis of the Brazilian case has strong parallels with Banaszak's (2009) study about feminists working within the US federal bureaucracy, thus effectively bridging the scholarship on social movements and states in the North and South of the Americas. Students of other regions and of other social movements will also be able to relate to Mische's analysis of attempts to ban partisan identities in the Brazilian student movement, and will benefit from her agency-centered model for understanding the tensions and ambiguities in the interactions between political parties and social movements. Consider, for example, the relationship between parties and the Civic

Forum in the Czech Republic during democratization (Glenn 2003), and the links between social movements and rightist and leftist parties during the process of neoliberal reforms in India (Desai 2012). Mische's analytical framework also helps to understand other cases in Latin America. To give just one example, there are strong parallels with the ambiguous but continuous process of distancing between the Chilean student movement and traditionally allied political parties (von Bülow and Bidegain, forthcoming).

Similarly, Rossi's conceptual framework will be useful for scholars who seek to explore the link between micro decisions and macro changes in repertoires in other social movements. This framework could help explain, for instance, why and how some of the guerrilla strategies formulated by Ernesto "Che" Guevara for rural Bolivia and Congo were adapted to its urban use by sectors of the Black Panthers Party and, later, the Black Liberation Army in the United States (Young 2006; Bloom and Martin 2013; Freedman 2013). It can also help understand the combination of collaborative and contentious strategies in the interplay between the landless peasants' movement and Brazilian party politics (Vergara-Camus 2009). Taken together, these chapters demonstrate that it is impossible to understand social movements, in Latin America and elsewhere, without considering how they interact with other political and social actors and state institutions in both routine and contentious ways.

Protest and Environmental, Economic, and Political Opportunities

While the first group of chapters moves beyond traditional formulations and boundaries, the second group of authors focuses on a debate that has a long (and contentious) history in social movement studies. These chapters explore the relationship between protest and economic, political, and environmental change. Of course, this is not a new topic in the Latin American literature, much of which sought to understand the relationship between collective action and authoritarianism in the 1970s and 1980s, and, later, the impacts of transitions to democracy.

In this book, we present two contributions on this debate. The chapter by Paul D. Almeida focuses on the effects of a still understudied dimension of the political context on social movements: the role of threats in explaining collective action. While acknowledging that both opportunity and threat may—in complex environments—activate episodes of collective action, this chapter offers new insights by offering a novel typology of threats. Based on extensive knowledge of various Central American cases of mobilization, the author distinguishes among threats of state repression, state-attributed economic problems, and environmental harms. Such a broad approach to threats allows us to move forward in understanding the impacts of the political context on social movements. At the same time, it underscores the dynamic character of collective action. The chapter ends with a call for more research on the timing of threats as catalysts for mobilization.

Ligia Tavera Fenollosa's chapter offers a framework for analyzing the unintended outcomes of social movements, a goal that has been overshadowed by the literature's focus on assessing intended impacts. Based on an analysis of the 1985 Earthquake Victims Movement in Mexico City, the author argues that this movement's success in meeting its stated goals is only part of the story. Most interesting is how the movement contributed to Mexico's democratization process, even though this was not on its explicit agenda. Thus, in this chapter the political context simultaneously influences and is influenced by social movements in unexpected ways that require, as the author argues, distancing ourselves from a movement-centered perspective and thinking of social movements as historical events.

These arguments travel well beyond the geographical limits of Latin America. For instance, the chapter by Almeida presents a welcome call for a more nuanced analysis of the relationship between protest and political context, which can and should be taken seriously by the literature on the topic. An analysis of a variety of threats can help to better explain the emergence of many social movements against mining, transgenic agriculture, nuclear projects, and dams in contemporary Latin America. The analysis of the role of environmental threats can also help explain the emergence of environmental movements elsewhere. For instance, the *Ekoglasnot*, a movement that became the first important defiance to the national Communist regime in Bulgaria (Petrova 2004). Tavera Fenollosa's call for thinking about social movements as historical events presents yet another example of a contribution to a broad debate, which is in no way restricted to the case of Mexico City. Studies of democratization processes in Eastern Europe, the former Soviet Union, and Northern Africa, also show the relevance of taking an eventful perspective in social movement studies (Beissinger 2002; della Porta 2014).

New Organizational Repertoires

The third debate approached in this book focuses on changes in organizational ecologies and networks of social movements within and across national boundaries. Two chapters address the processes of transnationalization and diversification of organizational forms, and the challenges and opportunities these present for social movements and other civil society organizations.

Adrian Gurza Lavalle and Marisa von Bülow bring together their previous research on organizational ecologies and on transnational networks, respectively, to analyze the intermediation roles of what they call "institutionalized brokers." In spite of the recent interest in the mechanism of brokerage in contentious politics, the creation of specific organizations in charge of intermediation within and beyond civil society has not been the object of systematic research. The authors argue for a dynamic approach to brokerage as a process, in order to better understand how it shapes relationships among actors through time. Thus, the chapter advances a research agenda that seeks to acknowledge the challenges and trade-offs of intermediation within expanded organizational ecologies.

The chapter by Rose J. Spalding builds on the growing interest in the creation and functioning of transnational networks. More specifically, it contributes to recent efforts at better understanding how and why actors move through multiple scales by introducing two mobilization processes: the "domestic loop" and the "deleveraging hook." The first shows how domestic networks bring home discourse and framing infused with international learning, thus advancing our knowledge about the national impacts of transnational activism. The second examines activist efforts to address the clash between democratic decision-making and externally enforced neoliberal rules. Based on the author's extensive knowledge of Central America (and more specifically of the anti-mining mobilizations in El Salvador), the chapter also contributes to better understanding the problems that routinely emerge in North–South movement alliances. It argues for conceptual refinement of the debate about the roles of actors in such alliances, differentiating between types of international nongovernmental organizations.

Both of these chapters build on the international literature and move forward by proposing new concepts and typologies that can be useful in thinking about other empirical cases. For instance, in their analysis about institutionalized brokers, Gurza Lavalle and von Bülow mention how organizations during the civil rights movement in the United States played similar types of brokerage roles. In spite of the recent interest in the study of brokerage in Latin America, this is neither a new topic, nor one that is restricted to the region. Spalding's analysis builds on previous attempts to study the ways in which national actors strategize and build coalitions beyond national borders. Thus, the framework proposed builds on Keck and Sikkink's "boomerang" (1998), Tarrow's "rooted cosmopolitans" (2005), della Porta and Caiani's "paths to Europeanization" (2009), and von Bülow's "pathways to transnationality" (2010), and contributes to this literature by further specifying actors and processes. As they put forward new typologies of institutionalized brokers and transnational processes, these chapters present research agendas that open doors for thinking about organizational power and coalition building in different contexts.

***

This book seeks to foster a greater dialogue among scholars that study different regions of the world. The various chapters of the book express an underlying common interest of the authors in developing a dynamic-relational approach to the study of social movements. However, this book does not propose a unique vision. Rather, it enriches the field with innovative ideas that travel well to other regions and cultures.

The book closes with a chapter by Margaret E. Keck, in which she discusses the potentialities of this research agenda. The author connects the ideas put forward separately in the chapters, and, in doing so, masterfully moves forward in the dialogue we propose to generate.

References

Abers, Rebecca Neaera, 2000. *Inventing local democracy: grassroots politics in Brazil.* Boulder: Lynne Rienner.

Abers, Rebecca Neara and von Bülow, Marisa, 2010. "Apresentação. Dossiê Movimentos Sociais e Ação Coletiva." *Revista Brasileira de Ciência Política,* 3, pp. 13–21.

Almeida, Paul D., 2007. "Defensive mobilization: popular movements against economic adjustment policies in Latin America." *Latin American Perspectives,* 34(3), pp. 123–39.

————, 2014. *Mobilizing democracy: globalization and citizen protest.* Baltimore: Johns Hopkins University Press.

Almeida, Paul D. and Johnston, Hank, 2006. "Neoliberal globalization and popular movements in Latin America." In: Hank Johnston and Paul D. Almeida eds. *Latin American social movements: globalization, democratization, and transnational networks.* Boulder: Rowman & Littlefield, pp. 3–18.

Álvarez, Sonia, Dagnino, Evelina, and Escobar, Arturo eds, 1998. *Cultures of politics, politics of culture: re-visioning the Latin American social movements.* Boulder: Westview.

Auyero, Javier, 2003. *Contentious lives: two Argentine women, two protests, and the quest for recognition.* Durham: Duke University Press.

Avritzer, Leonardo, 2002. *Democracy and the public space in Latin America.* Princeton: Princeton University Press.

Baiocchi, Gianpaolo ed., 2005. *Militants and citizens: the politics of participatory democracy in Porto Alegre.* Stanford: Stanford University Press.

Banaszak, Lee Ann, 2009. *The women's movement inside and outside the state.* New York: Cambridge University Press.

Bandy, Joe and Smith, Jackie eds, 2005. *Coalitions across borders: transnational protest and the neoliberal order.* Lanham: Rowman & Littlefield.

Beissinger, Mark, 2002. *Nationalist mobilization and the collapse of the soviet state.* New York: Cambridge University Press.

Bloom, Joshua and Martin, Waldo E., 2013. *Black against empire: the history and politics of the Black Panther party.* Berkeley: University of California Press.

Boschi, Renato, 1987. "Social movements and the new political order in Brazil." In: John Wirth, Edson De Oliveira Nunes, and Thomas Bogenschild eds. *State and society in Brazil: continuity and change.* Boulder: Westview, pp. 179–212.

Brysk, Alison, 1994. *The politics of human rights in Argentina: protest, change, and democratization.* Stanford: Stanford University Press.

Calderón, Fernando ed., 1986. *Los movimientos sociales ante la crisis.* Buenos Aires: Universidad de la Naciones Unidas–CLACSO–IISUNAM.

Collier, Ruth Berins, 1999. *Paths toward democracy: the working class and elites in western Europe and South America*. Cambridge: Cambridge University Press.

Corradi, Juan E., Fagen, Patricia Weiss, and Garretón, Manuel Antonio eds, 1992. *Fear at the edge: state terror and resistance in Latin America*. Berkeley: University of California.

Dagnino, Evelina, 1994. *Os anos 90: política e sociedade no Brasil*. São Paulo: Brasiliense.

———, 2003. "Citizenship in Latin America." *Latin American Perspectives*, 30, pp. 221–25.

della Porta, Donatella, 2014. *Mobilizing for democracy: comparing 1989 and 2011*. New York: Oxford University Press.

della Porta, Donatella and Caiani, Manuela, 2009. *Social movements and Europeanization*. Oxford: Oxford University Press.

della Porta, Donatella and Tarrow, Sidney, 2005. *Transnational protest and global activism*. Lanham: Rowman & Littlefield.

Desai, Manali, 2012. "Parties and the articulation of neoliberalism: from 'the emergency' to reforms in India, 1975–1991." In: Julian Go ed. *Political power and social theory* (23). Bingley: Esmerald, pp. 27–63.

Doimo, Ana Maria, 1995. *A vez e a voz do popular: movimentos sociais e participação política no Brasil pós-70*. São Paulo: ANPOCS/Relume-Dumará.

Eckstein, Susan ed., 1989. *Power and popular protest*. Berkeley: University of California Press.

Escobar, Arturo and Álvarez, Sonia eds, 1992. *The making of social movements in Latin America: identity, strategy, and democracy*. Boulder: Westview Press.

Foweraker, Joe, 1995. *Theorizing social movements*. London: Pluto Press.

Freedman, Lawrence, 2013. *Strategy: a history*. New York: Oxford University Press.

Garretón, Manuel Antonio, 2002. "La transformación de la acción colectiva en América Latina." *Revista de la CEPAL*, 76, pp. 7–24.

Giugni, Marco, 1997. "Federalismo e movimenti sociali." *Rivista Italiana di Scienza Politica*, 26(1) pp. 147–70.

Glenn, John K., 2003. "Contentious politics and democratization: comparing the impact of social movements on the fall of communism in Eastern Europe." *Political Studies*, 51(1) pp. 103–20.

Gohn, Maria da Glória, 1997. *Teoria dos movimentos sociais: paradigmas clássicos e contemporâneo*. São Paulo: Loyola.

Grimson, Alejandro and Pereyra, Sebastián eds, 2008. *Conflictos globales, voces locales: movilización y activismo en clave transnacional*. Buenos Aires: UNRISD–Prometeo.

Hochstetler, Kathryn, 2002. "After the boomerang: environmental movements and politics in the La Plata River basin." *Global Environmental Politics*, 2(4) pp. 35–57.

Jelin, Elizabeth, 1990. *Women and social change in Latin America*. London: Zed Books.

Jelin, Elizabeth ed., 1985. *Los nuevos movimientos sociales*, 2 vols. Buenos Aires: Centro Editor de América Latina.

Johnston, Hank and Almeida, Paul D. eds, 2006. *Latin American social movements: globalization, democratization, and transnational networks*. Lanham: Rowman & Littlefield.

Keck, Margaret E. and Sikkink, Kathryn, 1998. *Activists beyond borders: advocacy networks in international politics*. Ithaca: Cornell University Press.

Klandermans, Bert, Kriesi, Hanspeter, and Tarrow, Sidney, 1988. *From structure to action: comparing social movement research across cultures*. Greenwich: JAI.

Kriesi, Hanspeter, Koopmans, Ruud, Duyvendak, Jan Willen and Gugni, Marco eds, 1995. *New social movements in Western Europe: a comparative analysis*. Minneapolis: University of Minnesota Press.

Kunrath, Marcelo, 2011. "Apresentação. Dossiê Movimentos Sociais." *Revista Sociologias*, 13(28) pp. 14–16.

Lucero, José Antonio, 2008. *Struggles of voice: the politics of indigenous representation in the Andes*. Pittsburgh: University of Pittsburgh Press.

Mainwaring, Scott, 1987. "Urban popular movements, identity, and democratization in Brazil." *Comparative Political Studies*, 20(2) pp. 131–59.

Mainwaring, Scott and Viola, Eduardo, 1984. "New social movements, political culture, and democracy: Brazil and Argentina in the 1980s." *Telos*, 61, pp. 17–52.

McAdam, Doug, McCarthy, John and Zald, Mayer, 1996. *Comparative perspectives on social movements: political opportunities, mobilizing structures, and cultural framings*. New York: Cambridge University Press.

McAdam, Doug, Tarrow, Sidney and Tilly, Charles, 2001. *Dynamics of contention*. New York: Cambridge University Press.

Oxhorn, Philip, 1995. *Organizing civil society. The popular sectors and the struggle for democracy in Chile*. Pennsylvania: Penn State University Press.

Petrova, Dimitriva, 2004. "Bulgaria." In: Detlef Pollack and Jan Wielgohs, eds. *Dissent and opposition in communist Eastern Europe: origins of civil society and democratic transition*. Aldershot: Ashgate, pp. 161–84.

Pleyers, Geoffrey, 2010. *Alter-globalization: becoming actors in the global age*. Cambridge: Polity.

Poulson, Stephen C., Caswell, Cory P. and Gray, Latasha R., 2014. "Isomorphism, institutional parochialism, and the study of social movements." *Social Movement Studies*. DOI: 10.1080/14742837.2013.878246.

Rhodes, Sybil, 2006. *Social movements and free-market capitalism in Latin America: telecommunications privatization and the rise of consumer protest*. Albany: State University of New York Press.

Rice, Roberta, 2012. *The new politics of protest: indigenous mobilization in Latin America's neoliberal era*. Tucson: University of Arizona Press.

Roberts, Bryan R. and Portes, Alejandro, 2006. "Coping with the free market city: collective action in six Latin American cities at the end of the twentieth century." *Latin American Research Review*, 41(2) pp. 57–83.

Roberts, Kenneth M., 2008. "The mobilization of opposition to economic liberalization." *Annual Review of Political Science*, 11(1), pp. 327–49.

Rossi, Federico M., 2015. "The second wave of incorporation in Latin America: A conceptualization of the quest for inclusion applied to Argentina." *Latin American Politics & Society*, 57(1), pp. 1–28.

Rossi, Federico M. and della Porta, Donatella, 2009. "Social movement, trade unions and advocacy networks." In: Christian W. Haerpfer, et al., eds. *Democratization*. Oxford: Oxford University Press, pp. 172–85.

Sader, Eder, 1988. *Quando novos personagens entram em cena: experiências, falas e lutas dos trabalhadores da grande São Paulo (1970–1980)*. São Paulo: Paz e Terra.

Schneider, Cathy, 1995. *Shantytown protest in Pinochet's Chile*. Philadelphia: Temple University Press.

Silva, Eduardo, 2009. *Challenging neoliberalism in Latin America*. New York: Cambridge University Press.

Silva, Eduardo ed., 2013. *Transnational activism and national movements in Latin America: bridging the divide*. London: Routledge.

Slater, David ed., 1985. *New social movements and the state in Latin America*. Amsterdam: CEDLA.

Tarrow, Sidney, 2005. *The new transnational activism*. Cambridge: Cambridge University Press.

———, 2012. *Strangers at the gates: movements and states in contentious politics*. New York: Cambridge University Press.

Vergara-Camus, Leandro, 2009. "The politics of the MST: autonomous rural communities, the state, and electoral politics." *Latin American Perspectives*, 36(4), pp. 178–91.

von Bülow, Marisa, 2010. *Building transnational networks: civil society and the politics of trade in the Americas*. Cambridge: Cambridge University Press.

von Bülow, Marisa and Bidegain, Germán (forthcoming). "It takes two to tango: students, political parties and protest in Chile 2005–2013." In: Paul Almeida and Allen Cordero, eds. *Handbook of social movements across Latin America*. New York: Springer.

Walton, John and Shefner, Jonathan, 1994. "Latin America: Popular protest and the state." In: John Walton and David Seddon, eds. *Free markets and food riots: the politics of global adjustment*. Oxford: Blackwell, pp. 97–134.

Warren, Sarah D., 2012. "Latin American identity politics: redefining citizenship." *Sociology Compass*, 6(10) pp. 833–44.

Yashar, Deborah, 2005. *Contesting citizenship in Latin America: the rise of indigenous movements and the postliberal challenge*. New York: Cambridge University Press.

Young, Cynthia A., 2006. *Soul power: culture, radicalism, and the making of a US third world left*. Durham: Duke University Press.

PART I
Beyond Contentious
Versus Routine Politics

Chapter 2

Conceptualizing Strategy Making in a Historical and Collective Perspective

Federico M. Rossi

Introduction[1]

In this chapter, I propose two concepts with the aim of contributing to a better understanding of historically rooted and collective processes of strategy making and performing that transcend the overemphasis of the specialized literature on contentious and public action (Goldstone 2003; Abers and Tatagiba, this volume). These concepts are *repertoire of strategies* and *stock of legacies*. I propose these concepts in this chapter as a complement to Charles Tilly's "repertoire of contention." The implications of incorporating a focus on strategies are central for social movement studies because they lead us to pay attention to actors and their intentions, and the interactions among the intentions of a variety of deliberate actors (Jasper 2012, p. 30). Moreover, with these concepts I aim to recover Machiavelli's analysis of strategies through a historical understanding of the construction of strategies.

In this chapter I claim that when studying the interaction of any social movement with the state, allies, and antagonists, the public performances identified by a "repertoire of contention" approach is just part of the story. There are many other activities performed by social movements that are part of their strategic quest for influencing political decisions that are neither contentious nor public. However, I do not propose as an alternative to reduce the analysis to the study of micro-tactics. The complete story is built by the multiple and simultaneous strategies that guide and give meaning to each tactical action performed by the collectives that constitute a movement.

1 I would like to acknowledge the comments and suggestions to previous versions of this chapter provided by Stephanie Arnett, Donatella della Porta, Jeff Goodwin, Hank Johnston, Margaret Keck, John Markoff, Mattea Musso, David Ortiz, Philippe Schmitter, Sidney Tarrow, Marisa von Bülow, and an anonymous reviewer. Thank you so much for your contributions. I presented earlier versions of this chapter at the XXIV Convegno della Società Italiana di Scienza Politica in Venice (September 16, 2010), the Center for the Study of Social Movements, University of Notre Dame (May 4, 2012), and the Pittsburgh Social Movement Forum, University of Pittsburgh (November 2, 2012).

I illustrate both concepts with an analysis of the *piqueteros* (picketers) or unemployed workers' movement of Argentina. This movement is famous for its use of roadblocks, marches, and encampments, even though they strategized much more than these three types of protest. My empirical findings are based on the print editions of 12 newspapers, hundreds of documents produced by the *piqueteros*, and nearly 40 open-ended interviews with all the main *piquetero* leaders, key allies (human rights activists, priests, and so on), key state brokers (ministries, mayors, and so on), national and provincial parliamentarians, and journalists, conducted over three fieldwork periods in Argentina between 2007 and 2009, which also included direct observation.

Tactics, Strategies, and Contention

Social movement scholars have accorded a great deal of importance to the study of tactics and strategies (Gamson 1975; Piven and Cloward 1977; McAdam 1983; Fantasia 1988; Staggenborg 1991; Ganz 2000). However, until the 2000s, theorizing on this topic was limited, and research almost exclusively focused on protest events, overlooking other forms of claim making and collective action (Taylor and Van Dyke 2004, pp. 267–68; Smithey 2009; Maney et al. 2012: xiii–xvi).

In addition, most of the literature on strategies/tactics does not draw a conceptual distinction between "strategy" and "tactic" (Jasper 2004: 14, n.1; Taylor and Van Dyke 2004). Still, there have been some interesting recent efforts to clarify the differences (Fligstein and McAdam 2011; Maney et al. 2012; Meyer and Staggenborg 2012; Doherty 2013). Nepstad and Vinthagen (2012) have proposed the clearest distinction between tactic and strategy. These authors suggest a "Clausewitz-inspired understanding" that could help scholars: "... we define *tactics* as the means and plan to win a single campaign (one battle) and *strategy* as the plan of how to win the struggle (the war). Thus, tactics involve the small-scale repertoire and subgoals of the movement, while strategy is about how a movement reaches its goals" (Nepstad and Vinthagen 2012, p. 282, n.1). In order to avoid any conceptual confusion, I draw on the difference between tactic and strategy proposed by Nepstad and Vinthagen.

A fundamental approach to strategizing is Tilly's concept of "repertoire of contention." His concept has allowed us to study contentious and public events and their slow pace of change as part of what is known as "contentious politics." Tilly (1995, pp. 26–27) defined the repertoire of contention as a limited set of actions based on a relatively deliberate process of choice, in which social relations cluster together in recurrent patterns based on social and cultural capital accumulated through struggle. As he clearly said: "In stressing open, collective, discontinuous contention, the analysis neglects individual forms of struggle and resistance as well as the routine operation of political parties, labor unions, patron-client networks, and other powerful means of collective action, except when they produce visible contention in the public arena" (Tilly 1995, pp. 32). In other words, his definition is unambiguously limited to disruptive acts performed in the public space (Tilly 1986, pp. 3–4; 2008, pp. 203–04). This focus means that Tilly's definition does not allow for the study of a case of mobilization that did not happen. For example, one that was planned and organized by the members of a movement but never carried out. In this way, the narrative built would neglect that a public action emerges because several other non-public actions were performed and led to a contentious result. As a result, Tilly's conceptualization alone is unable to explain two crucial aspects of the dynamics of interaction of social movements: first, situations where contention does not emerge, and second, the relationship between the public and contentious events generally described by the media and most narrations and those that were not reported because they were not performed in the public space. The full picture of the strategic dynamics of interaction of social movements with the state, allies, and antagonists emerges if we broaden our scope beyond the contentious and public dimension of social movements only.

In contrast, with the goal of developing an agency-based approach to social movements, Jasper (2004, 2006, 2012) proposes the study of tactical options as a result of concrete dilemmas faced by agents. Jasper (2004, p. 4) suggests that we need "… to understand what happens at the micro level of individuals and their interactions in order to improve our theories at the macro level …" For this purpose, he proposes a series of "strategic dilemmas/trade-offs" that would allow us to understand the daily decisions of individuals without having to recourse to rational choice theory. The main issue with the concept of "strategic dilemmas/trade-offs" is that it suggests the universality of micro short-term tactical decisions. As a result, this perspective successfully eliminates several limitations of rational choice theory, but still lacks "… an understanding of how much dilemmas are interrelated and how their solutions are constrained" (Meyer and Staggenborg 2012, p. 6). An additional problem with this approach is that although sometimes an action seems to be logical when its effects are retrospectively analyzed, the "… social agents have 'strategies' which only rarely have a true strategic intention as a principle" (Bourdieu 1998, p. 81). It is, thus, necessary to trace the history of the strategy/tactic that is being performed to provide a contextualized meaning of it.

A crucial difference between Jasper's and Tilly's approaches to the study of tactical/strategic action is the answer they offer to a classic problem posed by Marx (1926[1852], p. 23) in remarkable terms: "Men make their own history, but not just as they please. They do not choose the circumstances for themselves, but have to work upon circumstances as they find them, have to fashion the material handed down by the past. The legacy of the dead generations weighs like an alp upon the brains of the living." While Jasper (2012) disregards the contextual factors as irrelevant, considering that this could take us to a return to structuralism, other authors, such as Bourdieu (1998), Tilly (1986, 2006, 2008), and Meyer and Staggenborg (2012), consider that what limits actors' free choice of strategies is crucial. The question with Jasper's view is that it omits the limitations posed to human agency by historical legacies of past struggles, which provide a meaning to and guides, limits, and enriches each short-term tactic. Whereas how to resolve the relationship between strategies chosen by collective actors and the legacies of past struggles was one of Tilly's main concerns.

In brief, while Jasper (2004, 2006, 2012) has been producing some of the most interesting conceptual ideas on small, short-term, and individually based tactics, Tilly (1986, 1995, 2008) made the most important conceptual contribution to the study of large, long-term, and collectively based repertoires of contention. However, while Jasper offers a universalistic approach to tactics, Tilly's historical approach only focused on public and contentious actions. Thus, there is a clear gap between public collective disruption and small tactical decisions.[2] In order to fill in this gap, I emphasize a historical and collective approach to politics to analyze the background of strategies. Then, a conceptualization of collective action that falls outside the realm of public protest needs to be incorporated into the current debates in the literature. In this chapter I propose a conceptual solution to this gap in the literature that would allow us to explain the historically rooted dynamics of *strategic* interaction between social movements and allies and antagonists.

Let us first look at the main characteristics of the case that will illustrate my conceptual proposal—the *piqueteros*.

The *Piqueteros*: The Unemployed Workers' Movement of Argentina

Throughout the 1990s, neoliberal reforms implemented in Argentina included hundreds of privatizations and resulted in de-industrialization and unemployment on a massive scale. These reforms downsized the work force of the largest state-owned company, the corporation Treasury Petroleum Fields (YPF), reducing the number of workers from 51,000 in 1989 to less than 11,000 in 1992. At the same time, YPF transferred oil fields deemed unprofitable to the provinces or closed them entirely. The social consequences of this decision were quickly felt in those petroleum enclaves that had been fully dependent on YPF. In 1996, the first *pueblada* (social uprising) was organized in the province of Neuquén to demand alternative industrial solutions in order to restore local employment levels. As no solution was offered, in 1997 a second *pueblada* took place, after which the national government started providing unemployment subsidies (Sánchez 1997; Auyero 2003).

De-industrialization particularly affected suburban areas such as La Matanza in Greater Buenos Aires. La Matanza is the most populated suburban area of Argentina with more than one million inhabitants. Historically an industrial district, after 1990 all the larger factories began to close—among them those of the automobile industry such as Volkswagen, Chrysler, Borgward, and MAN (Merklen, 2005, p. 54, n. 23)—which meant the loss of many jobs and the collapse of entire communities. Local Christian and left-wing activists reacted to this critical situation by building a movement of unemployed poor people.

---

2   For a review of some efforts to solve this gap, see Abers and Tatagiba (this volume).

In 1996, the first mobilization against unemployment was organized in Greater Buenos Aires. Party militants of the Maoist Communist Revolutionary Party (PCR), the Trotskyist Movement towards Socialism (MAS), and the Marxist-Leninist Communist Party of Argentina (PCA) organized the "March Against Hunger, Unemployment, and Repression" in La Matanza. In 1997, the first pickets in Greater Buenos Aires to succeed in getting unemployment subsidies were organized (Svampa and Pereyra 2003). Since then, the main immediate goal of the protestors, known as the *piqueteros*, has been to reinstate full employment for the urban poor. This goal has been related to the quest for the reincorporation of urban poor people into Argentina's socio-political arena (Rossi 2013b, 2015).

Multiple ideologies are present within the *piquetero* movement, and in order to understand the complexity of this movement it is also necessary to comprehend the ideological and organizational divisions within the left in Argentina. Although the number of organizations that compose the movement has gradually expanded, its original basis was in three main groups that share a common identity of "unemployed workers": (1) the Liberation Theology-based *Federación de Trabajadores por la Tierra, Vivienda y Hábitat* (Workers' Federation for Land, Housing, and Habitat, FTV); (2) the Maoist *Corriente Clasista y Combativa* (Classist and Combative Current, CCC); and (3) the Guevarist and autonomist *Movimientos de Trabajadores Desocupados* (Unemployed Workers' Movements, MTDs).

An important part of the *piquetero* movement originates in the same groups that coordinated urban land occupations in Greater Buenos Aires in the 1980s. Of these organizations, the FTV has the strongest links to this past experience. In 1981 and 1982, activists from Christian-based communities (CBCs), with the support of the local bishop, organized the first massive urban land occupations in Quilmes (Fara 1985). This was done via CBC-related human rights organizations, and the process initiated in Quilmes later spread to La Matanza (Merklen 1991). These two main CBC-organized land occupations, and their later expansion, became the seeds for the future growth of the FTV. The FTV now operates in those same neighborhoods where the original organizations staged their land occupations. In other words, the same people that occupied land in the 1980s were those who created the FTV, building upon the legacy left behind by CBC actions.

The Maoist CCC was created in 1996 as part of a long process of reconfiguring the left after democratization. The first major event against neoliberal reforms was the Federal March of 1994. This national mobilization was coordinated by left-wing and Peronist labor federations, as well as left-wing parties such as the Trotskyist MAS and the Maoist PCR. Increased cooperation in the wake of the Federal March led to the creation of the CCC by connecting the PCR with some members of the MAS.

In 1996, the PCR also helped to spread contention from the province of Jujuy to neighboring Salta with the creation of the *Unión de Trabajadores Desocupados* (Union of Unemployed Workers, UTD) of Mosconi in association with a network of former YPF workers. Simultaneously, another process of reorganization was taking place. In La Matanza, some PCR leaders had been involved in 1980s land occupations that were similar to those led by the CBCs, the precursor groups of the FTV. The outcome was a territorialized approach just like the one taken by the FTV. The creation of the CCC–Unemployed Workers Sector as one of three divisions of the CCC was the result of the PCR's redefinition of poor people as constituting "The same components that characterize the [working] class: those in work, those who have retired, and the unemployed" (national leader of the CCC, interviewed September 17, 2007).

Finally, the third main sector in the movement is the one related to Guevarist and autonomist ideologies. Since democratization, a group of left-wing organizations had systematically failed to organize employed workers at the factory level. This led them to work at the territorial level with popular sectors mostly ignored by the Peronist General Labor Confederation (CGT). The future MTDs were conceived in 1995 thanks to support that the human rights organization Mothers of the Plaza de Mayo Association gave to certain informal groups working in shantytowns. In La Matanza, the MTD of La Juanita was established, and in Florencio Varela, a former guerrilla member and a local Catholic priest, among others, started another MTD. From the beginning, the heterogeneity of this *piquetero* sector led it to splinter into new organizations.

The Repertoire of Strategies Concept

The *piquetero* movement is well known for its repertoire of contention. It is, indeed, this contentious dimension—and specifically its regular use of pickets—that earned this movement its name of *piqueteros* (picketers). A journalist presenting the movement to an English-speaking audience described the main characteristics of the *piqueteros* as follows:

> Very noisy and equally efficient, the *piquetero* movement in Argentina is well organized. They come in hundreds—men, women, and children—to demonstrate. About once a week, and sometimes more, and most of the time without any warning, they block some of Buenos Aires' main streets, causing major traffic obstructions (...) and forcing the city to organize itself in order to avoid total chaos. (...) Although some pickets are organized to show support to the Kirchner administration, the *piquetero* movement is mostly one of protest against the government (*Piquetero Movement – Argentina*, 00.00 to 1.12 minutes, http://www.youtube.com/watch?v=AKE1fIrtMR4, accessed October 10, 2012).

This same journalist goes on to explain the steps taken by the movement in a public action directed at the state:

> These *piqueteros* were marching towards the Plaza de Mayo, Buenos Aires' main square, in front of the House of Government. They were stopped by the police a few hundred yards before reaching the plaza. They decided to camp

out where they were until the president agreed to get them what they wanted: a job. (...) And so they did for 35 hours until the government finally agreed to their demands. The picket has become the most prominent way of protesting nowadays in Argentina—a common method, indeed, and a legal one, at that. But not a popular one (*Piquetero Movement – Argentina*, 1.13 to 1.49 minutes, http://www.youtube.com/watch?v=AKE1fIrtMR4, accessed October 10, 2012).

In fact, as this narrative illustrates, the repertoire of contention of the *piquetero* movement has been composed predominantly of roadblocks, marches, and encampments.[3] This dimension of politics is the one that had been the main focus of most of Tilly's (1986, 1995, 2006, 2008) research, and is the one that led to his formulation of the extremely useful concept of "repertoire of contention."

However, even this highly contention-prone movement engages in informal collaboration strategies and in bridge building with government officials, and these initiatives cannot be understood through the concept of repertoire of contention. They were the result of strategic decisions to avoid pursuing contentious actions. When an analysis of the history of the *piqueteros*—and any other social movement—is widened beyond contentious and public politics, a double logic of interaction emerges that embraces both public militancy and less public strategic retrenchment. If we were to reduce the analysis to the repertoire of contention, these other strategies would be missed.

Therefore, two questions arise as critical for improving the explanations of strategy making and performing by social movements: *How can we analyze the interaction of a social movement with the state, allies, and antagonists without reducing the analysis to its public and contentious dimensions only?* And, *how can we put strategy making in historical perspective?* The answers to these questions lie in the existence of two types of repertoires being simultaneously performed by the same movement. On the one hand, there is Tilly's repertoire of contention, which is public, militant, and glacially slow to change. This is corroborated by the *piquetero* movement's repertoire, which remained steadfast in its use of roadblocks, marches, and encampments. However, the narrative somewhat changes when the history of the movement is analyzed using an interpretative Weberian approach (*verstehen*) based on in-depth interviews with movement leaders and state brokers and direct observation of movement activities. If Tilly's sources were supplemented with the ones I suggest in this chapter, the analysis of the movement would gain access to public, semi-public, and private events that are both contentious and non-contentious. These events broaden the scope of collective action and need to be theorized to help explain what happens in social movements when contentious events are not taking place. I suggest that the concepts "repertoire of strategies" and "stock of legacies" bring into the analysis elements intentionally excluded from the concept of "repertoire of contention."

---

3   Between 1997 and 2012, the print media reported 19,811 roadblocks/pickets, the vast majority of them organized by the *piqueteros* (Ichaso 2013).

The basic idea is to consider contentious and routine repertoires simultaneously, not limiting the analysis to the in-the-public-space aspects of the movement, and achieving a fuller depiction of historical events. Thus, these concepts allow for explaining aspects that the previous concept was ignoring.

By repertoire of strategies I mean a historically constrained set of available options for non-teleological strategic action in public, semi-public (evolving across specific groups), or private arenas. This concept differs from the repertoire of contention in three main ways. First, the repertoire of strategies is more dynamic. Second, it is not solely contentious nor always public. It includes Tilly's forms of public disruption as well as non-contentious private actions such as informal meetings with politicians, audiences with the president, and so on. I use the term "strategy" and not "tactics" because movement actors choose a contentious and public action versus another form of action as part of the movement's long-term goals and a wider understanding of the social reality. Each strategic choice will necessarily include many tactical decisions to achieve the goal. The third difference is that the repertoire of strategies is mostly defined in its relationship to medium- and short-term changes in the political context, while the repertoire of contention is associated with longer-term changes.

Like Bourdieu (2000, p. 145), I look at action as the product of the accumulation of historical legacies.[4] Though acknowledging the contextual constraints on actors' choices, my approach has two fundamental differences with Bourdieu. First, collective actors, not individual agents, perform repertoires of strategies. Second, my definition is rooted in a perspective that is less structuralist than Bourdieu's, allowing for spaces for rupture and dislocation. On the other hand, I draw upon one of the attributes of Bourdieu's "habitus": that the actor's choices are not necessarily coherent (Bourdieu 2000, p. 160). Therefore, the definition of repertoire of strategies is sustained by the idea of the restricted nature of the available options perceived as feasible by the actor. While for Bourdieu the individual agent is structurally predisposed to selecting a particular strategy, I emphasize that strategic choice is the result of a historically constrained set of available and concatenated options (which I call the stock of legacies—more on this shortly). To sum up, the accumulation of strategies by a collective actor builds repertoires based on evaluating (whether correctly or not) their (and/or others') past strategies and, thus, opting to emulate, readapt, or reject them in a (socially delimited) conscious and oblivious fashion.

The concept of repertoire of strategies has two specific attributes that differentiate it from that of ideologies: It only represents the strategic options chosen, and, though being modular, it is rooted in time and space. It allows for the selection of strategies (contentious or otherwise), in public, semi-public, or private arenas, and thus offers a tool for improving the analytical connection

---

4　Emirbayer (2010) points out some similarities between Tilly and Bourdieu concerning the contextual constrains for action that are linked to the analysis I am presenting here.

among multiple types of simultaneous actions pertaining to the same actor. In other words, the repertoire of strategies has a historical origin and tradition that can explain it, but it can, and generally is, redefined by other actors coming from diverse ideological positions and different historical moments. This variety can be clearly seen in Table 2.1, which shows the main national *piquetero* social movement organizations (SMOs), their variety of ideologies, repertoire of strategies, and shared repertoire of contention. Various organizations have similar ideological traditions, such as *Barrios de Pie* (Standing Up Neighborhoods) and the *Movimiento Independiente de Jubilados y Desocupados* (Independent Movement of the Retired and Unemployed, MIJD), and use a different repertoire of strategies, while other organizations with different ideological traditions, such as the MTD "Aníbal Verón" and the UTD of Mosconi, use the same repertoire of strategies. Also, some strategies are widely used, such as *"basismo"* (territorially based grassroots assemblies) and "trade unionist" practices, while other strategies are restricted to one or a few organizations, such as "witnessing" and "NGO-ization." Therefore, there is no straightforward relationship between ideology and repertoire of strategies.

Table 2.1   Main *piquetero* SMOs, ideologies, repertoire of strategies, and repertoire of contention, 1996–2009

Piquetero social movement organizations	Ideology	Predominant repertoire of strategies	Predominant repertoire of contention
Barrios de Pie	National-populist	*Basismo* Multi-class popular front State colonization	Encampment March Roadblock
Coordinadora de Trabajadores Desocupados (CTD) "Aníbal Verón" (Movimiento Popular Revolucionario [MPR] "Quebracho")	National-populist	Moderate *foquismo* Witnessing	Encampment March Roadblock
Corriente Clasista y Combativa (CCC)	Maoist	*Basismo* Insurrectional alliance with the right Trade unionist	Encampment March Roadblock
Frente Popular "Darío Santillán" (FPDS)	Autonomist	Autonomist-introspective *Basismo*	Encampment March Roadblock
Federación de Trabajadores por la Tierra, Vivienda y Hábitat (FTV)	National-populist and Liberation Theology	*Basismo* Multi-class popular front State colonization Trade unionist	Encampment March Roadblock

Piquetero social movement organizations	Ideology	Predominant repertoire of strategies	Predominant repertoire of contention
Movimiento Independiente de Jubilados y Desocupados (MIJD)	National-populist	Insurrectional alliance with the right Witnessing	Encampment March Roadblock
Movimiento "Evita"	Left-wing Peronist	*Basismo* State colonization	Encampment March Roadblock
Movimiento Sin Trabajo (MST) "Teresa Vive"	Trotskyist	Morenist entryism Presentialism	Encampment March Roadblock
Movimiento de Trabajadores Desocupados (MTD) "Aníbal Verón"	Guevarist	Moderate *foquismo* Trade unionist	Encampment March Roadblock
Movimiento de Trabajadores Desocupados (MTD) of La Juanita	Social-democratic	NGO-ization	Encampment March Roadblock
Movimiento de Trabajadores Desocupados (MTD) of Solano and allies	Autonomist	Autonomist-introspective *Basismo*	Encampment March Roadblock
Movimiento de Trabajadores Desocupados "Teresa Rodríguez" (MTR) – Coordinadora de Unidad Barrial (CUBa)	Guevarist and Trotskyist	Moderate *foquismo* Trade unionist	Encampment March Roadblock
Movimiento Territorial Liberación (MTL)	Marxist-Leninist	Multi-class popular front Trade unionist	Encampment March Roadblock
Polo Obrero (PO)	Trotskyist	Morenist entryism Presentialism	Encampment March Roadblock
Unión de Trabajadores Desocupados (UTD) of Mosconi	Syndicalist	Moderate *foquismo* Trade unionist	Encampment March Roadblock

Notes: The time period does not imply that the organizations have applied these strategies continuously, but rather represents only the period during which the listed repertoires were considered predominant.

As stated, repertoires of contention and repertoires of strategies are intimately related. Table 2.1 shows that the use of the same contentious action by several organizations in a movement may result from different repertoires of strategies. Alternatively, the use of different contentious methods may result from the same strategy. In other words, repertoire of contention and repertoire of strategies refer to things happening within the same movement that are related but different. Let us look at some of the strategies for the *piquetero* movement to see why these actions were taken, how they were connected to previous ones, and how they are similar or different to previous and contemporary actions.

Multi-Sectoral Strategies

Among their several strategies, the *piqueteros* adopted three types of multi-sectoral strategies between 1996 and 2009. By multi-sectoral strategies I mean different versions of a strategy based on the idea that in order to achieve the desired political goals, it is crucial to join efforts with diverse segments of society and/or political groupings. Multi-sectoral strategies are not always contentious and involve many not-so-public actions.

A first type of multi-sectoral strategy is the "multi-class popular front," which implies, in the Argentine context, that left-wing parties and organizations should accept alliances with Peronist organizations (Justicialist Party [PJ], CGT, and so on), particularly with their more progressive wings.[5] Before being adopted by the *piqueteros* in relation to Peronist political, social, and labor organizations, this strategy was used in Latin America in the quest to unify the left during the Spanish Civil War (1936–39). It was mostly successful in Chile, while in Argentina, it emerged in the 1950s in the context of the debates about Peronism after the dissolution of the Comintern (Angell 1998). The use of this strategy by the *piqueteros* can be noted in their relationship with President Néstor Kirchner's Peronist government (2003–07). While the *Movimiento Territorial Liberación* (Liberation Territorial Movement, MTL) (linked to the PCA) was internally divided as to whether or not to support the government, the FTV and *Barrios de Pie* were allies of the government as part of what they conceived as a multi-class popular front.[6]

A second type of multi-sectoral strategy is the "insurrectional alliance with the right" promoted by the CCC (of the PCR), but also in a less structured fashion by the MIJD. Since its beginnings, the PCR has rejected armed struggle as promoted by guerrilla organizations. At the same time, it has had a long-standing relationship with some sectors of the armed forces. This has been sustained as part of their strategy of building an insurrectional alliance with the right. This strategy

---

5   Such alliances include multiple classes from the point of view of the *piquetero* organizations that enter into them, because, while they perceive themselves as composed of the working class (or the popular sectors), Peronist organizations reject any classist distinction, and Peronism is characterized by the integration of trade unions, national industrialists, and some middle classes (Rossi 2013a).

6   The main leader of the party behind *Barrios de Pie* explained to me the multi-class popular front strategy during the Kirchner administration in the following way: "… this is not our government, it is an alliance government. (…) It is a heterogeneous government with various interests that in some cases are counter-interests. So it is natural that there are several conflicts within the government. This is neither a reactionary nor a revolutionary government. It is just an alliance government…" (Interviewed September 20, 2007).

seems similar to the popular multi-class front that other *piquetero* organizations promote, but differs in some crucial respects: It is electorally abstentionist, and it is inspired by the Maoist 1940 anti-Japanese united front (Mao 1965[1940], p. 422). Thus, until 2009 the CCC promoted a protracted struggle in a multi-sectoral coalition with Peronist organizations with the expectation of leading to a popular insurrection that would bring down the regime.

The multi-sectoral alliance used by the CCC is based on the PCR politburo's interpretation of the Peronist PJ as the equivalent of the Chinese Kuomintang party due to its high level of internal heterogeneity, which opens up the possibility of exploiting the divisions among PJ elites in the same way as Mao Zedong proposed to do with the Kuomintang in 1940 (Mao 1965[1940], p. 427). To achieve this goal, they seek the support of the right-wing factions of the PJ and middle-size rural producers, while establishing long-term personalized contacts with PJ mayors. This coalition played a salient role in the 2008 rural lockout against a tax increase on the export of commodities.

A third type of multi-sectoral strategy is what I call "state colonization." *Barrios de Pie* adopted this strategy from 2003 to 2008, when it was a member of the governmental coalition. Using a multi-class popular front strategy in combination with Ernesto "Che" Guevara's beehive tactic, *Barrios de Pie* encouraged their members and leaders to actively participate in as many electoral, appointed, or technical positions that they could possibly negotiate with the PJ and the other coalition members in the national government, while also taking up as many local and provincial posts as possible. In this sense, this strategy implies accepting the Peronist organizations as tools that are useful, while simultaneously considering as crucial the access to gatekeeper positions of the state. As a result, in the province of Buenos Aires *Barrios de Pie* achieved middle-range positions in the Ministry of Human Development and in several municipalities. They also succeeded in securing several provincial sub-secretariats as well as national ones in the Ministry of International Relations and the Ministry of Social Development, and since 2007 have also had a few members elected to the national parliament, among other posts. Amid all the *piquetero* organizations, *Barrios de Pie* is the one that, until 2008, had achieved the greatest penetration of their members into the state apparatus. This was emulated by the FTV, although with much less success. The FTV suffered from internal indiscipline and co-optation as a consequence of imitating state colonization. Finally, the *Movimiento "Evita"* adopted the strategy, with a focus on the province of Buenos Aires, by formally participating in the functional structure of the PJ.

In brief, the three types of multi-sectoral strategies are diverse according to whether they adopt an internal or external relationship with the government or party, as well as according to which wing of the PJ or CGT they choose to ally themselves with. In the same sense, while the insurrectional alliance implies a non-electoral approach, the CCC, MIJD, and most of the *piqueteros* always play a role directly or indirectly during electoral periods (clientelism, protests, boycotts, and so on). This is different from the multi-sectoral coalition with the left-wing sectors of the PJ and state colonization strategies, which involve inclusion in the government coalition and access to parliamentarian and/or other kinds of electoral positions. Lastly, state colonization is focused on penetrating the state rather than the allied organizations.

Witnessing Strategy

The predominant repertoire of strategies of the *piqueteros* is much richer than these three multi-sectoral strategies and includes other, very different, strategies such as the one I have called "witnessing." This strategy is a way of showing the oppression of the political system through the personal experiences of the leaders of an organization. This strategy has been widely used around the world and can be traced to various adaptations, such as Gandhism and the Palestinian Intifada. In the *piquetero* movement, two organizations make systematic use of this strategy, in two variants. The *Coordinadora de Trabajadores Desocupados "Aníbal Verón"* (Coordination of Unemployed Workers "Aníbal Verón," CTD) of the *Movimiento Popular Revolucionario "Quebracho"* (Popular Revolutionary Movement "Quebracho," MPR) uses it for insurrectional purposes, while the MIJD uses it for electoral goals. These differences are not ideological, as they can both be considered national-populist anti-imperialist groups; the repertoire of strategies is what differentiates them. On the one hand, the CTD "Aníbal Verón" (MPR "Quebracho") uses violence against private property, as during the 2007 burning of the Neuquén Popular Movement's party office. This protest was not carried out undercover, but was openly played out in front of the media, followed by a public declaration at the location of the event by one of its leaders, thereby fulfilling his goal: to be immediately sent to jail.

On the other hand, the MIJD has made use of symbolically disruptive tools, such as setting up a popular soup kitchen in the richest neighborhood of Buenos Aires, organizing the participation of one of the MIJD leaders as a contestant on a prime-time television dance show, and protesting in front of McDonald's branches for the supply of 1,000 Happy Meals for the children of MIJD members. Raúl Castells, one of the main leaders of the MIJD, summarizes their strategy: "The Coca-Cola marketing strategists said that a message has to be recurrent and witty (…) We want socialism: this is our recurrent message. And we'll make it witty. The traditional left is dead boring. They have 100 years of history and people pay less attention to them than to a flock of sparrows" (*La Nación*, July 29, 2007). In the 2007 election the MIJD used this accumulated media coverage for electoral purposes by presenting Castells as a presidential candidate under a newly created MIJD ballot, which ended up garnering 54,893 votes (0.3 percent). In 2011, the MIJD could improve its electoral results, winning its first seat in the House of Representatives.

The CTD "Aníbal Verón" partially differs from the MIJD because it is abstentionist, and thus considers its witnessing strategy as part of an insurrectional path that has the potential to set a revolutionary process into motion, as explained by one of the CTD leaders:

> We still believe in the power of the people, which has to do with a strategy that calls for the need to get the people out in the streets. And additionally we don't believe that "the people" or "people" are closed categories because this would mean denying the [socio-economic and cultural diversity of] Argentina. In other words, the issue with the electorate, with the public opinion polls and these kinds of things, is what they conceal: the existing political proscription (Interviewed December 27, 2008).

While for the MIJD the perspective is based on a pragmatic understanding of the mass media, as Castells explains:

> The goal of our political struggle is socialism, but we don't have the economic resources [to promote our ideas] and because of this we use the mass media to spread our ideas. It was one thing to start a social revolution 100 years ago, but it's quite another to do it now, when almost every house has a television and seven million people have Internet access (...) For us, the issue is not who are the owners of the media, but who are its consumers. Otherwise, we would not bother with this program because the journalist is tied to the government, or that other one because it's part of an international monopoly that subjugates us. If we saw things this way we would not use any mass media because there are no big TV channels owned by the workers, no cooperative newspapers or influential radio stations that are part of the popular struggle. For us, this [the mass media] is not the interlocutor, but the one who is listening to it or reading it (*Página/12*, May 20, 2007).

To sum up, in both cases the purpose is to repeatedly access the media in the face of a lack of economic resources to generate their own propaganda. They promote their voice by presenting themselves as witnesses of the oppression of the system. In this way, both organizations hope to increase the number of sympathizers and gain empathy for their organizations and their message by partially relying on the mass media as a vehicle for the dissemination of their ideas and the recruitment of activists.

Trade Unionist Strategy

Just a few of the strategies are directly related to the repertoire of contention. In the *piquetero* movement, only the "trade unionist" and "moderate *foquismo*" strategies are directly associated with the use of the picket. The trade unionist strategy can be defined as Sorelian. In this strategy, while there is systematic use of radical methods, claims are intentionally moderate (Sorel 1999[1908], p. 201). Sorel (1999[1908], p. 118) talks of the general strike as a *myth* in which major transformation is comprised. The success of the *piqueteros'* strategy is based on another myth, one that has the same power and logic as the general strike: the total picket. In other words, the importance of small protest events, like pickets, is crucial for expanding insurrection based on the idea of wide-ranging economic collapse as the general strike would imply. In Sorel's words:

> It is possible, therefore, to conceive socialism as being perfectly revolutionary, although there may only be conflicts that are short and few in number, provided that these have strength enough to evoke the idea of the general strike: all the events of the conflict will then appear under a magnified form and, the idea of catastrophe being maintained, the cleavage will be perfect. Thus the objection often urged against the revolutionaries may be set aside: there is no danger of civilization succumbing under the consequences of a development of brutality, since the idea of the general strike may foster the notion of class struggle by means of incidents which would appear to bourgeois historians as being of small importance (1999[1908], p. 182).

In other words, the trade unionist strategy can be defined as a systematic use of the mythical disruptive power of the *total picket* for moderate aims by vertical organizations that seek to enter into negotiations and make use of institutional and rhetorical trade unionist tools.

The main leader of the UTD of Mosconi argued that, after a decade of struggle, they had improved the hourly rate of pay for newly re-employed workers in the petroleum enclave where this *piquetero* organization is located. This achievement has been called the *"piquetero* hour" (a 350 percent increase on the hourly rate). This trade unionist achievement was the result of improving the picketing strategy in Mosconi by completely blocking the entrances to the local branches of transnational petroleum companies. However, the trade unionist strategy is not only related to the use of the picket as a protest tool, but to the wider influence of the trade unions' logic within the *piquetero* movement. Reproducing the bureaucratic organization of most unions in Argentina, the FTV is a wholly top-down and personalized organization with power concentrated in its main leader and building a loosely structured network across the country.[7] As the FTV is controlled by the national leader's group and minimum standards of democracy have not been respected, a number of internal conflicts have occurred within the FTV over its lifetime. This also explains the unsuccessful attempts by MTL and *Barrios de Pie* activists to achieve leadership posts inside the FTV (Armelino 2008).

---

7 According to Barker et al. (2001, p. 20), "Bureaucratic organization involves a hierarchy of offices, with decision-making concentrated at the top, and command following down. Members are either directly excluded from decision-making, or only indirectly consulted through intermittent elections to top offices, occasional conferences, and ballots. Officials are commonly appointed rather than elected. Channels of communication are top-down and monopolized by the leadership."

Moderate Foquismo Strategy

There is another strategy that consists of a different use of the picket by the *piqueteros*. Moderate *foquismo* implies the use of radical methods for moderate goals. *Foquismo*, or the *foco* theory of guerrilla warfare, was developed by Ernesto "Che" Guevara as an armed strategy for expanding conflict through a small group of men and women. Its adaptation to nonviolent use in a democratic setting for immediate reformist goals is what I call "moderate *foquismo*." This strategy prevails among some organizations. It is attached to a vanguardist conception of politics and implies the construction of a site or "*foco*" of conflict and its diffusion by what he called the "beehive effect" (Guevara 1997[1963], p. 389). In Guevara's words:

> Let's consider how a guerrilla *foco* could start (...) Relatively small nuclei of people choose favorable sites for the guerrilla war, be it with the intention of triggering a counterattack or to bide time, and then start to act. The following must be very clearly established: in the early stages, the relative weakness of the guerrilla is such that it must only work on putting down roots, getting to know the environment, making connections with the population and strengthening the places that will eventually become its support bases (1997[1963]: 387).

This strategy predominated among some *piquetero* organizations in Greater Buenos Aires, Mar del Plata, and Cipolletti. Territorially, they created *focos* of organization with local networks by taking control of *juntas vecinales* (neighborhood associations in poor districts and shantytowns). Later, when the political opportunities were interpreted as favorable due to the increase in unemployment and the lack of access to unions to mobilize workers, the network activated the *focos*, now renamed as MTDs. Contentiously, the *Movimiento de Trabajadores Desocupados "Teresa Rodríguez"* (Movement of Unemployed Workers "Teresa Rodríguez," MTR), the CTD "Aníbal Verón" and the MTD "Aníbal Verón" had focused on systematic pickets at specific locations in Buenos Aires, and particularly the Pueyrredón Bridge (the main southern entrance to the city of Buenos Aires) as a moderate *foquismo* strategy.

NGO-ization Strategy

Other strategies that compose the repertoire of the *piqueteros* do not have a contentious dimension. For instance, the "NGO-ization" strategy means the moderation of claims and contentious strategies in a process of collaboration with middle-class foundations and companies for project-focused agendas of action relying on donors. NGO-ization is the strategy that has been used by one small organization only—the MTD of La Juanita, a pioneer in the formation of the *piquetero* movement. After rejecting the claim for unemployment subsidies as a source of clientelism, this organization initiated a strategy of gradually mutating into an NGO, working under the same logic as any post-1990 professionalized NGO. It started to get funding from international donors and allied with private companies and middle-class parties.

The Stock of Legacies Concept

The repertoire of strategies represents the predominant set of strategies used by a movement in a specific time period. But, *what delimits the actors' perception of the availability of strategies in their repertoire?* As in the case of the repertoire of contention, there are elements that limit what the repertoire can contain. While the repertoire of contention changes very slowly, linked as it is to macro-transformations such as regime changes, the repertoire of strategies is more dynamic, which implies that its demarcation is based on actors' participation in a historical accumulation of events, experiences, and intentional learning processes that build a "stock of legacies." *By stock of legacies I mean the concatenation of past struggles, which, through the sedimentation of what is lived and perceived to be lived as well as what is intentionally learned, produces an accumulation of experience that adds or eliminates specific strategies from the repertoire of strategies as both a self-conscious and oblivious process.*

The concept is inspired on Schutz's (1967, pp. 76–77) concept of "stock of experience." According to Schutz (1967, pp. 77–78), a "meaningful lived experience" is the reflective product of each individual's flowing stream of experience that builds a stock of knowledge, that which enables each person to guide his or her conduct in the course of their life. In a stock of legacies, the actor opts for actions based on a set of identified available options that are open to innovation. But this process of selection is not that of an entirely free agent, nor is it the result of a coherent deliberation. Rather it is limited by socialization, from among (mis)perceived accumulated available options, and within a restricted set of legacies that enrich or impoverish the range of the stock. The stock of legacies offers a complementary explanation to the purely structural limitations to innovations suggested by Tilly (1986, p. 4, 390–91; 2006, pp. 42–45, 48–49; 2008, pp. 203–04), which tend to make it much easier to explain the stability of repertoires than changes to them.

The stock of legacies materializes as an empirical question when trying to understand, for instance, why the *piquetero* movement only emerged with particular intensity in certain places. An ex-priest and main leader of one of the pioneer *piquetero* organizations explained this situation to me in the following way:

Q: How do you explain that in Greater Buenos Aires there seems to be three main places where everything emerged …?

A: The experience of struggle. Despite the crises, which always happen, the lessons of past experience always linger. In other words, you don't go back to zero. You don't go back to the beginning. Situations recur, but with the accumulation of learnt experience. The southern zone [of Greater Buenos Aires] was combative in the 1970s; these were industrial areas, with a relatively high level of industrialization. All this was later dismantled, but the experience of struggle and resistance still lingers, and it re-emerges every now and then—as if going into crisis mode (Interviewed September 28, 2007).

This "experience of struggle" that "always lingers" was echoed by many others I interviewed. The words of the ex-priest poignantly captures the stock of legacies concept.

Piquetero's *Stock of Legacies*

Three main national legacies comprise the overall stock of legacies of the *piquetero* movement. In each SMO the influence of each legacy varied, which explains many of the strategic options chosen in concrete historical situations, as well as investing them with a sense of Weberian *verstehen*.

The first element in the movement's stock of legacies is the experience of the armed struggle of the urban guerrillas and the consequences of repression under both democratic and authoritarian regimes between 1975 and 1989. This legacy has a dual basis. On the one hand, it arises out of the trauma produced by the last authoritarian regime and the effect that this had on the perceived strategic alternatives within the left's re-evaluation of democracy (Carr and Ellner 1993). This is due to a phenomenon that Roberts (1998, pp. 41–42) also identified in Chile and Peru, what he called the left's affirmative and disconfirming experiences of their respective last authoritarian regimes. In Argentina, many of the *piquetero* leaders had disconfirming experiences as guerrilla veterans and now value some aspects of democracy, even if they are divided about its short-, medium-, and long-term value. On the other hand, the legacy of armed struggle is based on attempts by former guerrilla groups and left-wing Peronists to politically reorganize in Greater Buenos Aires between 1981 and 1987. This produced a legacy of organizational and contentious action from former groups of urban guerrillas within a protracted and self-restrained disruption strategy. Signs of this legacy can be seen in the vanguard organizational models used and the moderate *foquismo* strategy that predominates in the *piquetero* movement in south Greater Buenos Aires and in parts of the province of Salta.

The second shared legacy is the CBCs' practice of *basista* organization and their urban land occupations between 1979 and 1982, and their re-emergence in the 1990s. As stated by Cerrutti and Grimson (2004) and Merklen (2005), the territorialized mobilization that characterizes the *piquetero* movement is, in part, the historical continuation of the land occupations promoted by the CBCs in the period of democratization. This legacy explains why in some Greater Buenos Aires districts the *piquetero* movement quickly emerged as an organized process.

Finally, the third shared legacy is trade unionism, which is the result of the accumulated experience of syndicalist and communist unionism since the late nineteenth century and Peronist unionism since the 1950s.[8] This has resulted in a large accumulation of former factory union delegates, who in some cases became the main leaders of various *piquetero* organizations, for example the CCC, PO, MST "Teresa Vive," MTL, UTD of Mosconi, MTD of La Juanita, and CTD "Aníbal Verón" (MPR "Quebracho"). The CCC and MTL, for instance, define themselves as politico-syndical organizations, and one national leader of the MTL explains "… that [it] was a very important element for those of us who were trade union delegates and knew how trade unions worked, [because] we transferred all our experiences into the organization of the unemployed movement" (Germano 2005, p. 142).

With these new concepts in our toolkit, events similar to the ones described by the journalist quoted above can be reconstructed with the incorporation of additional events that were performed in different arenas, but as part of the same set of events that (sometimes) includes contentious politics. In other words, the two repertoires are interrelated, but they have crucial differences that allow for explaining different phenomena. In addition, each micro and daily tactical trade-off can only be meaningful when viewed as part of a repertoire of strategies and a repertoire of contention, the specific context in which these repertoires are used, and the perspective for the future that they imply.

Explaining Innovation in the Repertoires of Strategies

Some strategies have a long tradition with international roots, such as the three multi-sectoral strategies analyzed. But others are specific to Latin America, like *"basismo,"* which entails a strategy of territorial organization of the popular sectors in Argentina. As the name implies, this strategy is meant for building "from below" several territorially based nodes of action sustained on assembly-based methods of organizing in urban and suburban poor areas. *Basismo* is also an example of a strategy that originated as part of the repertoire of a specific ideological group,[9] but has then been widely adopted by others, such as autonomists (*Frente Popular "Darío Santillán"* [Popular Front "Darío Santillán," FPDS], MTD of Solano), Maoists (CCC), national-populists (*Barrios de Pie*), and Peronists (*Movimiento "Evita"*). Yet, with other strategies that compose the *piquetero* repertoire, the opposite happens. One example is "Morenist entryism," an adaptation by Nahuel

---

8   Argentina has the highest rate of unionization in Latin America, reaching 50.1 percent at its peak, versus, for instance, 24.3 percent in Brazil (Roberts 2002, p. 15, table 1).

9   As Prévôt-Schapira (1999, p. 228) explains, *"Basismo* was forged in activist Christian engagement." In Argentina, the development of *basismo* was linked to the legacy of Peronism and its relationship with "integrist" and ultramontane Catholicism.

Moreno of Leon Trotsky's notion of the united front.[10] In Argentina, after the coup against Juan Domingo Perón in 1955, the Trotskyist party Workers' Word used this strategy in order to infiltrate and command Peronist unions (Tarcus 1996, p. 117).[11] The post-democratization Morenist entryism strategy within the *piquetero* movement can be defined as the quest to penetrate other popular organizations with the goal of disputing the hegemony of the labor movement from inside its constituent organizations and build a vanguard that can guide the unemployed and employed workers towards a classist united front.[12] The PO did this by coordinating seven meetings of the National Assembly of Employed and Unemployed Workers (2001–05), as well as the *Bloque Piquetero Nacional* (National Piquetero Block) coalition (2002–05, until the PO was expelled). Despite this strategy having been useful for the PO, it did not spread outside the Trotskyist *piquetero* organizations. How and why some of these strategies have diffused across countries, historical periods, and ideological traditions while others have had more limited take-up is a relevant Tillyian question that, in the case of the repertoire of strategies, has a non-Tillyian answer.

Because the repertoire of strategies is less structurally determined than the repertoire of contention, its transformations happen as a result of debates that are permanently renewed among the *piquetero* leaders, as well as the party, union, and intellectual elites related to them.[13] These debates sometimes set into motion some modifications that are partially based on experiential learning. In other words, the repertoire of strategies does not evolve through slow and gradual changes at the state and regime levels, but rather through teaching and learning, intergenerational transmission, trial and error, emulation, and so on. In empirical terms, this means that innovation in repertoires of strategies and their diffusion can take place much quickly and easily than in repertoires of contention.

One way this occurs is through emulation and teaching. Figure 2.1 shows the front cover of a training course handbook for activists organized by the FPDS in 2009. Activists and intellectuals used this handbook to teach members of the FPDS autonomist ideas about the strategic relationship with the state, as well as giving examples of successful struggles in Latin America. There are many other situations like this one, where strategies are transmitted and created in semi-public

---

10   Trotsky had also developed his idea of a united front as an adaptation of a previous strategy. His idea was based on Friedrich Engels' proposal of infiltrating the German Social Democratic party with socialist officials (Tarcus 1996, p. 326).

11   Since the last re-democratization, Moreno (1980, pp. 179–84) reformulated parts of his strategy because Peronism was legalized and many left-wing organizations were into demise under the authoritarian regime of 1976–83.

12   Morenist entryism is used outside Argentina because it was widely taken up by Trotskyist groups after Moreno presented his strategic approach to the International Committee of the Fourth International (Leeds 1958).

13   Several examples of intentional production of strategies by intellectuals in Asia, Africa, and Latin America can be found in Baud and Rutten (2004).

Figure 2.1   **Front cover of a handbook for the *Frente Popular Darío Santillán's* Fourth National Camp for the Training of Activists, November 2009**

Source: Political Training School of the FPDS.

or private gatherings (see note 13). Among the *piqueteros*, it is not only the FPDS that organizes training gatherings. Since 2012 the *Movimiento "Evita"* has operated a house on an island in the delta of Buenos Aires to train young members on ideological and strategic issues. This interest on strategic and ideological training is not unique to the *piqueteros*. In Brazil, since 2005 the Landless Rural Workers' Movement (MST) has offered courses to their own members and activists from all around the world at the "Florestan Fernandes" National School, located on the outskirts of São Paulo.

A second way that the expansion of repertoires is accomplished is through what I call "resignification"—where the original strategy is taken up by another group with different political goals and inserted within a different set of legacies.[14] One interesting case of innovation in this sense is what I term *"basista* empowerment," that is, the syncretic resignification of *basismo* and World Bank inspired entrepreneurial social policies of empowerment in the post-neoliberal context by left-wing or national-populist organizations. In the case of the *piqueteros*, the *Movimiento "Evita"* and *Barrios de Pie* specifically used it. In the words of the General Secretary of the youth branch of the *Movimiento "Evita"* and Sub-secretary of Youth in the government of the province of Buenos Aires:

> The popular organization determines the possibility for participants' appropriation of public policy decisions and of the allocation of resources. And this generates a much more solid relationship of public policy [with the beneficiaries] that makes this process more difficult to reverse. When a person in a cooperative builds fifty houses, how can you tell him that he no longer has his job? On the other hand, when the houses are built by a company, the company just submits another tender to the state. This does not produce a relationship of power in which the active participants are the people. We call this social policy as Evita [Perón] called it: "the organized popular force," "the popular power" (Interviewed August 8, 2007).

A third source of enrichment of the repertoires of strategies is transnational mutual influence among social movements. Movement leaders and members participate in many gatherings and meetings with other movements that tend to build a "community of practice" (Wenger 1998). In the case of the *piqueteros*, the community of practice acts as a source of transnational reproduction of patterns and strategies. For instance, the mutual influence and connections between the

---

14   Freedman (2013, pp. 252–53, 400–04) offers a detailed narration of how this process works across diverse ideological traditions (like the contentious strategies borrowed by Engels from Claus von Clausewitz), as well as within more proximate ideological traditions, such as the diffusion of *foquismo* from "Che" Guevara's original formulation to its urban use by sectors of the Black Panthers Party in the US. Freedman's book can be also seen as an illustration of the importance of reading and writing as a conscious process of learning and resignifying strategies as I am conceptualizing it.

piqueteros in Argentina and the landless peasants' movement in Brazil is a source of some commonalities. FTV leaders told me that urban land occupations in the 1980s were inspired by the CBC experience in Brazil (cf. Isman 2004, pp. 108–09). Brazil's MST has permanent contacts with the MTR and its divisions (the FPDS, mainly), the MTD of Solano, the MTD of La Juanita, and the UTD of Mosconi through the brokerage of the Mothers of the Plaza de Mayo Association. These links led the MST to create its own movement of unemployed workers in Brazil, as was explained to me by national leaders of the MST in São Paulo. In addition, the CCC has links with the Poor Peasants League, the Maoist social movement organization of the Brazilian landless peasants' movement. Finally, the World Social Forum was mentioned several times as a space for mutual learning and connection. However, though these connections all have significant effects, they are only partial sources for the expansion or contraction of the repertoire of strategies.

In brief, experiential accumulation intentionally and unintentionally expands or restricts the repertoire of strategies, and thus plays a decisive additional role in the comprehension of the interactive process of change and continuity. Actors reduce or expand their repertoire of strategies by defining their past actions and how they are linked to their present choice of strategic options. This can empirically take place through a Tillyian logic of repertoire of contention (through slow and gradual changes at the state and regime levels), but also through systematic reading/ studying (which happens among many philosophically or ideologically minded groups), trans-generational intentional transmission (when the older leaders give courses and informally transmit their experience and knowledge to younger and less experienced members), and so on. In other words, the repertoire of strategies is delimited by non-rationalistic principles as a result of the stock of legacies, as well as the configuration of the political context.

Conclusion

The process of interaction of a movement with allies and antagonists cannot be fully understood or explained through the study of its contentious dimension only. If we limit our analysis to the public and disruptive dimension of social movements, we see less than half of the picture. Even though pickets and intense contentious dynamics were part of the *piqueteros'* struggle for the inclusion of the urban poor as citizens and workers in the socio-political arena, this struggle also involved an extensive use of non-public and non-contentious strategies. These strategies were only partially new, as the *piqueteros* were preceded by a long history of left-wing, Christian, and Peronist struggles in Argentina. This stock of legacies can also explain why the *piqueteros* decide to use one strategy or another, and when to apply it, in their ongoing quest to end neoliberalism.

The story of the *piqueteros* shows the utility of retaining Tilly's tradition of contextualized political analysis. Adding in the context and the long-term roots of strategies allows us to avoid universalizing that which is time-space specific, and pushes us to ask how and why certain strategies enter the predominant repertoire of a movement while others do not. Simultaneously, and in order to avoid the structuralist trap, I have proposed a collective and historical understanding of strategy making and performing that lends more weight to actors than does Tilly's repertoire of contention (Krinsky and Mische 2013).

The concepts of repertoire of strategies and stock of legacies can be used to analyze other social movements elsewhere. The identification of a predominant repertoire of strategies allows for the identification of elements fundamental to a social movement that could not have otherwise been perceived in the tracing of its narrative. First, it allows us to explain what is happening when the repertoire of contention is not deployed, narrating a much more dynamic and rich process of strategic action than is possible through the concept of repertoire of contention alone. Second, it opens the door to analyzing the internal complexity of the movement. In other words, even though there are more than 15 national organizations within the *piquetero* movement that carry out roadblocks, marches, and encampments, they do not share a common repertoire of strategies and frequently perform different strategies in the same situation, sometimes mutually learning, but in many other situations developing autonomous strategies that are a result of the stock of legacies specific to their organization. This internal richness would have never been apparent if the analysis had been reduced to the Tillyian approach alone. And third, the conceptualization of strategy making I have proposed helps to close the gap in the social movement literature between an approach that proposes the micro analysis of tactical trade-offs and the macro analysis of repertoires of contention. Instead, I offer a collective and historically rooted understanding of strategy making.

As shown in this chapter, the concepts of repertoire of strategies and stock of legacies help to bridge the artificial distinction between contentious and routine politics, observing the picture as a dynamic interaction involving the selective use of strategies based on inherited legacies that limit the perception of available options for action. In addition, the configuration of the political context and the innovative capacity of actors to perform actions that—though not always fully logical—are the result of intentionally attempting to produce a public, semi-public, or private event, leads to an analysis of strategies that may or may not involve disruption. In this way, Tilly's approach can be complemented in the analysis of the strategic actions of social movements across time.

References

Angell, Alan, 1998. "The left in Latin America since c. 1920." In: Leslie Bethell ed. *Latin America: politics and society since 1930.* Cambridge: Cambridge University Press, pp. 75–144.

Armelino, Martín, 2008. "Tensiones entre organización sindical y organización territorial: la experiencia de la CTA y la FTV en el período postcrisis." In: Sebastián Pereyra et al., eds. *La huella piquetera. Avatares de las organizaciones de desocupados después de 2001.* La Plata: Al Margen, pp. 141–83.

Auyero, Javier, 2003. *Contentious lives: two Argentine women, two protests, and the quest for recognition.* Durham: Duke University Press.

Barker, Colin et al., 2001. "Leadership matters: an introduction." In: Colin Barker, et al., eds. *Leadership and social movements.* Manchester: Manchester University Press, pp. 1–23.

Baud, Michiel and Rutten, Rosanne eds, 2004. *Popular intellectuals and social movements: framing protest in Asia, Africa, and Latin America.* Cambridge: Cambridge University Press.

Bourdieu, Pierre, 1998. *Practical reasons: on the theory of action.* Stanford: Stanford University Press.

———, 2000. *Pascalian meditations.* Stanford: Stanford University Press.

Carr, Barry and Ellner, Steve eds, 1993. *The Latin American left: from the fall of Allende to the perestroika.* Boulder: Westview Press.

Cerrutti, Marcela and Grimson, Alejandro, 2004. "Buenos Aires, neoliberalismo y después. Cambios socioeconómicos y respuestas populares." *Working Paper Series #04–04d.* Center for Migration and Development–Princeton University.

Doherty, Brian, 2013. "Tactics." In: David Snow, et al., eds. *The Wiley-Blackwell encyclopedia of social and political movements.* Oxford: Wiley-Blackwell, pp. 1315–21.

Emirbayer, Mustafa, 2010. "Tilly and Bourdieu." *The American Sociologist,* 41(4), pp. 400–22.

Fantasia, Rick, 1988. *Culture of solidarity: consciousness, action, and contemporary American workers.* Berkeley: University of California Press.

Fara, Luis 1985. "Luchas reivindicativas urbanas en un contexto autoritario. Los asentamientos de San Francisco Solano." In: Elizabeth Jelin, ed. *Los nuevos movimientos sociales.* Buenos Aires: Centro Editor de América Latina, pp. 120–39.

Fligstein, Neil and McAdam, Doug, 2011. "Toward a general theory of strategic action fields." *Sociological Theory,* 29(1), pp. 1–26.

Freedman, Lawrence, 2013. *Strategy: a history.* New York: Oxford University Press.

Gamson, William, 1975. *The strategy of social protest.* Homewood: Dorsey Press.

Ganz, Marshall, 2000. "Resources and resourcefulness: strategic capacity in the unionization of California agriculture, 1959–1966." *American Journal of Sociology,* 105(4), pp. 1003–62.

Germano, Carlos ed., 2005. *Piqueteros. Nueva realidad social.* Buenos Aires: ACEP-Konrad Adenauer Stiftung.

Goldstone, Jack ed., 2003. *States, parties, and social movements.* New York: Cambridge University Press.

Guevara, Ernesto "Che." 1997[1963]. *Obras completas.* Buenos Aires: MACLA.

Ichaso, Josefina, 2013. *Indicadores de conflictividad social 1980–2012.* Buenos Aires: Centro de Estudios para la Nueva Mayoría.

Isman, Raúl, 2004. *Los piquetes de La Matanza: de la aparición del movimiento social a la construcción de la unidad popular.* Buenos Aires: Nuevos Tiempos.

Jasper, James M., 2004. "A strategic approach to collective action: looking for agency in social movement choices." *Mobilization*, 9(1), pp. 1–16.

———, 2006. *Getting your way: strategic dilemmas in the real world.* Chicago: University of Chicago Press.

———, 2012. "Choice points, emotional batteries, and other ways to find strategic agency at the micro level." In: Gregory M. Maney et al., eds. *Strategies for social change.* Minneapolis: University of Minnesota Press, pp. 23–42.

Krinsky, John and Mische, Ann, 2013. "Formations and formalisms: Charles Tilly and the paradox of the actor." *Annual Review of Sociology*, 39(1), pp. 1–26.

Maney, Gregory M., et al., 2012. "An introduction to strategies for social change." In: Gregory M. Maney et al., eds. *Strategies for social change.* Minneapolis: University of Minnesota Press. xi-xxxviii.

Mao, Tse-Tung, 1965[1940]. "Current problems of tactics in the anti-Japanese united front." In: Tse-Tung Mao ed. *Selected works of Mao Tse-Tung.* Beijing: Foreign Language Press, pp. 421–30.

Marx, Karl, 1926[1852]. *The eighteenth brumaire of Louis Bonaparte.* New York: International Publishers.

McAdam, Doug, 1983. "Tactical innovation and the pace of insurgency." *American Sociological Review*, 48(6), pp. 735–54.

Merklen, Denis, 1991. *Asentamientos en La Matanza: la terquedad de lo nuestro.* Buenos Aires: Catálogos.

———, 2005. *Pobres ciudadanos. Las clases populares en la era democrática Argentina, 1983–2003.* Buenos Aires: Gorla.

Meyer, David and Staggenborg, Suzanne, 2012. "Thinking about strategy." In: Gregory M. Maney et al., eds. *Strategies for social change.* Minneapolis: University of Minnesota Press, pp. 3–22.

Moreno, Nahuel, 1980. *Tesis sobre las revoluciones del siglo XX. Actualización del programa de transición.* Buenos Aires: Antídoto.

Nepstad, Sharon Erickson and Vinthagen, Stellan, 2012. "Strategic choices in cross-national movements: a comparison of the Swedish and British plowshares movements." In: Gregory M. Maney et al., eds. *Strategies for social change.* Minneapolis: University of Minnesota Press, pp. 263–84.

Piven, Frances and Cloward, Richard, 1977. *Poor people's movements: why they succeed, how they failed.* New York: Vintage.

Prévôt-Schapira, Marie-France, 1999. "From utopia to pragmatism: the heritage of basismo in local government in the greater Buenos Aires region." *Bulletin of Latin American Research*, 18(2), pp. 227–39.

Roberts, Kenneth M., 1998. *Deepening democracy? The modern left and social movements in Chile and Peru.* Stanford: Stanford University Press.

———, 2002. "Social inequalities without class cleavages in Latin America's neoliberal era." *Studies in Comparative International Development*, 36(4), pp. 3–33.

Rossi, Federico M., 2013a. "Peronism." In: David Snow et al., eds. *The Wiley-Blackwell encyclopedia of social and political movements*. Oxford: Willey-Blackwell, pp. 925–28.

———, 2013b. "*Piqueteros* (workers/unemployment movement in Argentina)." In: David Snow et al., eds. *The Wiley-Blackwell encyclopedia of social and political movements*. Oxford: Wiley-Blackwell, pp. 929–32.

———, 2015. "The second wave of incorporation in Latin America: a conceptualization of the quest for inclusion applied to Argentina." *Latin American Politics and Society*, 57(1), pp. 1–28.

Sánchez, Pilar, 1997. *El cutralcazo: la pueblada de cutral co y plaza huincul*. Buenos Aires: Agora.

Schutz, Alfred, 1967. *The phenomenology of the social world*. Evanston, IL: Northwestern University Press.

Smithey, Lee A., 2009. "Social movement strategy, tactics, and collective identity." *Sociology Compass*, 3(4), pp. 658–71.

Sorel, Georges, 1999[1908]. *Reflections on violence*. Cambridge: Cambridge University Press.

Staggenborg, Suzanne, 1991. *The pro-choice movement: organization and activism in the abortion conflict*. New York: Oxford University Press.

Svampa, Maristella and Pereyra, Sebastián, 2003. *Entre la ruta y el barrio: la experiencia de las organizaciones piqueteras*. Buenos Aires: Biblos.

Tarcus, Horacio, 1996. *El marxismo olvidado en la Argentina: Silvio Frondizi y Milcíades Peña*. Buenos Aires: El Cielo por Asalto.

Taylor, Verta and Van Dyke, Nella, 2004. "Get up, stand up": tactical repertoires of social movements." In: David Snow et al., eds. *The Blackwell companion to social movements*. Oxford: Blackwell, pp. 262–93.

Tilly, Charles, 1986. *The contentious French*. Cambridge: Harvard University Press.

———, 1995. "Contentious repertoires in Great Britain, 1758–1834." In: Mark Traugott ed. *Repertoires and cycles of collective action*. Durham: Duke University Press, pp. 15–42.

———, 2006. *Regimes and repertoires*. Chicago: University of Chicago Press.

———, 2008. *Contentious performances*. New York: Cambridge University Press.

Wenger, Etienne, 1998. *Communities of practice: learning, meaning, and identity*. Cambridge: Cambridge University Press.

Chapter 3

Partisan Performance:
The Relational Construction of Brazilian
Youth Activist Publics

Ann Mische

Introduction[1]

In June 2013 the Brazilian streets exploded into protests, as a series of small demonstrations against transportation fare increases shifted dramatically in scale, with millions of people in the streets of over 100 cities at the peak of the movement on June 20. Protestors voiced a wide array of partially overlapping grievances—from precarious public services and ragged urban infrastructure to exorbitant expenditures on megaprojects, government corruption, police violence, unresponsive bureaucracies, poor quality education, and LGBTQ rights. While the rallies electrified the nation and brought many previously nonpoliticized people to the streets, they were also perplexing and troubling, particularly from the point of view of more traditional movement activists. One of the hallmarks of the rallies was the insistent—at times, virulent—rejection of political parties (and by association, most of the traditional social movements, civic organizations, and labor unions in Brazil) as legitimate participants, let alone as representatives or carriers of the demands of the protests. Partisan actors were shouted down, pushed off the streets, and at times, subjected to physical violence by their fellow protestors. Many long-time activists feared that this rejection of partisanship was an indicator of right-wing or even "fascist" tendencies in the movement. Others celebrated the spontaneity and horizontalism of the protests, with their rejection of centralized leadership and bureaucratic organization.

Opposition to partisanship in Brazil was not a "new" phenomenon in the June 2013 protests, although these episodes were startling in their intensity and vehemence. Anti-partisan sentiment in Brazil has a long and complicated

1   This chapter adapts, condenses, and theoretically reformulates some of the material presented in Partisan Publics: Communication and Contention across Brazilian Youth Activist Networks (Princeton University Press, 2008). It is used here with the permission of Princeton University Press. I would like to thank Marisa von Bülow, Federico Rossi, Mimi Keck, Ana Velitchkova, and an anonymous reviewer for their comments on earlier versions of this chapter.

history. The military dictatorship from 1964–1985 reigned in partisanship via a tightly controlled two-party system, while discouraging political activity on the part of the population, under the motif, "workers work, students study, and the government governs." As Brazil returned to multiparty democracy in the 1980s and 1990s, it remained characterized by a weakly institutionalized political party system, low levels of party identification, and strong distrust of politicians among the general population (Mainwaring 1999; Mainwaring and Scully 1995). At the same time, however, partisan activism on the left – and particularly the growth of the Workers' Party (PT) as a player in local, state and national politics – played a critical role in the construction of the social movement field in the 1980s, and perhaps more indirectly, in the construction of the broader field of civil society in the 1990s (Meneguello 1989; Keck 1992; Dagnino 1994, 2002; Doimo 1995; Sandoval 1998; Hochstetler 2000; Baiocchi 2003, 2005; Mische 2008). In part this was due to the strong coupling of partisan, labor, popular, student, and civic activism in the 1980s—a relationship that I argue began to unravel around the time of the 1992 impeachment movement, when the relation between partisan and civic activism became much more troubled and ambivalent.

This chapter highlights this ambivalence and puts it in historical perspective, taking an ethnographic look back at the construction of widely differing "publics" of youth activism in the 1980s and 1990s. During the mid-1990s, I spent over two years in São Paulo doing participant observation, interviews, network surveys, and archival research on Brazilian youth politics (for a more detailed account of this research and of the groups described below, see Mische 2008). In these publics, young activists struggled with the changing relationship between partisan identities and those of the other partially overlapping groups in which they participated, concurrently and over time (including the student movement, the Catholic youth pastoral, NGOs, antidiscrimination groups, professional associations, and business groups). Partisan affiliations were one component of those multiple identities, although certainly not the only ones in play. Yet I found that partisan relations—and attempts to manage these—cut across and influenced the dynamics of almost all of the other sectors, deeply informing the pragmatics of political talk and action within and between groups. Either partisan battles were being fought up front, as in many student movement events; or they were shoved underground, as in some of the pre-professional or business settings; or they formed a kind of overarching bridge, as in many of the church-based popular movements.

This leaves us with a somewhat puzzling phenomenon: Parties were everywhere in an emerging civil society—particularly among its most active practitioners—but to be partisan in the mid-1990s was often seen as being anti-civic. While it may be analytically possible to separate "civil" society from "political" society, as some democratic theorists have advocated, in practice it was often the same people who were involved in both. The challenge was not so much how to separate these distinct logics, but how to negotiate their often tense and ambiguous interface, as this played out in different kinds of movement settings and encounters.

To understand these dynamics, I argue for a reformulation of the concept of "publics" as *performative* as well as relational constructions. The publics that these young people were building during the period of democratic reconstruction were complex and multivalent, with many more identities and projects *potentially* in play than could be expressed in any given encounter. Participants had to negotiate which subset of their multiple identities could be expressed in particular interaction settings, and which needed to be put in the background or suppressed. I argue that youth activist publics in the 1980s and 1990s generated very different *styles of communication* in response to the challenges posed by their own relational complexity, contributing to the varying relationships to partisanship that I observed in my ethnographic work.

In what follows, I first highlight the problematics involved in the ambivalent relationship between partisan and civic engagement during Brazil's period of democratic reconstruction. I then propose a revised understanding of publics not as spaces of free expression, but rather of performative and relational *suppression* that enables and inhibits certain modes of political communication. I argue that this reconception allows us to analyze (but not resolve) the tensions between civic and partisan relations, while understanding their political generativity. I demonstrate the usefulness of this framework by analyzing five distinct (and sometimes contending) publics of Brazilian youth activism in the 1980s and 1990s: the traditional student movement, the Catholic youth pastoral, and the movements of black, professional, and business-oriented students. I end with a discussion of how this reconceptualization of publics contributes to a new understanding of the role of partisanship in civic life.

Partisan and Civic Engagement in Democratic Reconstruction

Partisanship and civic dialogue are often seen as two mutually opposing modes of communication. Proponents of deliberative democracy and a normatively oriented civil society decry the instrumentalism and strategic manipulation that is often associated with partisan politics (Cohen and Arato 1992; Bohman and Regh 1997; Cohen and Rogers 1998). F Advocates of civic engagement often celebrate extrapolitical forms of association—such as clubs, parents' groups, sporting activities, or faith communities—while neglecting or downplaying more explicitly political channels of institutional influence (Putnam 1993, 2000). Meanwhile, more hardnosed political analysts criticize the idealism of deliberative democrats, insisting on what they see as entrenched influences of interest and power in real political process (Elster 1998).

At issue here is how we combine our civic commitments with partisan and particularistic pursuits. As citizens, we are torn between competing involvements. On the one hand, we are concerned with the good of the whole—whether this is defined as the neighborhood, the polity, the nation, or the global community. On the other hand, we also experience commitments to various "parts" of this whole—the product of our participation in multiple social networks. These can represent private concerns about individual or family well-being, but can also refer to larger collectivities—religious, racial, ethnic, or national groups, for example, as well as other community, professional, commercial, or political interests. These commitments are not necessarily compatible with each other, and sometimes enter into direct contradiction, making it difficult to see how they all add up to a common "civic" good.

Disagreements over the common good often crystallize into larger ideological and tactical alliances that we come to know as political parties. In post-authoritarian politics, as countries move from decades of dictatorship into a somewhat shaky return to democratic institutions, partisanship poses a particular set of challenges and conundrums. Political parties are a necessary vehicle for citizen access to and participation in institutionalized politics—or rather, they can be. Historically, they have often been the vehicles for patronage politics, corruption, regional feuds, and pacts between elites (Mainwaring and Scully 1995; Mainwaring 1999). In a country such as Brazil, with an extremely low level of trust in public officials and politicians in general, the word "political," let alone "partisan," has often been turned into an ethical condemnation (an association that the dictatorship was all too eager to reinforce). This condemnation shadows the political class as a whole, even those who are trying to reform the political system in terms of access, ethics, and ideas.

Scholars working in a Habermasian tradition (Cohen and Arato 1992; Avritzer 2002) have argued for a strong distinction between the instrumental logic of political society—that is, political parties and other means of access to the institutional power of the state—and the discursive or communicative logic of the "public space" (even while arguing that there needs to be more connection between these). This perspective tends to celebrate the emergence of "autonomous" social movements and neighborhood associations in Brazil during and after the democratic opening as a sign of Brazil's strengthening civil society (Sader 1988). However, this work often elides the fact these emerging forms of social organization in the 1980s were permeated through and through with partisan associations. Brazil returned to a multiparty system in 1980 just as opposition leaders were returning from exile, contributing to a sudden flourishing of small opposition parties, notably the Workers' Party (PT), as well as other labor, socialist, and eventually communist parties. These were by and large parties of ideas, which demanded a higher degree of commitment and active engagement than was customary in Brazilian politics (Mainwaring 1999).

As a result, the country saw a rush of grassroots party-building at the same time as it experienced an explosion of urban and rural popular movements, which had started under the protective umbrella of the Catholic Church. It was not simply the case that the parties allied with the popular movements, or even that they went to the popular movements to colonize or recruit (although this did happen in some cases). Rather, many leaders in labor and popular movements went to the party; in the case of the PT in particular, they were building the party at the grassroots level. During the same period, Brazil's centralized student organizations, such as the National Student Union (UNE), as well as local university and high school organizations, returned to legality and strove to rebuild themselves, with strong ties to the partisan factions of the left. While this period of institutional reconstruction was certainly contentious, it was also extremely energetic and forward moving. Partisan participation served both a bridging and a bonding function in youth politics (Putnam 2000); it helped to give narrative and network cohesion to expanding activist communities, at the same time as these activists built organizations and formed alliances across institutional sectors. To be partisan was understood by activists to be an expression of citizenship, a contribution to the rebuilding of democratic institutions in Brazil.

The 1992 mobilizations for the impeachment of President Fernando Collor de Melo marked a turning point in the relationship between partisan and civic discourse. With the country mesmerized by the civic outpouring of opposition to the Collor government, and further disillusioned by fresh evidence of corruption among Brazil's political leaders, the impeachment deepened the gap between ideas of partisanship and civic virtue, despite the fact that partisan mediation played an important role in the convergence of the movement against Collor (Mische 2008). The "civic" discourse moved from the popular movements and NGO community into the modernizing business and professional sectors, which began to talk about "business citizenship" (*cidadania empresarial*). This was reinforced by liberalizing efforts of the Cardoso regimes to shift some social services to NGOs and other third-sector organizations. Some of these actors were much less accepting of the strongly politicized understanding of citizenship offered by the popular movements of the 1980s, grounded in notions of social rights, community empowerment, and influence on the state (Dagnino 2002, 2005).

During the 1990s, Brazilian youth politics saw the emergence of several different kinds of innovative student groups that challenged the highly adversarial, overtly partisan dynamic of Brazil's traditional student movement. These challengers included groups engaged in anti-discrimination struggles (particularly the black student movement), in pre-professional activism (especially the movement of "course executives"), and in business entrepreneurship (via the "junior enterprises"). In different ways, these groups tended to see partisanship as an impediment to effective political communication, and as a result, pushed partisan identities to the background of their publics-in-formation. However, I would argue that such attempts to banish partisan identities were a problem for youth activists in the 1990s, even though they made those attempts in the name of enhancing the quality of democratic communication. While they did sometimes succeed in having richer discussions, they risked the paralysis and depolitization that can result from the loss of the more challenging and provocative forms of democratic participation, particularly those committed to expanding social and political inclusion. At the same time, these young activists had put their finger on a sore spot for democratic politics: How do you maintain partisan commitments while also engaging in the more exploratory and reflective talk that keeps political communication from degenerating into rigid posturing and manipulation?

Communication in Publics: A Relational-Pragmatic Model

In order to understand this problem, we need to conceptualize publics in such a way as to challenge the strong divide between instrumental and communicative forms of action. I argue that partisan and civic modes of communication can in fact be closely interconnected. While partisanship can contribute to polarization, manipulation, distrust, and communicative stalemate, it can also be a force for bridging and bonding, for cross-sectoral dialogue, and for civic-institutional creativity. Parties can bring dispersed constituencies and sectors together, create forums for debate, and provide the competitive impetus and vision for institution building in the public arena. Rather than seeing a collaboratively oriented "public sphere" (or "civil society") in opposition to the competitive dynamics of institutionalized power politics, we should focus on the ways in which people and organizations move between multiple modes of political communication in different kinds of public encounters. That is, we need to examine how people *perform* their varied identities—partisan, civic, religious, racial, professional, family, and others—in particular relational settings.

To help us understand the interconnections between partisanship and civic life, I propose what I call a "relational-pragmatic" model of political communication, drawing on theories of public performativity as well as recent work linking networks and cultural process. In a series of recent works, Jeffrey Alexander (2004, 2008) suggests that the concept of performativity can help us to understand how ritual and strategy are fused in modern life, as well as when attempts at fusion fail. Alexander argues that with the increasing complexity, fragmentation, and contentiousness of modern life, culturally resonant performances are simultaneously more difficult and more necessary for creating strong and powerful bonds between public leaders and their audiences. I agree with Alexander's assertion that the multiple publics that compose social life involve complex performances that fuse ritual and strategy. However, I am less interested in the relation between leaders and followers *per se* than in the *styles of communication*, as well as the *changing relationships*, that emerge in different contexts of performative interaction. People perform not just for somewhat removed, although potentially critical, audiences, but for real or potential co-performers—often on the same stage—who may or may not accept the proposed definition of the situation and adjust their own performances accordingly.

Recently, students of political culture have begun to focus attention not just on cultural representations (whether understood as symbols, codes, schemas, or narratives), but rather on how these are filtered through what Goffman (1974, 1981) calls the "footings" of performative interaction. Footings are shifting forms of alignment, posturing, and self-projection within talk that construct shared framings of "what is going on here" within a given interaction setting. Footings define the changing participation roles of the interaction partners (for example, as speaker, recipient, or audience), as well as embed them (grammatically, semantically, and institutionally) in larger temporal and relational contexts. Such footings can be contested and negotiated, but also collectively encouraged and enforced. Building upon Goffman's work, Nina Eliasoph and Paul Lichterman define "group styles" as "recurrent patterns of interaction that arise from a group's shared assumptions about what constitutes good or adequate participation in the group setting" (Eliasoph and Lichterman 2003, p. 737; Eliasoph 1998; Lichterman 2005, 2012). Styles represent shared assumptions about "what talk is for," that is, the appropriate footings for participants within a given conversational setting.

To some extent, styles of talk are shaped by the avowed purpose or task of the communicative encounter. A recreational encounter among friends will evoke a different set of footings than a religious service, a scholarly seminar, a protest rally, or a political party congress. However, while the modes of communication that predominate in a given setting often follow established scripts or institutional templates, styles are not determined by the task or the institutional setting. Rather, those tasks and purposes themselves must still be constituted interactionally, through the shared performances of the participants. As Goffman has shown us, it takes shared dramaturgic work to define a given setting as work or play, as public or private, or as enacting one of our multiple identities over another. Moreover, actors can contest the joint definition of the situation or break the institutionalized frame; style and task do not necessarily walk hand in hand. Styles that are developed and honed in one setting can be carried by actors to new settings, in which they do not always "fit" the predominant definition of collective purpose or task. For example, in the Brazilian case, young activists who developed their leadership skills in the highly collaborative, self-reflective settings of the Catholic youth pastoral often found themselves at a stylistic disadvantage when they moved into the competitive, maneuver-driven settings of the traditional student movement.

Styles are not only constitutive of tasks, but also of social relationships. As Paul McLean (2007) demonstrates, past, present, and proposed ties with others are often at stake in our performative interaction with others. Through our communicative practices, we align ourselves with and against different sets of others, thus performing our interpersonal relationships as well as our group affiliations. The shifting enactment of those relationships is a critical dimension of style. Because of this, styles do not only respond to tasks and templates of institutional contexts, but also to the relational composition of the given encounter.

I propose that we incorporate a stronger relational and pragmatic component to our understanding of political communication: *Communicative styles develop out of the social and cultural challenges of local configurations of relations.* A student or religious group, for example, will need to find a way to coordinate, manage, foreground, or background the multiple possible identities that participants bring into any given interaction setting, via their overlapping affiliations in other kinds of groups. We can refer to these as "styles" because they are patterned and recognizable, to participants as well as to relevant sets of non-participants. However, their good exercise is also a *skill* that can be deployed more or less effectively by individuals and adapted to new settings as they arise. As actors carry these skills in new settings, they in turn help to build new relations—and constitute new kinds of institutional intersections—in the broader field. This dynamic can be summarized in the following model (see Figure 3.1):

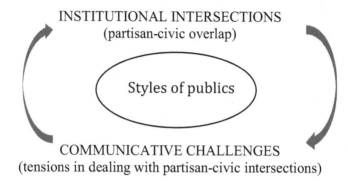

INSTITUTIONAL INTERSECTIONS
(partisan-civic overlap)

Styles of publics

COMMUNICATIVE CHALLENGES
(tensions in dealing with partisan-civic intersections)

Figure 3.1   Communication in Publics: A Relational-Pragmatic Model

Styles are important because they inform the performances that constitute different kinds of publics. They underlie choices about what dimensions of shared relations and projects should be expressed or suppressed in public settings. While these "choices" often have routine, taken-for-granted, or institutional dimensions, they can also consist of strategic or negotiated responses to the array of relations potentially in play within a given setting. In such publics, actors tied by multiple relationships selectively activate and deactivate various strands of their identities—including their partisan identities—as they communicate, build relations, and pursue joint actions. This model in turn leads us to reformulate our notion of publics to highlight their character not simply as forums for free expression, but rather as fundamentally shaped by the *suppression* of certain kinds of identities and relations.

Relational Enactment and Suppression in Complex Publics

The term "public" is ubiquitous in studies of civil society and civic association. Building on Habermas's seminal study of the transformation of the bourgeois public sphere, scholars have looked at publics as arenas for more or less free and open-ended flows of ideas and debate, related to shared understandings of the "common good" (Habermas 1989; Calhoun 1993). Publics, Habermas noted, took shape in eighteenth-century urban coffee houses and salons, in which people came together in unaccustomed combinations, often mixing class, professional, and regional backgrounds. Many scholars have since taken issue with exclusionary aspect of such publics, pointing out the marginalization of actors along gender, class, and racial lines (Ryan 1990; Fraser 1992; Honig 1992). Still, the ideal of free spaces for open-ended rational-critical debate among heterogeneous actors has been a seminal theme of recent theories of civil society and deliberative democracy.

While building on this ideal, I believe we should challenge and reframe the conventional notion of publics so as to focus on the relational mechanisms by which they are constructed. A number of scholars have offered reformulations of the notion of publics so as to link them with theories of social networks. For example, Margaret Somers (1993) describes regional variation in citizenship practices as resulting from different historically grounded "relational settings," combining network, institutional, and cultural configurations. Likewise, Mustafa Emirbayer and Mimi Sheller (1999) conceive of publics as "interstitial networks of individuals and groups acting as citizens," involving "open-ended flows of communication that enable socially distant interlocutors to bridge social-network positions, formulate collective orientations, and generate psychical "working alliances," in pursuit of influence over issues of common concern (Emirbayer and Sheller 1999, p. 156). Publics are relational constructions with subaltern, intermediate, and elite manifestations, some of which involve face-to-face interaction while others are more distant in time and space.[2]

While highlighting the relational dimension of publics, these approaches accord with conventional accounts in conceiving of publics as forums for the free expression of ideas. However, we cannot understand such public expressions without tending to their flip side: the suppression of identities and relations that makes such communication possible. I am not here referring to the common, and quite important, critique of the concept of the public sphere for being exclusionary, in the sense that certain groups, individuals, or categories are either explicitly or implicitly prevented from participation. Rather, I argue that the composition of the public in itself depends upon the suppression of many of the multiple identities and involvements that participants could, potentially, bring into play. Such suppression is in fact crucial to Habermas' idea of the rational-critical public sphere, in which universalizing arguments are seen as more important than particularistic identities or interests. However, the communicative practices involved in such suppression have rarely been brought to the fore of thinking about public debate. The particularistic identities and interests of participants in a coffee house or salon do not magically disappear; they are momentarily, provisionally suppressed by the actors themselves, who restrain themselves from bringing them into public

---

2 For a review of some recent relational approaches to sociology from the point of view of network analysis, see Mische 2011; see also Emirbayer 1999. For relational approaches to citizenship, civil society, and publics, see Somers 1993, 1998; Mische 1996, 2003; Mische and Pattison 2000; Ikegami 2000, 2005; Smilde 2004, 2007; Fishman 2004; Baiocchi 2005; von Bülow 2011; Abers 2000; Abers and Keck 2013.

display (although as Goffman would note, the cynicism or sincerity of this restraint may vary).[3]

Far from debates about democratic theory, Harrison White and his colleagues have offered a less normative description of publics as short-term buffer zones that ease transitions between more specialized, longer-term "network-domains."[4] White builds on Goffman's work on interaction in public spaces by describing how participants in publics become decoupled from other identities and involvements, in bubble-like interactions that alter the experience of time. Within a public, participants experience a momentary sense of connectedness due to the suspension of surrounding ties. "The social network of the public is perceived as fully connected, because other network-domains and their particular histories are suppressed. Essential to its mechanism is a decoupling of times, whereby time in public is always a continuing present time, an historic present" (White 1995, p. 1054).

In this view, publics are not just "networks," and nor are they simply "spaces of debate"; rather they are liminal settings of interaction that momentarily suspend participants from their ongoing involvements and allow for relational mixing as well as movement into new forms of involvement. A public in Goffman's most limited sense might not involve debate at all; it might involve a ritual tipping of hats in a public square, the tense silence of an elevator, or the observant detachment of a crowded subway, in which everyone is momentarily connected and equalized for the short span of the ride. On the other hand, publics also may consist of more discursive contexts such as cocktail parties, salons, public ceremonies, deliberative assemblies, protest rallies, or Mardi Gras celebrations, which also bring usually segmented groups and individuals together in unaccustomed combinations. As Mische and White (1998) elaborate:

> [Publics] function by reducing the uncertain and problematic nature of such spaces by positing minimally recognizable identities, maximally decontextualized from the complex array of relations and story sets that each actor brings to the occasion. Publics create temporary social scaffoldings in which fully connected actors (who may be tied either through equivalence or hierarchy) engage in

---

3   Goffman (1959) notes that performances vary on a spectrum from sincere to cynical. In publics, some actors might, accordingly, cynically conceal their personal or partisan motivations while professing concern for the common good; or they might sincerely believe that they are acting on behalf of the larger collectivity, rather than promoting their personal point of view. Most performances, Goffman would agree, fall somewhere in the middle.

4   A "network-domain," in White's sense, links networks and discourse by referring to specialized sets of ties and related stories that keep those ties moving forward through a continuous process of reflection and updating. With the complexity of modern life, we are continuously forced to switch back and forth between multiple network-domains, thus evoking the need for the buffering transition zones of publics. See White 1995, 2008; Mische and White 1998; Godart and White 2010; Fontdevila 2010.

highly ritualized interactions. ... Time is provisionally suppressed in publics, decoupling actors from the multiple temporalities in which they are embedded (Mische and White 1998, p. 705).

In this perspective, "nothing happens" in a public, or at least, nothing that evokes surprise or high stakes uncertainty among participants. The ritualization of the public and the suspension of outside identities and relations help to keep the bubble intact, at least until participants switch back into more specialized network-domains. Yet this claim of the inconsequentiality of publics is somewhat disconcerting. While we can relatively easily see this frozen quality in a subway, a cocktail party, a salon, or even a carnival parade—in which pragmatic or instrumental pursuits are clearly suspended—it is less obvious at a protest rally or deliberative assembly, in which participants are ostensibly trying to accomplish something. However, even contentious public gatherings aimed at challenging the status quo have a suspended, ritual character. Activists know that at a well-organized rally, there are no surprises. Factional in-fighting is kept carefully in check and a highly ritualized script is worked out ahead of time.

Squaring this perspective with deliberative assemblies is a bit harder, since such assemblies are, after all, supposed to deliberate, that is, to decide what to do, to make something happen. Certainly there must be stakes in such deliberation; as Mansbridge (1983) shows in her seminal study of town meetings and consensual workplaces, deliberative settings are often permeated with overt or latent contention. But But even in the most idealized conceptions of deliberative democracy, private or particularistic stakes must be carefully suspended as participants focus on the collective good. Note again that even the strong versions of "democratic publics" depend on suppression, a fact not underlined by most democratic theorists.

In contentious real life deliberations, such suppression is even more vital, as participants struggle to construct a sometimes tenuous and fragile sense of common ground and shared purposes amidst heterogeneous identities and projects. In addition to suppression, some kind of unifying ritual is necessary to achieve the decontextualization and simplification of identity needed to provisionally detach people from their ongoing purposes and involvements and thereby make deliberation possible. Such ritual may consist of formal rules of order, of an opening prayer, pledge, or song, or of a potluck supper or a trip to the bar after the meeting (as they say in Brazil, "everything ends in pizza"). While the idea of ritual does not fit comfortably with the idea of "rational-critical debate," it would be hard to find successful deliberative publics that do not have either a strong or weak form of ritual integration.

I depart to some degree from the perspective of White and his colleagues by considering publics as not necessarily inconsequential, but rather as places where things do potentially happen. Identities and projects are elaborated, decisions reached, and alliances forged within the liminal bubbles of publics. We can see a touch of the classic division between expressive and instrumental action in White's conception of publics, although White along with Habermas would insist that this is an historical, and not just an analytical, division. Both argue that the invention of relatively free-form, open-ended forums of conversation and debate, detached from instrumental purposes or stakes, was only made possible with the institutional differentiation (or "decoupling") of modernity. Nevertheless, when we look explicitly at *political* communication, ideas and purposes are very much connected. In fact, the linking of ideas, purposes, and actions—especially in situations of varied stakes and power relations—is what politics is about.

Political communication is facilitated when actors can carve out spaces "in between," that is, not dominated by single identities or membership blocks, but positioned at the intersections of multiple identities, projects, and forms of political intervention. I define such publics as *performatively constructed spaces in which actors temporarily suspend at least some aspects of their identities and involvements in order to generate the possibility of provisionally equalized and synchronized relationships.* In such settings, provisional homogeneities are constructed along a reduced identity dimension, in which some subset of the possible ties in play is (at least partially) backgrounded or suppressed. This suppression can be intentional and explicit, such as when the rule of "no partisan talk" or "leave religion at the door" is a clearly acknowledged and sanctioned group norm. Or it can be implicit and informal, negotiated and reinforced interactionally but never arriving at the level of a conscious directive. These interstitial spaces buffer relations between individuals and collectivities that otherwise may be engaged in particularistic and contending projects. They often draw upon ambiguity and ritual in order to find points of connection that generate productive relationships and new forms of joint action.

To call such publics "equalized" and "synchronized" does not mean that power differentials, cultural conflicts, or contending projects are eliminated from the political domain. As many scholars have pointed out, such divisions are an essential and irreducible dimension of political life (Young 1990, 2000; Fraser 1992; Benhabib 1996; Gutmann and Thomson 1996; Gutmann 2002). Nevertheless, productive communication does sometimes take place across such divides, and this communication drives both the construction of civic institutions as well as new kinds of public collaboration and coalition-building. Such communication is possible through the cultural and performative work that actors invest in constructing a provisional homogeneity out of complex and possibly contentious relations.

However, these moments of intensified cross-sectoral dialogue (or "civic unity") are extremely fragile and fraught with latent conflict. Suppressed identities, purposes, and relations do not magically disappear. They are present in a state of latency that always has the potential to break through into public expression. Mische and White (1998) describe such eruptions of latent or suppressed relations in a public as "situations," which are analogous to what Goffman (1974) calls "breaking frame." A private argument can loudly spill over into a subway car or elevator; a political faction can unexpectedly denounce co-organizers at a protest rally; neighborly rivalries can tumble into view in a town assembly. Suddenly stakes are heightened and outcomes thrown into a state of radical uncertainty. These performative breaches can be repaired through ritual, coercion, mediation, or some combination of these. Such repair efforts may restore the public to its previous stability, or alternatively reconfigure its component relations and send communication in a new direction.

This conception of publics makes a general theoretical contribution in understanding how multiple relations and identities become activated and deactivated in the performative play of public settings. But more specifically for the purposes of this chapter, it allows us to analyze the ways in which political actors navigate among the partisan and civic components of their multiple affiliations as they build relationships and pursue projects in a complex field. By focusing on the performative enactment of different identities and relations within complex publics, we move beyond the instrumental-expressive divide and show how partisanship and civic life are intertwined. In the empirical discussion below, I show how political actors enact their partisan (and other) relations in different ways, variously expressing and suppressing these identities as they wrestle with the complexities of relation-building in particular settings and situations.

Wrestling with Partisanship in Emerging Publics

In the Brazilian youth activist publics that I studied in the 1990s, activists needed to devote considerable communicative work to the selective activation and deactivation of the multiple identities and relations that were potentially in play. Many activists had multiple affiliations across different political sectors, including the student movement, church-based groups, urban popular movements, socialist organizations, NGOs, labor unions, and professional or business groups, often accompanied by participation in contending political parties and factions. However, in the different institutional contexts of youth activism, varying subsets of those relations were highlighted, while others were downplayed. In what follows, I will discuss how young people involved in different configurations of overlapping publics—student, Catholic, black, professional, and business—wrestled with the tensions between their civic and partisan engagements, as they responded to their own internal relational complexity as well as their positioning in the multisectoral field.

Student Publics: Unity and Compartmentalization

Within the field of Brazilian youth politics in the 1990s, the traditional student movement, with its capstone centralized organization, the National Student Union (UNE), represented the symbolic embodiment of the partisan style of organization. The publics of UNE (congresses, councils, encounters) were dominated by highly adversarial modes of communication, revolving around internal competition among partisan factions for control of the organization. At the same time, as a highly visible organization with a storied, treasured past, UNE aspired to be a player in the national arena of *civic* organizations. UNE prided itself in taking part in many civic movements and consultative councils, in addition to serving as a launching pad for young leaders into political careers. Because of this civic and political visibility, control of the organization was a high stakes prize among the youth wings of the political parties (and party factions) of the left, with leadership distributed by a system of proportional representation, determined by hard fought elections (and intensely negotiated electoral alignments). As a result, partisan identities were highly salient in student publics, with partisan affiliations tightly fused with the student identity. Many students reported that it was nearly impossible to have any active voice or position in the student movement without being affiliated with a political party.

From interviews and surveys conducted during student movement events in the mid-1990s, I found that many participants had a wide array of affiliations beyond the traditional student organizations. Among 21 respondents at a meeting of UNE's directorate in 1996, all belonged to political parties (and party factions), arrayed along the spectrum of extreme to center left. About half participated in professional and/or socialist organizations, and about 20 percent had concurrent or past participation in popular movements, labor unions, church-based groups, NGOs, and/or research organizations. While these other kinds of groups were not completely invisible at student events, they were often relegated a more marginal role, as partisan contestation (and the negotiation of electoral "slates") took front and center. At the raucous and colorful congresses of UNE, participants' multiple affiliations were funneled into a much narrower focus on student and partisan identities, with other affiliations either suppressed or relegated to a secondary, segregated status (for example, to side forums dedicated to professional, black, or Catholic groups). In moments of high partisan tension, participants ritually declared their unity "as students," synchronizing their voices in the historic chant of "UNE SOMOS NOS, NOSSA FORÇA E NOSSA VOZ" ("UNE is us, our force, and our voice").

Historically, UNE had had an uneasy relationship with its own strong partisan orientation, as it tried to reconcile its combination of partisan and civic logics. When UNE was in the process of reconstituting itself in the *abertura* period (after having been brutally crushed by the dictatorship in 1968), the UNE directorate explicitly addressed the issue of its relationship with political parties, which themselves had just been relegalized in 1980. A statement of the directorship in 1980 reflects this tension:

> 1. The directorate reaffirms that, in principle, UNE is an organization representing all Brazilian students, independent of race, color, sex, ideology, or religious belief; being, therefore, *unitary, apartisan, not submitting itself to any Party, and to none of them affiliated.*

2. For this reason, UNE does not delegate to any Director or student the power to represent it within the structure of the Parties. On the other hand, *UNE defends and stimulates the participation of students, including its Directors, in political parties*, as an individual option, as a form of contribution to the democratic struggle of the Brazilian people (Resolution of the UNE directorate, UNE document, December 6, 1980, emphasis added).

Here we see the civic (as opposed to partisan) status of UNE swinging on an analytical hinge: UNE *as an organization* was non-partisan, representing all students; however, UNE's leaders, *as citizens* were permitted and in fact encouraged to participate in parties as part of their democratic duties. In other words, UNE is apartisan, but its directors are not. This subtle compartmentalization of the identity of the organization from that of its members enabled one form of what I call "partisan bridging" (Mische 2008), that is, the leveraging of (partially) suppressed partisan identities to build other kinds of relationships in a civic arena. This discursive maneuver allowed UNE to qualify its own actions as civic, rather than partisan, thus enabling its very partisan activists to construct bridges on behalf of UNE with other kinds of civic actors in Brazil. As this document indicates, in the 1980s partisan activism was conceived by many activists as fundamentally civic and democratic—an association that would become more difficult in the 1990s.

How do these dynamics reflect the model of publics that I have theorized above? The complex set of institutional intersections within student publics required leaders to manage a *student* organization with a long history of *civic* engagement, even as they were involved in a complex web of *partisan* competition. These three primary identities co-existed uneasily, with considerable internal dissension about how much weight should be given to each. The communicative challenges of maintaining a unitary, centralized institution claiming to represent all Brazilian students in the face of fierce factionalism required a form of identity play in which activists switched back and forth among those three identities in both strategic and ritualized ways. Negotiations between these three identities took center stage in student publics, suppressing the activation of more specialized identities (for example, professional, religious, race, or gender) by relegating them to a marginalized position. The resulting style was highly competitive internally yet euphoric in its declarations of unity. Most political elaboration took place inside factions, while student congresses turned into vehicles for discursive positioning and backstage negotiations. Meanwhile, student leaders engaged in ritualized celebrations of the unified and apartisan UNE, "present in all of the great moments of Brazilian history."

Catholic Youth Publics: Integration and Autonomy

A quite different relationship to partisanship can be seen in the Catholic Youth Pastoral (*Pastoral de Juventude*), the other major form of youth activism to emerge in the late 1970s and early 1980s. Stylistically, the Catholic youth publics were almost diametrically opposed to those of the student movement; they were consensus-oriented, highly self-reflective, and committed to an inclusive, dialogic internal pedagogy. Building on the earlier "Catholic Action" movement of the early 1960s (with its praxis-oriented methodology of "See, Judge, Act"), the youth pastoral expressed the Catholic Church's growing commitment during that period to social justice, human rights, and the poor, as manifested by its support for urban and rural popular movements as well as movements for democracy and human rights. As with the student movement, the youth pastoral was in ascension at the same time that Brazil saw an explosion of popular movements (in which many of the Catholic youth leaders played important roles), as well as the return to a multiparty system. Many Catholic activists were deeply embedded in densely overlapping movement and partisan networks, particularly in the urban peripheries. As a result, they wrestled self-consciously with the relationship between their religious, popular, and partisan activism.

In 1995, I surveyed 27 youth leaders at a São Paulo regional assembly of PJMP (the *Pastoral de Juventude do Meio Popular*, one of the more radical branches based in the "popular milieu," or poor urban neighborhoods). I found that nearly all of the young people had begun their participation prior to the impeachment movement, mostly in the heady partisan days of the 1980s. More than half had formal partisan affiliations—almost all of them with the Workers' Party (PT)—and most of the rest declared themselves to be PT sympathizers. Most also participated in urban popular movements for education, health, transportation, or housing, and about a third also had concurrent or past participation in student groups, NGOs, antidiscrimination organizations, and/or labor unions.

The more collaborative style of Catholic Youth Pastoral (in comparison to the student movement) was facilitated by the fact that most activists were associated with the same party. Internal factional divisions were downplayed as activists used both self-reflection and religious ritual to integrate their "intermediary" identities (as they referred to them) with their Catholic activism. Most of those who were involved in political party activism saw this as a natural extension of their Catholic and popular movement involvements, although it did generate enough tension to warrant special reflection sessions in several of the youth encounters I observed (that is, small breakout groups charged with discussing "the relationship of the pastoral with political parties"). For the most part, the challenge was framed as that of "integrating" their multiple involvements as they worked together on the collective project of "building the Kingdom of God on Earth."

Historically the challenges of linking faith and partisanship had been the subject of considerable reflection and debate. In the following discussion text elaborated by a team of PJ youth leaders in São Paulo in 1982, we can hear the bold assertion of a biblically supported link between the religious and partisan components of their identities:

> The God of the Old Testament and the God of Jesus is a PARTISAN GOD ...
> By the life of Jesus, it is clear that God TOOK A SIDE (*"tomou partido"*) in the

grand conflict that existed in society; He took a side for JUSTICE, the POOR, the EXPLOITED (PJMP discussion booklet "Pedagogia e Projeto," 1982, capitalization in original).

The text uses the Portuguese phrase *"tomou partido,"* which translates best as "took a side," but uses the same word for "party." Clearly there is an attempt to reclaim the words "partisan" and "party," cleansing them of connotations of corruption and manipulation, and infusing them with moral righteousness and political commitment.   In the early 1980s, discussions of this sort were still taking place under the official auspices of the Catholic Church, at least in more progressive centers such as São Paulo, where seminars producing such booklets were supported by the Archdiocesan coordination of the youth pastoral. However, by the mid-1980s, the young militants who were articulating the more radical versions of the youth pastoral began to enter into direct conflict with the local Church hierarchy, which was concerned with what they saw as the co-optation of their leadership by the vanguardist political factions of the left. To combat this, the clerical advisers of the youth pastoral offered a forceful call for a respect for the *autonomy* of the various spheres of actions—a mandate which is, at least on the surface, in direct contradiction with the desire for integration:

> Political militancy should *respect the specificity and autonomy of the pastoral,* as the pastoral should respect the autonomy and structure of the popular movements, unions, and parties. It would not be good if these were tutored by the Church, if the bishop or priest were to control what the intermediate organizations do or think. ... On the other hand, we need to *avoid the error of instrumentalizing the pastoral,* which could lead to the mistake of ... reducing the pastoral to the youth wing of the party (PJ clerical advisor's booklet, "Os Cristãos e a Militância Política," 1988, emphasis added).

To sum up the model of publics in play here, institutional intersections within Catholic youth publics required leaders to combine their *religious* commitments with participation in the *popular* movements, at the same time as they threw themselves into intense *partisan* activism. The leaders of the youth pastoral saw these as different dimensions of the same struggle, although they wrestled with the communicative challenges of integrating these in their daily lives. Recognizing that the institutional logics (and practical demands) of these three forms of activism could overtake and undermine each other, they talked often and forcefully about the autonomy of these different "spheres." In fact, the oft-noted danger of having religious faith overrun by the partisan logic seemed to reinforce the internal valorization of their consensual, self-reflective style. This style suppressed competition and schooled young leaders in a form of political intervention oriented toward dialogue and inclusion. But just as the student movement's stress on unity marked internal fissures that threatened to divide it, the youth pastoral's frequent reference to autonomy points to a trouble spot—the difficulties in practice of maintaining a separation between these logics in a relational context that was so densely interwoven.

Challenger Publics: Problematization, Taboo, and Rejection

When I did my field research in the 1990s, the student and Catholic publics were highly institutionalized, with well-established, routinized procedures for dealing with their own internal heterogeneity. While the tensions between their partisan and civic identities did not disappear, they were performatively managed by young activists in relatively stable and predictable ways. However, in the 1990s a number of student groups emerged in the universities that challenged the primacy of UNE (and other traditional student organizations), criticizing their highly competitive orientation, as well as the lack of attention to racial, gender, and professional identities. Sometimes these groups drew directly on the more collaborative repertoire of the Catholic youth pastoral (in which some of the activists got their start), but they also introduced new, hybrid ways of building publics. Here I focus on the ways in which they wrestled with their own relational complexity as they worked to build these challenger publics, and in particular, how they responded to the tension between the partisan and civic components of their activism.

Black University Scholars

One of the challenges to traditional student activism in the 1990s came from a group that called itself the National Coordination of Black University Scholars (CONUN). CONUN emerged as a caucus of black students within the congresses of UNE that questioned the lack of attention to racial issues in student politics, going on to organize a number of successful national seminars thematizing the problem of race in the academy. In my survey of leaders at a national planning meeting, I found that a large proportion were long-time activists; among the 20 respondents, more than two-thirds began their participation in the highly partisan 1980s. More than half got their start in religious groups (mostly the Catholic youth pastoral), and about half had concurrent or prior participation in political parties, NGOs, and popular movements. Among those with partisan affiliations, about 80 percent were associated with the PT, with the rest scattered across a variety of parties of the left and center-left.

Despite these multiple involvements, they gathered in the meetings of CONUN *as black activists*, attempting to redress the neglect of racial issues within the traditional student movement, as well as within the academy more generally. They focused on the unifying identity of race while working hard to suppress the partisan and ideological identities that actively divided them in other contexts. Over several years of meetings, the student leaders in CONUN had developed a particular style of public in which they constructed homogeneity around racial identities, subordinating partisan affiliations and using race to problematize their participation in other sectors. While it may seem obvious that black activists highlight race as a unifying identity, this was not, in fact, inevitable. These activists shared many other dimensions of their identities that were explicitly backgrounded during their encounters as CONUN. Moreover, the construction of "blackness" in Brazil was far more tenuous and contested than in the more racially polarized US, given Brazil's complex history of miscegenation and lack of state-codified racial categories, which has made racially-based organizing difficult for black activists (Marx 1998; Telles 2004).

Like other movements, the CONUN leaders had wrestled with issues of partisanship in black student politics. One of the coordinators, in São Paulo, Marcos, described long and tumultuous meetings resulting from ideological clashes between activists: "You have black militants linked to diverse parties and from time to time they confuse the ideas of the black movement with the partisan movement." However, he said that they had developed group norms and practices by which they held partisan rivalries in abeyance:

> *Marcos: The racial question is way above the ideological question*, at least for me, since I don't know any party that has this discussion solid, clear, with concrete proposals ... I have my ideology, but to the extent that I begin to discuss racial questions, *I am obliged to have a supra-partisan reading*, to locate the racial question as the principal axis of my discussion ...

> *AM:* How successful are you at this, because it can be very complicated ...

> *Marcos:* No, within our group this was always very clear. We have problems when we have an open event. ... To the extent that we have been meeting already for four years, some things have already become concrete within the group. People who arrive and who don't fit themselves within the rules of our group, these people tend to leave. Not that our rules are necessarily the correct ones (Interviewed October 16, 1995).

Marcos described the "rules of our group"—or in the terminology of this chapter, the communicative style that constituted the black student publics—as a conscious downplaying of partisan identity, in order to focus on questions of racial exclusion that were seen as supra-ideological (with "ideology" here serving as an indicator of partisan and factional alignment). That is, they highlighted their *racial* identities and used these to problemetize both their *student* and their *partisan* activism. Over time, they had worked out a conversational "footing" (to use Goffman's term) that allowed them to do this, even if hot-headed newcomers could occasionally arrive and disrupt that footing. They constructed publics that suppressed partisan and territorial disputes while building provisional homogeneity around a shared racial identity. The resulting style was self-reflective, purposeful, and yet still militant in its external positioning. While it had certain infrastructural fragilities (due in part to its rejection of the status of "organization"), the CONUN public constituted itself as rare forum of reflective, critical deliberation that challenged social exclusion while holding partisanship provisionally at bay.

Forum of Course Executives

A second form of challenge in the 1990s came from associations known as "course executives," organized in particular professional areas of study in the universities (for example, medicine, communications, agronomy, pedagogy). These organizations had survived during the 1970s as one of the few forms of student organizing permitted by the dictatorship, given their billing as "technocratic" versus "political" associations. However during the *abertura* period they became a base from which the more general student movement reorganized. During the 1980s, many of them took on explicitly politicized projects, concerned with social justice issues such as land reform, health care, expansion of public services, and professional reform in their own specialized fields. In 1992, a group of course-based activists founded the National Forum of Course Executives, in explicit challenge to the traditional style of student politics represented by UNE. The traditional student movement was critiqued by these activists as being overly competitive, bureaucratic, authoritarian, and distant from student concerns. In contrast, the Forum presented itself stylistically as consensus-oriented, flexible, non-hierarchical, and closely linked to the interests and identities of students.

In contrast to the long-term CONUN activists, the Forum participants tended to be more recent entrants. Among 31 respondents at a 1995 national planning meeting in São Paulo, two-thirds began their activism during or after the 1992 impeachment movement. In addition to their participation in "specialized" course-based organizations in their areas of study, many also participated in the "general" student movement at the university, state, and national level. As in CONUN, nearly half were affiliated with political parties, with another 25 percent expressing partisan sympathies. Of these, the great majority were associated with the PT, although a few were connected with other parties of the left. About 20 percent also had prior or concurrent involvements in other kinds of movements, including popular, NGO, and/or church-based activism.

As with CONUN, partisan identities were a delicate component of the Forum, requiring strong normative regulation. Despite the fact that almost three-fourths of the participants had partisan affiliations or sympathies, mention of political parties was almost completely taboo. The closest they came to mentioning parties was to condemn the "logic of dispute" within UNE.

When I discussed this with one of the Forum organizers (who was also involved in UNE leadership as well as the youth wing of the PT), he told me that avoidance of partisanship was part of a deliberate strategy to change the traditional adversarial style of student politics. He argued that this suppression of partisan identities allowed for the kind of political debate and elaboration of alternative proposals that was very difficult within UNE:

> *Jaime:* [The executives] constitute a space that is not as tense, where you don't have to vote on anything, in which you can discuss more calmly and without trying every moment to defeat the other. If you open your mouth in the congress

of UNE ... you have your label. PT, boom, he's PT, he's PT ... even if what you say makes sense, they are going to attack" (Interviewed November 29, 1995).

The suppression of partisan identity was made simpler by the predominance of PT activists in the Forum, although given intense factional disputes within the PT, this did not eliminate ideological disagreement. Nevertheless, Jaime admitted that it was sometimes difficult to carry out this separation of adversarial and consensus-oriented logics, given the fact that so many course-based leaders were also involved in partisan disputes in the general student movement. Many multiply affiliated activists preached non-partisanship in the course-based movement even while waging partisan battles just down the hall, so to speak, in the universities, or in the state and national student organizations. Jaime himself was deeply immersed in internal factional disputes within the PT as well as in attempts to wrest control of UNE from rival parties such as the PCdoB (Communist Party of Brazil), even as he served as one of the articulators of an alternative, consensus-based style of student politics.

In sum, the publics of the course executives highlighted their *professional* identities as an alternative form of *student* activism while suppressing any mention of *partisan* dispute, even though many participants were deeply engaged in such disputes. They built their provisional homogeneity around the rejection of adversarial logic, allowing them to build a public that generated a richer level of dialogue and exchange of ideas than occurred in many traditional student publics. However, this response to internal complexity posed its own communicative challenges: The Forum risked paralysis or collapse when faced with disagreements on issues requiring pragmatic or ideological closure. Fine-grained factional differences among the (mostly) PT activists made consensus hard to achieve and sometimes led to exhausting, long-circling discussions. Moreover, many activists wrestled with ambivalence about whether their purpose was to "dispute UNE" or formulate proposals to transform their professions (and thus their own role as socially engaged professionals). While the students hungered to "elaborate projects," the insistence on consensus process made such projects hard to elaborate. Partisan contention hovered just beneath the surface, making the Forum a more fragile and unstable public than its organizers acknowledged.

Junior enterprises
A third group of students, somewhat disconnected from the others, was also contesting space within the universities, engaged in building autonomous, student-run entrepreneurial groups ("junior enterprises") in which they could hone their professional skills while gaining early experience in the business world. Junior enterprises were mini-consulting firms within the universities in which students developed paid projects for external clients in their area of study, under the supervision of a faculty member. While the enterprises originated in the business-oriented fields of economics and administration, they were quickly spreading to other fields, ranging from engineering, statistics, and agronomy to

communications, psychology, and social science. While these may not sound like "movement" organizations, they referred to themselves in those terms (*movimento de empresas juniors*). I often heard more traditional student activists refer to the junior enterprises as rivals in local student politics, competing for resources and recruits as well as for the ideological "hegemony" of student politics. For the most part, the junior enterprises tried to keep themselves out of the fray, preaching a militant non-partisanship that gazed resolutely inward at the enterprises themselves.

Like the Forum activists, most participants were relatively recent entrants. Among 23 respondents at the monthly meetings of the State Federation of Junior Enterprises (FEJESP), over 85 percent had begun their participation in the 1990s. However, they had fewer overlapping involvements than either the Forum or CONUN activists, with very little experience of activism outside of the university, with the exception of the 1992 mobilizations for the impeachment. About 70 percent were involved in the junior enterprises alone, with no concurrent participation in any other sector. About a third had some past or present participation in the general student movement (mostly very light), and about 40 percent reported brief participation in the 1992 impeachment movement or other civic groups. Only one student reported any participation in a political party (sympathy with the Brazilian Social Democratic Party [PSDB]).

Several leaders of FEJESP insisted that in the junior enterprise, they never talked partisan politics. As one of the co-founders told me, "There were three things we didn't discuss: football, religion, and politics. Because it leads to fights, it's no use." This suppression of partisanship had been carefully institutionalized in both the formal rules and informal practices of the junior enterprises. Among other things, it required that the junior enterprises keep their distance from the other student organizations, which were often located in the same faculties, right down the hall. As Flávio, president of FEJESP during my fieldwork, told me:

> Flávio: *The junior enterprise is, in principle, completely apartisan.* The statute defines that we have no link with any political party, no link with religion, no link with any interest group ... we try to stay outside of partisan questions. I don't say political, because everyone is political, but outside of partisan questions within the [universities], in relation to the [student organizations], for example.

He argued that junior enterprises should not get involved in any political issues related to educational policy or university administration—they should leave that to the student movement groups and to UNE. However, they should (and did) get involved in things "that touch the pure interests of the junior enterprises," such as lobbying national congress for legislation that supported their organizations. There was some internal tension between their official "non-profit" status and their revenue-generating activity, with fierce internal debate about whether the students should be paid for their consulting services (personal remuneration was officially prohibited). In general, they downplayed the explicit profit motive and tried to frame the benefits to participants in terms of professional training and personal growth. Some leaders incorporated civic language from the non-profit sector, conceptualizing the junior enterprises as civil associations engaged in a form of university outreach to the community, along with occasional "social projects" in poor communities.

Overall, the publics constructed by the junior enterprises depended, like the others, on the suppression of various kinds of potential divisions. Most students concentrated their participation within the *business* sector, while characterizing the junior enterprises as *civic* organizations that trained them as young *professionals* via practice in running small enterprises. Their occasional affiliations in partisan, student movement, religious, or other groups had to be carefully left at the door. The publics of the junior enterprises were militantly apartisan and strove to maintain a collaborative and pragmatic style of communication. Narrow expressions of self-interest were suppressed, even while more instrumental calculations hovered beneath the surface. Participants generated provisional homogeneity around their shared identities as professionals-in-training engaging in civic outreach while preparing for the business world. However, the conception of civic engagement was quite thin, tied to a neo-liberal conception of the non-profit sector as charitable service providers at the edge of a competitive market, not engaged in a transformative project addressing social inequities and exclusions.

Conclusion: The Problematics of Partisan Suppression

The publics that I have described in this chapter are not rarefied zones of abstract and reasoned debate about the common good. They are complex, heterogeneous, and often contentious spaces in which people bring with them too many partially overlapping identities and projects to allow for smooth communication about ideas and action. How do they ever arrive at anything resembling understanding, or get anything jointly accomplished? I have offered the perhaps startling proposition that publics first of all require suppression. Not "free expression," not "publicity," not "unrestrained communication," but rather the provisional suspension of potentially distracting, disruptive, or divisive aspects of participants' multiple affiliations. While all communication requires selective attention and the backgrounding of irrelevant aspects of identities, I am not talking merely about the routine deactivation of non-relevant ties. Rather, publics require *the active suppression of situationally potent identities*. Publics are charged places "in between," in which interstitiality heightens the sense of both contingency (something else might happen) and of negotiated restraint.

Theorists of democratic communication implicitly acknowledge such restraint when they refer to "self-limiting civil society," the "economy of moral disagreement," "self-censorship," or the "focusing of debate on the public good." However, these theorists tend to see this kind of suppression primarily in relation to the tension between individual self-interest (or personal moral principles) and the broader public good. The activists that I studied were often negotiating among many different ways of pursuing what they thought of as "the common good," including, as they understood it, their partisan pursuits. These multiple involvements generated tensions, dilemmas and questions for their day-to-day practice: When is it important that I bring my identity as a black activist, as an agronomist, as a Communist, or as Catholic into play? When should I hold these in abeyance as I attempt to build bridges, elaborate projects, and set up institutions? When do these identities contribute to the public under construction, and when do they distract or disrupt? When should I fuse my multiple identities and projects, and when should I keep them carefully (if precariously) compartmentalized?

Within the bubbles of the five kinds of publics described here, participants constructed streamlined and reduced identities that decoupled communication from some subset of the identities that could, potentially be brought into play, given their multiple affiliations. Within student and Catholic settings, this had the effect of highlighting and valorizing partisan identities, although in tension with their own self-representations as being unified and autonomous. Within the black and professional student publics, students downplayed the partisan affiliations that actively guided their own interventions in other settings, as they attempted to create a space for other relations and projects to flourish. This did not entail a stark choice between being partisan or civic, but in negotiating which of their multiple identities, including partisan affiliations, could be "performed" within particular settings, and which had to be downplayed or suppressed. Within the business publics, there was an active rejection of partisanship, combined with a delicate balancing act between narrow self-interest and civic engagement.

While partisanship can clearly have distracting and destructive effects on democratic communication, it can also make important contributions to civic life. For this reason, we need to leave behind idealized, dichotomous views of political communication as being civic or partisan, consensual or competitive, or as Jane Mansbridge (1983) put it in her seminal study of democratic deliberation, divided between "unitary" and "adversary" democracy. We should focus, rather, on their somewhat troubled but still fertile coexistence. I have suggested that one way to avoid this dichotomy is to look at the performances of actors in complex publics. Rather than curtly condemning partisanship and singing the praises of a tamed and declawed "civicness," we should rather pay attention to the more subtle discursive switching that actors engage in as they move between different kinds of political settings, as well as between contending definitions of what those settings are about.

My research suggests that that the avoidance or rejection of partisanship by challenger groups in the 1990s generated new problems and tensions, even as it contributed to organizational innovation within student politics. As I listened to debates over Brazilian youth politics, including the often harsh criticisms of UNE coming from different sectors, I became increasingly wary of the blanket condemnations of partisanship that seemed to infuse many critiques. These criticisms neglected the more complex identity negotiations that most activists engaged in, of which partisanship was just one, albeit especially problematic, dimension. Student publics that managed this heterogeneity by forcing partisanship underground, such as the Forum of Course Executives, seemed oddly paralyzed, lacking in the strong public voice that they claimed to seek. And those that repudiated partisanship altogether, such as the junior enterprises, contributed to a thin and depoliticized understanding of citizenship, in line with recent concerns about the replacement of the democratic, inclusionary projects of civil society with neoliberal conceptions of civic engagement (Dagnino 2002, 2005). On the other hand, the entrenched partisan climate of UNE often proved alienating and counterproductive, discouraging dialogue and reflection on how best to reform the "unified" organization of which leaders were so proud.

This suggests that to be effective, political groups require a certain sort of *jogo de cintura*,[5] or what I call the "dance of democracy." This entails the ability to move back and forth among multiple identities—and the modes of confrontation and collaboration that they entail—in response to the relational challenges of particular situations. The pragmatic-relational model presented here conceives of publics themselves as performative constructions created by the deployment and recognition of certain *subsets* of identities, along a reduced dimension that is always *less* than the full array of identities that could, potentially be in play. Because some of these possible identities are held in a state of abeyance, they always hover around the situation in a state of potentiality, threatening to intrude in and disrupt the communication in process—that is, publics are always *more* than the identities in play. Thus to ensure dialogue in publics, political actors need to know how to provisionally background or downplay their partisan identities in order to be able to converse across conventional divides, as they build coalitions and engage new actors.

But this does not mean eliminating or crushing partisanship or denying it entrance into the public stage, as seemed to be the impetus in the June 2013 protests. The extreme partisan ambivalence and rejection expressed in the recent protests represents a real challenge to progressive movements, which need to rethink how they respond to a population that is brimming with social and political criticism, but deeply suspicious of institutional politics and organized groups of all sorts. Political parties can play an important role in transformative democratic politics and projects of social and economic justice. They can build bridges between popular movements and the state, articulate ties across diverse movement sectors, and formulate counterhegemonic projects and projects of institutional reform. The absolutist rejection of political parties (and of institutional politics more generally)—whether coming from the right or the left—risks leaving power in the hands of the most elite, corporatist (and corporate) sectors, reinforcing neoliberal tendencies and generating further disconnection and alienation from the broader population.

---

5   This is a popular Brazilian phrase which means "swing of the hips," referring to the ability to respond in flexible and improvisational ways to emergent situations, in order to dodge dangers and seize and generate opportunities, especially when access to resources and power is limited.

The challenge for activists is how to rethink parties, making them more dialogic, flexible, and responsive to emergent movements. Developing *jogo de cintura* entails the ability to move nimbly between confrontational and collaborative modes of political interaction; or in other words, activists must know how to take the partisan hat on and off. This is not to say that movements should be "controlled by" political parties, or even instigated by them. Colonization, corporatism, and opportunism are real problems, in Brazil and elsewhere. Broad-based movements for social change should maintain their relative autonomy; they should strive to be "supra-partisan" while also respecting and encouraging the participation of those who don't identify with parties at all. Likewise, parties need to be self-restrained and adopt a more humble role, relinquishing the self-promotional urge to always to be at the forefront as the "representative" of the people. Yet as "articulators"—that is, as channelers of discursive and institutional mediations—they can be essential players in a broader movement field.

Partisanship does not necessarily destroy civic dialogue; in fact, it can enrich and extend it. But for this to happen, leaders must be skilled not only in the articulation of joint projects and identities, but also in their provisional suppression. By looking carefully at these processes, here and elsewhere, we can show how the partisan can also be public, engaging the problems and the possibilities of democratic practice.

References

Abers, Rebecca Neaera, 2000. *Inventing local democracy: grassroots politics in Brazil.* Boulder: Lynne Rienner.

Abers, Rebecca Neaera and Keck, Margaret E., 2013. *Practical authority: agency and institutional change in Brazilian water politics.* Oxford: Oxford University Press.

Alexander, Jeffrey C, 2004. "Cultural pragmatics: social performance between ritual and strategy." *Sociological Theory*, 22, pp. 527–73.

———, 2008. *The civil sphere.* Oxford: Oxford University Press.

Avritzer, Leonardo, 2002. *Democracy and the public sphere in Latin America.* Princeton: Princeton University Press.

Baiocchi, Gianpaolo, ed., 2003. *Radicals in power: the workers' party (PT) and experiments in urban democracy in Brazil.* London: Zed Books.

———. 2005. *Militants and citizens: the politics of participatory democracy in Porto Alegre.* Palo Alto: Stanford University Press.

Benhabib, Seyla ed., 1996. *Democracy and difference: contesting the boundaries of the political.* Princeton: Princeton University Press.

Bohman, James, and William Rehg, eds. 1997. *Deliberative democracy: essays on reason and politics.* Cambridge, MA: MIT Press.

Calhoun, Craig ed., 1993. *Habermas and the public sphere.* Cambridge: MIT Press.

Cohen, Jean and Arato, Andrew, 1992. *Civil society and political theory.* Cambridge: MIT Press.

Cohen, Joshua and Rogers, Joel eds, 1998. *Associations and democracy (The Real Utopias Project, V.1).* Verso Books.

Dagnino, Evelina, 1994. "Os movimentos sociais e a emergência de uma nova concepção de cidadania." In: Evelina Dagnino, ed. *Anos 90: Política e sociedade no Brasil.* São Paulo: Brasiliense, pp. 103–55.

———, 2002. *Sociedade civil e espaços públicos no Brasil.* São Paulo: Paz e Terra.

———, 2005. "Citizenship and the social in contemporary Brazil." Paper prepared for *After Neo-liberalism? Consequences for citizenship,* Workshop #2 in the series Claiming Citizenship in the Americas, organized by the Canada Research Chair in Citizenship and Governance, Université de Montréal.

Doimo, Ana Maria, 1995. *A vez e a voz do popular: movimentos sociais e participação política no Brasil pós-70.* Rio de Janeiro: Relume-Dumará/ANPOCS.

Eliasoph, Nina, 1998. *Avoiding politics: how Americans produce apathy in everyday life.* Cambridge: Cambridge University Press.

Eliasoph, Nina and Lichterman, Paul, 2003. "Culture in interaction." *American Journal of Sociology,* 108, pp. 735–94.

Elster, Jon ed., 1998. *Deliberative democracy.* Cambridge: Cambridge University Press.

Emirbayer, Mustafa, 1997. "Manifesto for a relational sociology." *American Journal of Sociology,* 103, pp. 281–317.

Emirbayer, Mustafa and Sheller, Mimi, 1999. "Publics in history." *Theory and Society,* 28, pp. 145–97.

Fishman, Robert, 2004. *Democracy's voices: social ties and the quality of public life in Spain.* Ithaca: Cornell University Press.

Fontdevila, Jorge, 2010. "Indexes, power and netdoms: a multidimensional model of language in social action." *Poetics,* 38, pp. 587–609.

Fraser, Nancy, 1992. "Rethinking the public sphere: a contribution to the critique of actually existing democracy." In: Craig Calhoun ed. *Habermas and the public sphere.* Cambridge: MIT Press, pp. 109–42.

Godart, Frédéric C. and White, Harrison C., 2010. "Switchings under uncertainty: the coming and becoming of meanings." *Poetics,* 38, pp. 567–86.

Goffman, Erving, 1959. *The presentation of self in everyday life.* New York: Anchor Books.

———, 1974. *Frame analysis.* New York: Harper and Row.

———, 1981. *Forms of talks.* Philadelphia: University of Pennsylvania Press.

Gutmann, Amy, 2003. *Identity in democracy.* Princeton: Princeton University Press.

Gutmann, Amy and Thompson, Dennis, 1996. *Democracy and disagreement: why moral conflict cannot be avoided in politics, and what should be done about it.* Cambridge: Harvard University Press.

Habermas, Jürgen, 1989. *The structural transformation of the public sphere: an inquiry into a category of bourgeois society.* Translated by Thomas McCarthy. Cambridge: MIT Press.

Hochstetler, Kathryn, 2000. "Democratizing pressures from below? Social movements in the new Brazilian democracy." In: Peter R. Kingstone and Timothy J. Power, eds. *Democratic Brazil: actors, institutions, and processes.* Pittsburgh: University of Pittsburgh Press, pp. 167–82.

Honig, Bonnie, 1992. "Toward and agonistic feminism: Hannah Arendt and the politics of identity." In: Judith Butler and Joan W. Scott, eds. *Feminists theorize the political.* New York: Routledge, pp. 215–35.

Ikegami, Eiko, 2000. "A sociological theory of publics: identity and culture as emergent properties in networks." *Social Research,* 67, pp. 89–1029.

———, 2005. *Bonds of civility: aesthetic publics and the political origins of Japanese publics.* Cambridge: Cambridge University Press.

Keck, Margaret, 1992. *The workers' party and democratization in Brazil.* New Haven: Yale University Press.

Lichterman, Paul, 2005. *Elusive togetherness: how religious Americans create civic ties.* Princeton: Princeton University Press.

———, 2012. "Religion in public action: from actors to settings." *Sociological Theory,* 30(1), pp. 15–36.

Mainwaring, Scott. 1999. *Rethinking party systems in the third wave of democratization: the case of Brazil.* Stanford: Stanford University Press.

Mainwaring, Scott and Scully, Timothy R., 1995. *Building democratic institutions: party systems in Latin America.* Stanford: Stanford University Press.

Mansbridge, Jane J., 1983. *Beyond adversary democracy.* Chicago: University of Chicago Press.

———, 1986. *Why we lost the ERA.* Chicago: University of Chicago Press.

Marx, Anthony, 1998. *Making race and nation: a comparison of the United States, South Africa and Brazil.* Cambridge: Cambridge University Press.

McLean, Paul, 2007. *The art of the network: strategic interaction and patronage in renaissance Florence.* Durham: Duke University Press.

Meneguello, Rachel. 1989. *PT: a formação de um partido 1979–1982.* São Paulo: Paz e Terra.

Mische, Ann, 1996. "Projecting democracy: the construction of citizenship across youth networks in Brazil." In: Charles Tilly ed. *Citizenship, identity, and social history.* Cambridge: Cambridge University Press.

———, 2003. "Cross-talk in movements: rethinking the culture-network link." In: Mario Diani and Doug McAdam, eds. *Social movements and networks: relational approaches to collective action.* Oxford: Oxford University Press, pp. 258–80.

———, 2008. *Partisan publics: communication and contention across Brazilian youth activist networks.* Princeton: Princeton University Press.

————, 2011. "Relational sociology, culture, and agency." In: John Scott and Peter Carrington, eds. *The Sage handbook of social network analysis*. London: Sage, pp. 80–97.

Mische, Ann and Pattison, Philippa, 2000. "Composing a civic arena: publics, projects, and social settings." *Poetics*, 27, pp. 163–94.

Mische, Ann and White, Harrison, 1998. "Between conversation and situation: public switching dynamics across network-domains." *Social Research*, 65, pp. 295–324.

Morris, Aldon D. and Mueller, Carol eds, 1992. *Frontiers of social movement theory*. New Haven: Yale University Press.

Putnam, Robert D., 1993. *Making democracy work: civic traditions in modern Italy*. Princeton: Princeton University Press.

————. 2000. *Bowling alone: the collapse and revival of American community*. New York: Simon and Shuster.

Ryan, Mary P., 1990. *Women in public: between banners and ballots, 1825–80*. Baltimore: Johns Hopkins University Press.

Sader, Eder, 1988. *Quando novos personagens entrarem em cena: experiências e lutas dos trabalhadores da grande São Paulo 1970–80*. São Paulo: Paz e Terra.

Sandoval, Salvador, 1998. "Social movements and democratization: the case of Brazil and the Latin Countries." In: Marco G. Giugni, Doug McAdam and Charles Tilly, eds. *From contention to democracy*. Lanham: Rowman & Littlefield, pp. 169–201.

Smilde, David, 2004. "Popular publics: street protest and plaza preachers in Caracas." *International Review of Social History*, 49, pp. 179–95.

————, 2007. *Reason to believe: cultural agency in Latin American evangelicalism*. Berkeley: University of California Press.

Somers, Margaret, 1993. "Citizenship and the place of the public sphere: law, community, and political culture in the transition to democracy." *American Sociological Review*, 58, pp. 587–620.

————, 1998. "We're no angels: realism, relationality, and rational choice in social science." *American Journal of Sociology*, 104, pp. 772–84.

Telles, Edward E., 2004. *Race in another America: the significance of skin color in Brazil*. Princeton, NJ: Princeton University Press.

von Bülow, Marisa, 2011. *Building transnational networks: civil society networks and the politics of trade in the Americas*. Cambridge: Cambridge University Press.

White, Harrison, 1995. "Network switchings and Bayesian forks: reconstructing the social and behavioral sciences." *Social Research*, 62, pp. 1035–63.

————, 2008. *Identity and control: how social formations emerge*. Princeton: Princeton University Press.

Young, Iris, 1990. *Justice and the politics of difference*. Princeton: Princeton University Press.

————, 2000. *Inclusion and democracy*. Oxford: Oxford University Press.

Chapter 4

Institutional Activism: Mobilizing for Women's Health From Inside the Brazilian Bureaucracy

Rebecca Neaera Abers and Luciana Tatagiba

Introduction

After the Worker's Party began to govern Brazil's federal government in 2003, a number of researchers called attention to an increasingly visible phenomenon that contradicted prevailing conceptions of how social movements work: With the arrival in office of a party closely tied to social movements, many activists decided to take jobs in the new administration (Dagnino, Olvera and Panfichi 2006; Feltran 2006; Abers and von Bülow 2011; Silva and Oliveira 2011; Abers, Serafim and Tatagiba 2013). This process, it turned out, was not something entirely new in Brazil: The environmental (Alonso et al. 2007) and health movements (Dowbor 2012; Rich 2013), among others, had long histories of working inside government agencies to promote movement goals (Abers and von Bülow 2011; Dowbor 2012). The debate about this kind of institutional activism has for the most part focused on revealing its existence and discussing its implications for our understanding of where the boundaries between social movements and the state lie, if they exist at all. In this chapter, we hope to go a bit further, thinking about what it is that activists inside the bureaucracy actually do. In particular, we make two general arguments. First, this kind of activism involves an artisanal effort to promote change in rigid bureaucratic structures and under often powerful political constraints. Second, as they persevere under such frustrating circumstances, the activists we studied are not alone. Their connections to social movement networks provide both resources and obstacles for activism inside of the state.

We use the term institutional activism to describe what people are doing when they take jobs in government bureaucracies with the purpose of advancing the political agendas or projects proposed by social movements. This tends to be a less glamorous form of activism than the kinds of grand repertoires of protest normally associated with social movements. We are examining action at the micro-level, which may be neither heroic nor radically transformative. Instead, it involves a daily effort at experimentation and problem-solving, the results of which are not always immediately perceptible.[1] Although many bureaucrats are likely engaged in such purposeful problem-solving, our concern here is with how prior militancy in social movement networks affects those activities. Our main argument is that such connections help activists mobilize a variety of resources (knowledge, contacts, information, prestige, and so on) once they are working on the inside of the state, but also impose limits on what they can do.

To explore this issue, we conducted a case study of a unit within Brazil's Ministry of Health: The Technical Area for Women's Health. This is a sub-division of the Department of Programmatic and Strategic Action, which in turn is part of the Secretariat of Health Care, the biggest division within the ministry. The Technical Area's main job is to establish guidelines related to women's health that guide service providers within Brazil's national health care system. We took interest in this unit because it is the product of an important struggle within Brazil's feminist movement: the struggle against the historical tendency to reduce the scope of women's health to childbearing and motherhood. The creation in 1983 of the Program for Integrated Women's Health Care (PAISM—*Programa de Atenção Integral à Saúde da Mulher*) at a time when Brazil's military regime was still in power and the feminist movement was still incipient, is widely considered to be one of the earliest successes of both the feminist movement and of the health reform movement. PAISM has thus become a sort of founding myth for women's health policy in Brazil, a fact reflected in the substantial academic literature on the subject (Alvarez 1990; Costa 1992; Correa 1993; Osis 1998). Activism in the area of women's health involves multiple, partially overlapping social movement networks that are permeated by internal differences and conflicts. This heterogeneity means that if, on the one hand, institutional activists have access to a diversity of resources, on the other hand, their every move is likely to generate criticism from somewhere. The women's health agenda was forged out of the attempt to construct a dialogue between ideas about how to improve Brazil's health care system (promoted by the *sanitarista movement*, which we loosely translate as the public health movement) with feminist ideas defending women's autonomy over their bodies. The second group of ideas often puts feminist health advocates in direct conflict with a medical culture that had historically reduced women's health to reproductive issues and gave little credence to the empowerment of women in doctor-patient relations. These feminists also differed strongly amongst themselves with respect to what issues should be given priority in the defense of women's health.

Advancing movement goals by occupying government positions is a common practice in Latin American feminism, especially in recent decades. Sonia Alvarez's study of the movement argues that in the 1990s, governments began to respond to the women's movement by creating new agencies and policies for women's issues. Since they were often the only people with substantial experience and knowledge

---

1   This concept of action is influenced by the pragmatist approaches of authors such as Berk and Galvan (2009), Mische (2009), Emirbayer and Mische (1998), among others.

about those issues, prominent feminists were frequently invited to run those agencies. Like us, Alvarez suggests that the move into government positions did not necessarily imply that these activists were co-opted by patriarchal institutions: By taking up spaces traditionally occupied by men, they engaged in struggles to control how decision-making occurred (Lind 1995, p. 17 *apud* Alvarez 1998, p. 299).

What is it that activists do when they work inside the state? To explore this question, we conducted nine in-depth interviews with activists involved in women's health policy. The interviews were conducted in person or by telephone or Skype and lasted between one and two hours. This small number of interviews was supplemented by participant observation in meetings and office debates during the period of several weeks during which the interviews took place by both authors. We also conducted a detailed analysis of the large secondary bibliography on the issue, as well as commentary available in journalistic media. We focused on the period since 2011, when Dilma Rousseff became president and introduced a major change in women's health policy involving large scale investment in maternity wards throughout the country. In a context in which evangelical Christian politicians had increasing leverage in the president's political coalition, working as a feminist inside the state became increasingly difficult. This context allowed us to explore institutional activism under relatively adverse circumstances, highlighting the difficulties and conflicts activists face.

We started by interviewing all the women in policy-making roles currently working in the Technical Area for Women's Health who had prior experience in social movements. They included three women who had participated in feminist organizations and a leader of coalition promoting the "humanization" of childbirth. We also interviewed a staff member who had worked in the unit for many years and could tell us about its history. We then interviewed two feminist activists who had worked in the Technical Area under other administrations and two women who had followed the Area's evolution over time, one from within government (as a member of the health reform movement particularly involved in women's issues) and another involved in non-governmental feminist organizations. These interviews helped us compare the experience of the current activists with those in previous periods and to understand better the role of social movements in the construction of women's policy over time. To preserve their anonymity, the chapter will refer to them as Interviews 1 through 9.

Our intention in this investigation is both exploratory and reflexive: Both of us had much experience studying state-society activism in other policy areas such as the environment (Abers and Keck 2013; Abers 2000), urban policy (Abers 2000, Tatagiba 2011; Tatagiba and Blikstad 2011), and in participatory decision-making arenas such as public policy councils, river basin committees, and participatory budgeting. That research led us both to a question that neither of us had really explored systematically: What is the daily life of institutional activists actually like? Our hope was to get fresh insight into that question by exploring a policy field that was relatively new for us. Even though this strategy means that this chapter's results are preliminary, studying something new pushed us forward conceptually in ways that we hope will contribute to the construction of a research agenda around this little understood form of activism.

Our argument is organized in three parts. First we analyze the literature on social movements to identify how it has explored the relationship between movements and the state. We show that although recent works have rejected rigid dichotomies between states and movements, very few studies have actually examined activism inside the state. Second, we present our case study, examining the evolution of PAISM since its creation in 1984. Third, we examine the dynamics of institutional activism in the Dilma Rousseff government (2011 to the present), in which increasingly powerful conservative groups associated with the religious anti-abortion lobby have put major constraints on what feminists can do.

We argue that the participation in multiple networks over their lives provides institutional activists with resources that help them deal with the difficult job of promoting change from within state institutions. Those same networks, however, also constrain them in particular ways. Brazilian feminism is made up of diverse, heterogeneous, and highly competitive networks. When activists connected to particular groups take government jobs, the people with whom they shared a life of militancy provide them with support, but conflicts and disputes produce criticisms and challenges that other government officials do not face. This kind of friendly fire can put additional pressure on those who choose to work within the state and who already must deal with multiple constraints on their actions.

Activism Inside the State

Until recently, most of the North American and European literature on social movements ignored the possibility that activists might work from inside government bureaucracies. The literature on new social movements heralded the emergence of a "self-limited" civil society (Cohen and Arato 1991). The presumption was that proximity between bureaucracy and civil society would limit the latter's democratizing and transformative potential. The resource mobilization and political process literature showed more interest in relations with the state, but the latter was still largely understood to be an adversary. In his trend-setting classic, *From Mobilization to Revolution* (Tilly 1978, p. 52), for example, Charles Tilly distinguished between polity "members" and "challengers" and since then most studies of social movements in that tradition presumed that these engaged in "collective challenges" to the political system (Tarrow 1994, p. 4).

This did not mean that social movements never had allies within political institutions. Indeed, that possibility was an important component of theories of "political opportunity" which "lower the costs of collective action, reveal potential allies and show where elites and authorities are vulnerable" (Tarrow 1994, p. 18). Various studies showed how "sponsors" (Jenkins and Perrow 1977) within political institutions sometimes protected movements from opposition and promoted movement goals. Yet many studies presumed that any kind of alignment between movement and government goals would imply demobilization, bureaucratization, and de-radicalization (Piven and Cloward 1977). For Tarrow, the institutionalization of movement demands was a key reason that cycles of protest come to an end (Tarrow 1994, pp. 153–69).[2]

More recent research has suggested, however, that social movements normally combine outsider (protest-based) strategies with attempts to influence state institutions by getting involved in party politics, political nominations, and the actual design of policies. Goldstone (2003) argues that social movements often combine institutional and non-institutional strategies and, more generally, that policy and movements tend to mutually influence each other in complex ways. Others have suggested that the very notion of "non-institutional" strategies is problematic in advanced democracies where the classic social movement repertoire (such as marches and occupations) has become part of conventional politics (Meyer and Tarrow 1998). In a recent essay, McAdam and Tarrow (2010) point out that movements and electoral processes influence each other in a variety of ways, such as when social movements are closely tied to parties that achieve electoral power.

As Meyer (2005) notes, when governments respond to social movements by creating a new policy or even a new agency, movements themselves often gain a place at the negotiating table. Some studies suggest that outsider influence tends to be limited to public hearings or policy boards, while they remain excluded from policy-making processes that occur behind the closed doors of the bureaucracy (Ingram and Ingram 2005). Sometimes, however, movements gain access to those decision processes, such that "certain movements tend to become integrated into the decisional, regulatory, or implementation phases of the political process" (Giugni and Passy 1998, p. 82). These studies draw attention to the interior of the policy-making process which, in so many movement studies, is presumed to be the terrain of government actors alone.

Another way to examine movement participation in policy-making is to include social movements in the epistemic communities (Haas 1992), advocacy coalitions (Jenkins-Smith and Sabatier 1993), and policy networks[3] studied by the public policy literature. Meyer (2005) and Ingram and Ingram (2005) emphasize that policy networks often exclude social movement activists, working as stable "monopolies" that maintain the status quo. "Social movements can … influence policy by altering the composition of the relevant policy monopoly" (Meyer 2005, p. 18). Grattet (2005) examines cases where movements were able to influence policy reform by gaining such access to policy networks.

---

2 On the association between participation in governing and co-optation, see Selznick's (1949) classic work as well as Coit 1978; Gittell 1983; Marris and Rein 1967; and Piven 1970.

3 For reviews of the extensive policy network literature, see Rhodes 1997; Thatcher 1998; Dowding 2008; Bevir and Richards 2009, among many others.

While the above approaches think of social movements as components of networks, other recent work has defined social movements as networks in and of themselves (Diani 1992; Diani and McAdam 2003). This approach allows us to imagine that at least some nodes of a social movement network might be located within the state. As Abers and von Bülow (2011) argue, defining movements as networks means that the analyst cannot, *a priori*, exclude particular actors from a social movement because they occupy a government position. A network approach thus implies that sometimes social movements may actually encroach into the state, by way of their members.

Outside Latin America, few studies have explored what happens when movement activists actually occupy positions in government institutions. Interestingly, much of what has been written focuses on feminists. For example, Katzenstein (1999) studied feminist activists in military and religious institutions, examining how they helped change the internal dynamics and employment policies of the institutions in which they worked. Santoro and McGuire (1997) compare two US employment policies promoting racial and gender equality. They argue that many women and black politicians seek to "translate their ideological commitment into political action on behalf of a social movement" (Ibid., 505). In a study of Australia and Canada, Chappell (2003) examines what she calls the "femocrat strategy": occupying the bureaucracy to pursue feminist goals. She explores the tension between the autonomy institutional activists need to take advantage of opportunities for movement gains within the state and the pressure to be accountable to activists on the outside. She also explores the political and cultural differences between countries that affect how much influence and authority feminists can obtain within the state.[4] The state appears in these works as a political battleground in which struggles over the details of policy-making occur, although for the most part, the authors still presume that there is a clear distinction between the social movement (outside the state) and the work of feminist allies within it.

Banaszak's (2010) book on feminists working within the US federal bureaucracy is the only study we know of that systematically explores the strategies and tactics particular to feminist activism within the state from a social movement perspective.[5] The author contradicts prevailing presumptions that insider activists tend to moderate their goals: She finds that many feminists she interviewed became more radical over time, in some cases only converting

---

4   Other studies of feminists inside bureaucracies in Australia, where the term "femocrat" was coined, are Eisenstein (1990), and Sawer (1990), among others.

5   Interestingly, the book comes to conclusions quite different from some of her earlier work, such as Banaszak, Beckwith and Rucht (2003), which presumed that the relationship between the women's movement and the state reflected the institutionalization of the movement and the moderation of demands. The study also advances with respect to Banaszak (2005), where insider activists are seen to engage in confrontational action, but largely "off the job," for example by participating in protests.

to feminism after they started to work for government. She also challenges the idea that the incorporation of activists inside the state was a consequence of prior feminist victories: Feminists worked within the US government well before the second wave of feminism began and played a key strategic role in promoting the movement at its early stages. Understanding the boundary between states and movements as thus blurred, Banaszak puts into question the predominant understanding within the social movement literature that political institutions and government policies are externally generated "political opportunities" to which social movements react and adapt.

Banaszak's work is especially helpful in questioning the dichotomy between conventional and confrontational tactics, showing that activities commonly understood to be conventional or institutional—such as litigation and lobbying public officials—can be used for disruptive and radical ends, even from inside institutions. In the US, feminist lawyers working for government played a crucial role in promoting lawsuits for women's rights. Feminist government employees also often used their privileged access to information to the advantage of the movement, sometimes by supplying outsider activists with news about government activities. In agencies or administrations hostile to feminist causes, Banaszak describes how feminists engaged in even more subtle tactics, trying to make changes "under the radar," following orders as minimally as possible, while subtly adjusting the wording in legislation and policy documents, keeping the movement informed of efforts to reduce women's rights, among other activities.

All of these arguments corroborate many of the findings presented below, contributing to our understanding of how activists can use their location in the bureaucracy to promote feminist goals in ways that are often hidden to outsiders, including to other feminists. Like the literature coming from the advanced democracies, studies of Latin American social movements have also only just begun to pay more systematic attention to the relations between movements, governments, and parties. Until recently, in Latin America, the main influences on the social movement debate were different forms of Marxism and new social movement theory, with little room for political process theory (Davis 1999; Gohn 2000). Conceiving movements in terms of their "newness" made it particularly important to deny their links with mainstream political institutions. This literature emphasized dichotomies (such as between state and movement) in the effort to highlight the notion that "new" political subjects were engaged in "new" forms of political action. This resulted in what Hellman (1992) dubbed "autonomy fetishism": any kind of proximity between movements and the state or parties was equated with co-optation or subordination.

In Brazil, however, academic studies questioning "autonomy fetishism" started to appear as early as the mid-1980s. Boschi and Valadares (1983) explored how state action influenced movement strategies and results. Ruth Cardoso (1983) argued that movements often mixed institutional and non-institutional strategies, and (Cardoso 1987) called for a more dynamic analysis of the relationships between movements and institutional actors. Kowarick (1987) accused most Brazilian studies in the 1980s of a dichotomizing bias that conceived of movements and the state as two distinct, homogeneous fields in a natural, radical, and inexorable opposition. Democratization intensified the perception that social movements were engaging the state, rather than rejecting it. Alvarez and Escobar's influential anthology on Latin American social movements (Alvarez and Escobar 1992, pp. 328–29) proposed that the central question was no longer the role of movements in the democratic transition but rather the impacts of democratic politics on movement organizing processes and strategies. Foweraker (2001, pp. 842–43), argued that Latin American "social movements had to interact with the state, precisely because of the fragility of civil and social rights in those countries. Doimo (1995) lamented that the dichotomy between autonomy and institutionalization present in much of the Brazilian literature produced theoretical paralysis and led some scholars to question the very concept of social movement.

In the 1990s, a few authors noted that the proximity between movements and the state could lead to the migration of activists into government agencies. As has already been noted, Alvarez (1998) argued that when feminist victories led to the creation of new policies and programs for women's issues, feminists started working with the state, sometimes joining government agencies. Davis (1999, p. 598) argued that the "relatively fluid and interconnected relations *between* state and societal domains" (Ibid., 598.) produced activists with dual identities: "Some of the most mobilized societal actors in Latin America are in many cases also 'state' actors, that is to say, teachers and other public sector employees" (Ibid., 589–99).

For various reasons, this provocative agenda did not find fertile ground in the 1990s. Internationally, the new social movements literature moved increasingly towards an interest in civil society and deliberative democracy (Alonso 2009, p. 75). In Brazil, the vaguely expressed belief that protest movements were no longer important political actors and the fact that new experiments in participatory policy-making seemed particularly innovative, led studies about participatory policies to expand at the same rate that research on social movements declined (Doimo 1995; Gohn 2000). This thematic shift (Lavalle 2003) reduced the research agenda on the relationship between movements and the state to a narrow focus on participation in formal arenas such as the participatory budget and policy councils, in detriment to a broader exploration of the relationships between movements and the state outside those spaces. Only in the 2000s did social movements re-appear on the Brazilian academic scene as an actor in their own right (Silva 2010), this time with a strong emphasis on their relationships with the state. Some of this research was motivated by the increasing importance on the political scene of radical social movements with massive mobilizing capacities, such as the *Movimento dos Trabalhadores Rurais Sem Terra* (MST, Rural Landless Workers Movement). But the new focus was also influenced by the *turn to the left* in various Latin American governments, a phenomenon that pressured analysts to reconsider the axiom that the state was always an enemy (Arson and Perales 2007; Canon and Peadar 2012; Weyland, Madrid and Hunter 2010).

A key theme propelled forward by the electoral victories of political parties with strong social movement support is the migration of activists into government positions. This practice—which occurred even during the authoritarian period, when center-left parties won local elections, and which became common during the 1990s—expanded dramatically under Lula.[6] The phenomenon has put in check the idea that there are clear frontiers between state and society, or at least has revealed that those borders are much more porous than we might have thought. In an influential study of Latin American politics, Dagnino, Olvera and Panfichi (2006) challenge the presumption that civil society and the state are hermetically sealed spheres of action and argue that movement and state actors can share purposes and goals—what they call *political projects.* Sometimes, they suggest, people move from civil society to the state without necessarily abandoning their social movement agenda. Dowbor (2012) shows how the Brazilian health reform movement intentionally developed a strategy of occupying government positions to advance its political agenda. Rich (2013) has examined how federal AIDS bureaucrats work through civil society networks and even foster the creation of new civic groups to monitor the activities of sub-national politicians. Tatagiba and colleagues have argued that the São Paulo housing movement combined traditional protest practices, such as occupying buildings with attempts to influence policy by getting members jobs in the municipal government (Tatagiba 2011; Tatagiba, Paterniani and Trindade 2012). Silva and Oliveira (2011) examine the *Economia Solidaria* (solidary economy) movement in the state of Rio Grande do Sul, where the Workers Party has won elections both at the state level and in many municipalities. They focus on how the party mediated the relationship between movement and policy-making, as activists moved in and out of government depending on whether or not the party held office.

A study we co-authored with Liza Serafim (Abers, Serafim and Tatagiba 2013) compares state-society interactions during the Lula government in three policy sectors characterized by entirely different historical patterns of state-society relations: family agriculture, urban policy, and public security policy.[7] In that article we adapted Tilly's concept of "repertoire of contention" to argue that interactions between state and society actors are also encoded in historically constructed patterns which are often too complex to be routinely characterized on one side of the conflict/cooperation dichotomy. We showed that social movements do not only interact with the state through negotiation or protest, but also invest heavily in building state institutions themselves. One of the key mechanisms that propelled innovations in the form that state-society interaction took was

---

6 Under Lula, D'Araújo found that 43 percent of ministers in the first administration and 45 percent of those in the second had prior careers in which they were activists in some kind of social movements, compared to around a quarter of ministers under the previous two presidencies (2009, p. 117–20).

7 Other studies of activists in Workers Party governments include Feltran (2006) and Losekann (2009).

the migration of activists from movements into the state. Traditional protest practices were transformed when people on the state side invested in a more fluid and interactive negotiation processes; and personal ties were often mobilized to advance movement agendas inside government.

In this chapter, we delve further into the experience of institutional activism. For all that recent studies have called attention to the existence of activists on the inside of state institutions, little seems to be known about what those activists actually do, or how working within the state differs from activism on the outside. We know little about what kinds of resources institutional activists mobilize, what specific challenges they face, and how they try to overcome them. This chapter seeks to contribute to the debate by shedding light on these questions.

The Feminist Movement, the State, and Women's Health in Brazil

The construction of a women's health policy imbued with feminist ideals began during Brazil's dictatorship (1964–1985) and feminist ideas appeared in key policy documents as early as 1983. These early advances made women's health policy an important arena for the development of two important Brazilian social movements: feminism and the health reform movement. The 1980s were an ambiguous period in Brazilian politics, during which a slow, controlled transition to democracy kept alive many of the repressive policies of the authoritarian period at the same time that social movements gained voice and influence. Unlike other developing countries, the Brazilian government had declared in the 1970s that population growth was not a serious problem and did not introduce an official family planning policy (Osis 1998; Alvarez and Escobar 1992). But when General-President Figueiredo made a declaration that Brazil was in danger of a population explosion, feminists became concerned that the government wanted to increase control over women's reproductive decisions.

When the Ministry of Health approved a progressive women's health program in 1983—PAISM (*Programa de Atenção Integral à Saúde da Mulher*)—feminists were surprised. The program document had strikingly feminist wording, declaring that women had the right to decide how many children they desired and that women's health should be integrated, treating women in all their dimensions, rather than focusing only on their roles as mothers (Alvarez and Escobar 1992; Correa 1993; Osis 1998; Costa 2009). Professionals within the Ministry of Health influenced by feminist ideals at a time when feminism itself was still quite incipient in Brazil were responsible for this wording (Correa 1993; Interview 6, 7). Not long after the publication of the program, Ana Costa, one of its designers, moved to Goiânia, the capital of the Brazilian state of Goiás, and began to implement a policy along those lines for the state government. She collaborated intensely with feminists outside the state, many of whom worked or volunteered for small non-governmental organizations (Interviews 6, 7, and 9).

Two years after the creation of PAISM, the federal government created the National Council for Women's Rights, which, despite its governmental origins, became a major arena for feminist organizing (Alvarez 1998). In 1986, the Council organized the first (and only) National Conference for Health and Women's Rights which approved a "Letter from Brazilian Women to the Constitutional Assembly." This document reaffirmed the main ideas of PAISM (Costa 2009). By then, however, some of the problems that would plague the program over the next two decades were already visible: the lack of guaranteed financial and human resources, the need to restructure the nation's hospital network, and the resistance of many health professionals to a more integrated, preventative, and patient empowering approach.

The 1990s was not a particularly favorable period for improving on that situation. In addition to fiscal crisis and structural adjustment policies that drastically limited the government's capacity to advance any major social policy, it was hard to mobilize government commitment to the integrated approach. Ana Costa (n.d.; 2009) laments that in the 1990s, the department responsible for the program's implementation was once again renamed "maternal health," going against the attempt to broaden the scope of women's health policy. The idea of integrated health care "went back to being a civil society agenda" (Costa 2009). During this time, our interviewees noted, the presence of feminists inside the ministry of health also declined and by the mid-1990s, the Catholic Church seems to have had greater influence than the feminist movement, a fact reflected in the appointment of Zilda Arns, an activist closely connected to the church known for her work building programs for impoverished children, to coordinate the maternal health program, responsible for PAISM (Interview 9).

During this period, feminism consolidated and professionalized in Brazil, but also fragmented, as multiple groups claimed to speak for women's interests from different discursive standpoints (Alvarez 1998). In the area of women's health, a variety of networks appeared with different perspectives. One group was the National Feminist Network for Reproductive and Sexual Rights, also known as the Feminist Health Network, which worked on traditional feminist concerns such as reproductive rights, abortion rights, sexuality, and violence against women. This network had a long history of participating in government policy arenas, sitting on councils, as consultants, or even coordinating agencies. Another coalition, created in the mid-1990s was the Network for the Humanization of Childbirth (ReHuNa), founded by a mix of feminist and non-feminist health professionals seeking to combat the medicalization of childbirth and Brazil's extremely high caesarian section rates and to empower women's role in the birthing process. Other organizations, such as the Articulation of Brazilian Women, and the World Women's March, also worked on health issues, with a focus on the issues of poor women and closer connections to grassroots movements (Interviews 1, 3, 7, 8, 9).

These networks express the diversity of the women's movement in Brazil, in terms of agendas, organizational structures, party ties, and political influence. The networks are internally dense, but also interconnected, with many activists belonging to more than one of them. It was not uncommon over the period we studied for members of both the Feminist Health Network and the Humanization of Childbirth Network to work closely with, if not *in*, the Technical Area for Women's Health. Between 1998 and 2002, a new minister brought in professionals with connections to feminist movements and the Maternal Health sector was renamed "Technical Area for Women's Health," a change understood to mean a return to PAISM's focus on an integrated approach to women's health. The Technical Area designed a number of guidelines for the national health system that would be lauded by feminists. Brazilian law prohibits abortions except in two situations: rape and when the mother's life is at risk, but these exceptions were rarely carried out, in part because the health care system did not know how to deal with them. In 1998, the Area approved a rule for preventing and treating the consequences of sexual violence against women and adolescents that guaranteed the right to abortion in cases of sexual violence and provided financial support for those services. A year later, it published a technical manual on high risk pregnancy that provided guidelines on abortions when a mother's life was at risk. Under the coordination of Tania Lago, a feminist academic, the Area also played an important role in promoting normal child birth and reducing caesarian sections (Costa 2009; Interviews 1,6,7,9).

When President Lula came to office in 2003, PAISM got a further boost when his health minister named Maria Jose de Araújo, one of the founders of the Feminist Health Network, to be coordinator of the Technical Area. She led the effort to transform the program into a "policy." The difference would be that rather than having only a small staff and delimited responsibilities, a policy would have to be implemented throughout the ministry. PAISM was replaced by the PNAISM, the National Policy for Integrated Women's Health Care (*Política Nacional de Assistência Integral da Saúde*). The guidelines also incorporated new ideas, explicitly emphasizing that health policy should address the needs of a diversity of social groups such as black women, rural workers, lesbians, HIV positive women, and so on. The Technical Area would now be responsible not just for implementing particular projects but also for guaranteeing that the policy was implemented throughout the ministry, and, if possible, the health care system as a whole.

The Lula period is described by the feminists we interviewed as the heyday of women's health, a period when the ideal of "integrated" care was taken seriously. The new government made a broader commitment to women's rights when, in 2003, it created a special agency for women's policies, directly linked to the president's office and a year later held the first National Conference for Women's Policies. In the Technical Area for Women's Health, people connected to both the Feminist Health Network and ReHuNa were involved in policy-making, for example, by being hired as consultants in a 2006 effort to evaluate the first three years of the new Women's Health Policy (Interview 9). President Lula and the Health Ministers he hired also worked to make space within the government and in the public debate for the abortion issue, especially through public statements to the effect that the abortion was a public health problem that the nation needed to face.[8]

In 2010, Lula campaigned for his self-designated successor and ex-Chief-of-Staff, Dilma Rousseff to be elected president. Although Lula continued to have extremely high rates of popularity, Rousseff was little known to the public and perceived largely as a technocrat. Pulling off her election required the construction of a new coalition, part of which involved seeking out the vote of the powerful evangelical Protestant lobby in congress. Despite the symbolic gains of a woman president, this alliance did not bode well for feminist goals, especially with respect to the abortion issue. One institutional activist who worked in the government in both periods commented on how different the new climate was:

> Under Lula, we were not afraid to say, "I'll go after a deputy who defends abortion for us to work on an abortion bill." Now [under Rousseff], we can't make alliances with those who support abortion because we cannot make our position explicit. We have to stay on the fence the whole time... (Interview 3).

In addition to the greater influence of religious groups, another source of tension with feminists in the new government was the creation of a new program for reducing maternal mortality. During her campaign for the presidency, Rousseff promised to revolutionize childbirth policy in Brazil by creating the "Stork Network" (*Rede Cegonha*). Upon taking office, she announced that the government would spend nine billion reais (about US$4.5 billion), refurbishing and building maternity wards and guaranteeing high quality prenatal care and childbirth to women in the public health system. The Stork Network would be coordinated by the Technical Area for Women's Health. The Minister of Health invited Esther Vilela, one of the founders of ReHuNa and a long-time activist in the movement for humanized childbirth, to coordinate the program.

Activists linked to the Feminist Health Network denounced the program as a huge step backwards. As they saw it, after so many years of building a more integrated approach, women's health went back to a narrow focus on maternity. People connected to ReHuNa understood things differently. Although they too were discomfited by the silly name, the nomination of Vilela to the job meant that the idea of "humanization" and of an integrated approach was not to be abandoned. It would be first time major federal resources would go to policies promoting a vision of childbirth that prioritized women's empowerment. For the most part, feminists did not so much reject those ideas but rather questioned the emphasis on one component of women's health. Several interviewees also noted that many

---

8 For example, in his keynote speech at the 11th National Conference on Human Rights, in Brasília, Lula declared that abortion should be understood as a public health issue. See: http://g1.globo.com/Noticias/Brasil/0,,MUL923651-5598,00-LULA+DIZ+QUE+ABORTO+E+QUESTAO+DE+SAUDE+PUBLICA+E+DEFENDE+DEBATE+SOBRE+O+TEM.html (accessed on August 16, 2013).

(but not all) members of ReHuNa were feminists and that the idea of humanizing childbirth was consistent with feminist ideals. The feeling that conservative sectors had much more influence over the government agenda, however, made feminists pessimistic about the program and often led them to criticize the work of their erstwhile allies who now worked on the inside of the bureaucracy. This is the difficult context that we will explore in the next section.

Activism on the Inside: Women's Health Policy in the Rousseff Government

The Technical Area for Women's Health employs about 30 people in a single large room in the Department of Strategic and Programmatic Action, which also includes other thematically defined units, such as Men's Health, Children's Health, Adolescent Health, Mental Health, Health in the Penitentiary system, and so on. Until the creation of the Stork Network, the Area was mainly responsible for designing guidelines and programs that would steer service provision in the national health care system related to prenatal health, childbirth, contraception, maternal mortality, sexual rights, menopause, cancer, and violence against women. The Area personnel spend most of their time negotiating those rules and their implementation with other agencies in the Health Ministry, with state and municipal governments, and with other actors. The coordination of the Stork Network now looms large over those other responsibilities, although they still must work on other issues under their purview. Building and renovating maternity wards throughout the country are not directly under the Area's control, but its personnel define the basic operating rules, examine and approve building plans, carry out training programs, and coordinate regional planning and monitoring networks, among other related activities. The challenge for institutional activists committed to feminist ideas is to transform this kind of work into a vehicle for promoting women's reproductive and sexual rights.

According to the Area's website, the unit was created to implement the Integrated Women's Health Care Program (PAISM), discussed earlier, which it describes as:

> ... a historic document that incorporated feminist ideas into integral health care, including making the Brazilian state responsible for reproductive health. In this way the definition of priority actions was based on the needs of the female population, which implied a rupture from the model of infant and mother's health that had dominated until then.[9]

On face value, then, the Area would seem to be the uncontested territory of the feminist movement. However, as the last section suggested, the unit's activities

---

9   http://portal.saude.gov.br/portal/saude/visualizar_texto.cfm?idtxt=25236 accessed on March 18, 2013.

were subject to intense and multi-layered conflicts not only among feminists within and outside the agency, but also with conservative religious movements who have put increasing pressure on the Area to obstruct what they understood to be a pro-abortion stance. Key actors here are parliamentarians linked to Catholic and Protestant organizations and churches, who are members of the Parliamentary Front in Defense of Life. Those political leaders were among the key organizers of an umbrella organization, the National Movement of Citizenship for Life, created in 2005 and dedicated largely to campaigning for pro-life candidates and organizing annual marches in Brasília.[10]

Increasing Tensions over Abortion under Rousseff

Two recent conflicts help illustrate the tense and conflict-ridden conditions under which the activists we interviewed try to influence women's health policy. In December 2011, President Rousseff issued a Provisional Measure (*Medida Provisória*) creating a registry for pregnant women. Provisional Measures are temporary laws decreed by the president that must be approved by the legislature within four months. They have been used systematically by Brazilian heads of state in recent years as a means to advance the presidential agenda in the legislature (Pereira, Power and Rennó 2008; Negretto 2004). The proposal in this case was to guarantee prenatal visits and to provide modest financial support to help registered women get to monthly doctor's appointments and to the hospital to give birth. Although not against those goals, the feminist movement interpreted the requirement that women register as a veiled attempt to control their bodies, since the registry would allow others to know, for example, if a pregnancy ended (intentionally or not). Some noted that with the recent passage of a law that guarantees better access to public information, the names of women receiving the transportation support would be on the public record, further increasing social or even legal sanctions should women be identified later as "no longer pregnant" (Interview 3). The issue was made incalculably worse by the fact that its first published version—to which the specialists at the Women's Health Area had no prior access—included a reference to "fetal rights." This terminology signaled to feminists that the document had been written by people aligned with the anti-abortion movement. The Women's Health Area was only indirectly involved in writing the measure, which according to interviewees was drafted by people in a different secretariat of the ministry and in the Casa Civil, the agency responsible for coordinating the federal government. Women's Health Area personnel found inclusion of the anti-abortion terminology to be particularly baffling and were able to get it removed in a rectification of the decree a month later (Interview 1).

It was too late. Despite the removal of the terminology, feminists mobilized intensely against what they now called the "Fetus Measure" ("*MP do Nascituro*"). In a broad campaign on the Internet, women's groups claimed that the Measure

---

10   http://www.brasilsemaborto.com.br/ accessed on August 16, 2013.

threatened women's reproductive freedom.[11] According to some interviewees, President Rousseff's decision soon after to nominate renowned abortion-rights feminist, Eleonora Menicucci, to head up the Secretariat of Women's Policy was an attempt to rebuild trust with feminists after this incident.[12] The administration also decided to abandon the pregnancy registry and allowed the measure to expire at the end of the 120-day period, neither attempting to implement the policy nor insisting that the legislature vote it into law. Feminist blogs and websites celebrated the decision as a victory for the women's movement and a sign that the government had come to its senses.[13]

The second conflict quickly threw cold water on that celebration. In late May 2012, just a few days before the provisional measure expired, the abortion issue came up at national seminar on maternal mortality, held in Brasilia by the National Health Council.[14] Given the huge numbers of illegal abortions estimated to occur in Brazil, mostly under unsanitary conditions, abortion is one of the main causes of maternal mortality. In the months preceding the meeting, health ministry officials had been putting together a proposal for reducing abortion-related deaths by way of a "harm reduction policy." The idea, modeled on recent experiences in Uruguay, was that even though abortion is illegal in Brazil, health care providers should be understood to be responsible for providing women with information about the dangers of certain procedures. Such policies had been discussed previously in the health ministry and had a precedent in drug use policy in, for example, programs encouraging disposable needle use (Interview 1, 6). At the May meeting, the Secretary of Health Care declared to the press that the ministry was studying a

---

11   In January 2012, a number of feminist organizations, such as the World Women's March, the Articulation of Brazilian Women, and the Feminist Women's Health Network, published protest letters. See, for example, http://www.agenciapatriciagalvao.org.br/index. php?option=com_content&view=article&id=2595:feministas-exigem-a-retirada-da-mp-557-que-cria-o-cadastro-nacional-da-gestante&catid=52:pautas, accessed on August 15, 2013; http://www.feminismo.org.br/livre/index.php?option=com_content&view=arti cle&id=7277:nota-publica-pela-imediata-revogacao-da-medida-provisoria-no-557&catid=81:europe&Itemid=458, accessed on August 15, 2013; and http://www. viomundo.com.br/politica/rede-feminista-de-saude-e-contra-a-mp-557-por-razoes-tecnicas-eticas-politicas-e-conceituais.html, accessed on August 15, 2013.

12   Representatives of major feminist organizations commemorated the decision: See http://www.viomundo.com.br/politica/feministas-aplaudem-escolha-de-nova-ministra-da-secretaria-de-mulheres.html, accessed on August 15, 2013.

13   See: http://www.cfemea.org.br/index.php?option=com_content& view=article&id=3698:31-de-maio-sem-mp-557-vitoria-das-mulheres-brasileiras&catid=218:artigos-e-textos&Itemid=152 accessed on August 15, 2013; and http:// www.viomundo.com.br/politica/caducou-a-mp-557-vitoria-dos-movimentos-sociais.html accessed on August 15, 2013.

14   http://conselho.saude.gov.br/ultimas_noticias/2012/25_mai_maternidae_ maternal_seminario.html.

new policy along these lines.[15] According to one interviewee, this declaration was not what set off the crisis. The problems arose when the head of a pro-abortion non-governmental organization declared that his group had been hired to write a pamphlet on how to have a safe abortion. The ministry denied the declaration and the NGO retracted it, but again, it was too late.

The repercussions came a few days later, when the story came out on the front page of a major national newspaper (*Folha de São Paulo*, June 6, 2012). Religious groups flooded the ministry with emails and letters, and members of the "evangelical caucus" in the national congress began to file official requests for information about women's health policy.[16] On June 26, the Movimento Brasil Sem Aborto, mentioned earlier, initiated a Twitter campaign under the hashtag #BrasilSemAborto (Brazil without abortion).[17] The Technical Area began to spend huge amounts of time answering queries. Their every action was now under observation, with repeated queries coming in, for example, about why ministry officials had attended a meeting in Uruguay in which, the letter writers suspected, that country's pro-choice policies had been discussed (Interviews 1, 2, 3). The government announced soon after that it was abandoning the idea of "harm reduction." Words such as "abortion" and "misoprostol" (a medication used to cause abortions) were avoided from then on in government documents and declarations. Several interviewees noted that Menicucci, the Secretary of Women's Policy, stopped using those words too, despite the fact that in her earlier career, she had mobilized actively and openly in favor of abortion rights.

These are the conditions under which a group of activists who worked in the Women's Health Technical Area operated. The relationship between the activists inside the government and the feminist movement was tense. Several of those we interviewed expressed frustration with what they called "the feminist movement," perceived by some as obsessed only with abortion, to the exclusion of other women's issues (such as pregnancy and childbirth) and by others as intolerant and hierarchical, with little openness to younger activists (Interviews 1, 2, 4, 6). Although they often felt that (some) feminists outside the state questioned their "authenticity," all of the Area employees we interviewed clearly identified with feminist ideas, loosely understood. In particular, they unanimously expressed the idea that childbirth policy and the abortion issue could not be easily separated. The need to deal with the fact that many women arrive in health services desiring to end their pregnancies, or after recently having done so, seemed to be constantly on the mind of these professionals. As one participant remarked, at an informal

---

15   http://www1.folha.uol.com.br/cotidiano/1100945-governo-estuda-adotar-medidas-de-reducao-de-danos-para-aborto-ilegal.shtml.

16   http://www1.folha.uol.com.br/cotidiano/1101584-religiosos-criticam-projeto-de-reducao-de-danos-para-aborto.shtml, accessed on August 15, 2013.

17   http://www1.folha.uol.com.br/paineldoleitor/ultimasdasredessociais/1110787-campanha-contra-aborto-mobiliza-internautas-no-twitter.shtml, accessed on August 15, 2013.

meeting we observed during the field work, "As soon as a woman finds out she is pregnant, there is the possibility that she wants to terminate the pregnancy, and the professionals around her have a responsibility to protect her health if she decides to do so."

Artisanal Activism

Over the course of an ordinary working day, institutional activists in the Women's Health Area found themselves faced with the difficult task of delicately promoting this agenda in a context in which the government was treating the anti-abortion lobby with kid gloves. Seemingly simple activities—such as writing a handbook on procedures for pregnancy testing—were imbued with complexities. How should a health professional proceed with the test? Should results be given by a health professional or should women be allowed to receive them without having to speak to anyone? Should professionals inquire whether pregnancy is desired? What should they do if the patient expresses the wish to terminate the pregnancy? Trying to influence how health professionals make these hard decisions through the elaboration of a technical manual is activism at the most *detailed* level of policy-making. Activists sought to design training programs, write rules for building plans, or define wording protocols and decrees in ways that promoted particular ideological perspectives. Those projects were not necessarily in keen accordance with the official positions of the government hierarchy, but could not explicitly contradict higher level policies. This activist engagement in policy-making occurred under substantial pressure from various directions: Wording too strong would easily invite the ire of the evangelical caucus; wording too weak would inevitably bring on more criticism from feminists who were already quick to question the commitment of those working on the inside. The artistic balancing of these pressures is what we call *artisanal activism.*

To take one example, the pregnancy test manual under discussion at the time of our field work went through dozens of revisions, as the authors worked out carefully calibrated wording that would be approved for publication. Activists decided to move a statement that explicitly noted that conversations between health care workers should be confidential from the section about how to deal with unwanted pregnancies to a more general section that presented the conditions under which the test should be taken (Departamento de Ações Programáticas, in press: 9). This, according to one interviewee, was necessary to guarantee that no one would accuse them of promoting conversations about abortion in the doctor's office.

Along the same lines, the earlier version required health professionals to inform any patient with an unwanted pregnancy that should she come to have a medical emergency as a consequence of a (presumably illegal) abortion, she should "seek out the nearest hospital … without fear of punishment, since she will always be protected by professional secrecy." In the final version, that statement was cut. Instead, the activists added a section at the beginning of the handbook on how international law guarantees a women's right to reproductive self-determination. Now the document explicitly noted that international conventions require that women have access to the abortion services foreseen by national laws "and according to her free decision, without risk or discrimination" (Ibid., 7). The idea was to present a more neutral and authoritative source of support for their attempt to get health providers to, at least, conduct those abortions that are allowed by law (in the case of rape or danger to the mother's life). They also sought out (and obtained) the official support of two professional associations, one representing gynecologists and obstetricians, and the other representative obstetrical nurses. Both associations agreed to co-sign the document, which the bureaucrats hoped would dilute any criticisms against the Technical Area.

Activism within the bureaucracy—especially in politically charged environments such as this one—involved learning to deal with censures and limitations and with a bureaucratic structure that resists change. The staff member we interviewed who had worked longest in the ministry commented on how hard it was for social movement activists to adapt to this environment:

> When people from civil society come into the ministry they often get disillusioned because they encounter a reality that does not correspond with their desires ... Here sometimes you work and work and work for an idea that you believe in and you cannot implement it the way you believe in. And you need to adapt quickly. You suffer today and tomorrow you need to be here, ready for the next idea ... and there are people who cannot stand the heartbreak (Interview 5).

Several of those we interviewed complained about the extreme difficulty in getting simple decisions off the ground, such as to purchase plane tickets or pay stipends to hold a meeting. For some, such difficulties were almost too much to bear:

> I know I am not from this place and I won't stay very long ... my cholesterol went up from eating so much bureaucracy (Interview 1).

> Because you can stand it up to a point, the stagnation, the being in a place where you can't operationalize things. Bureaucracy, hierarchy, power play, all that is very strong ... I think there is a time for everything. I think I will go back to the movement, with this knowledge, with this vision (Interview 2).

But for the moment they were bearing it, and often came up with creative strategies for doing so. One of the activists we interviewed—who was particularly critical of the current policy—told us that she often "whispered in the ear" of her feminist friends outside the government to suggest that they bring up criticisms and questions that she herself was unable to raise (Interview 3). Creative solutions could sometimes be found for getting things done, for example, by transferring funds to non-governmental organizations that would be able to operate at a quicker pace (Interview 4).

Comments about frustrations were accompanied by affirmations that helped explain why these women kept on investing in the bureaucracy as a space for activism. For many, the "up" side lay in the power to intervene in public policies on a grand scale, to make an agenda move forward, even if not at the speed or intensity they had hoped for.

> I started to like making regulations ... at the time I thought, 'I cannot believe I am going to have the chance to transform all that we learned in practice, into a government regulation!' ... and we went there, and it wasn't easy, but we did it and that makes me want to do things that will make a difference out in the real world (Interview 1).

> I think it is strategic to be in the government, working with national policies that are going to make a difference for an immense population ... you know that what you are doing is making a difference. Of course I know my place; I say what I can say ... I do not do anything that is not authorized. But I think it is fundamental to have people with a different kind of experience, who are not technocrats, who know about social movements, inside the government. Because you bring this perspective ... of someone who is from the other side, to a space that tends to be very rigid and technocratic (Interview 3).

Career Trajectories and Activist Networks

The institutional activists we interviewed had long experience as participants in social movement networks outside the state. When they took government jobs, they brought with them different kinds of skills and resources for dealing with limitations and for pushing forward their diverse political agendas. One group began their activism as part of a medical practice committed to the principles of health reform. Others were feminists who for various reasons got involved in the debate about health care. Some were involved in both kinds of practices, such as one of the feminist professionals who worked in the Ministry of Health way back in the 1980s and helped put feminist ideas into PAISM. These different kinds of life histories brought with them different resources.

One group of activists we interviewed was deeply influenced by participation in feminist movements. One activist had participated for years in an organization dedicated to supporting HIV positive people, which eventually led her to get involved in a state-level network of feminist organizations. In that role, she participated in various campaigns, organized protests, and did other activities. Another had been active in the student movement in the 1970s and had worked for more than a decade at a feminist NGO. She represented that organization on a state government commission responsible for investigating maternal mortality. A third had little work experience outside government, but had gotten involved in a feminist youth network while in college to which she was still closely connected. The members of the network remained an important part of her private life, although as a member of the government she did not participate directly in the activities of civil society organizations. Indeed all three said that joining government necessarily implied breaking formal ties with "the movement."

A second group of activists had prior careers in professional movements in which *practicing* alternative models had been a key mode of action. Esther Vilela, the Coordinator of the Women's Health Area in the Rousseff Government had a career less associated with political movements than with a network of professionals seeking to transform the medical profession. Before working in government she worked for 20 years as a doctor and hospital administrator. Although Vilela was active on the national scene as a founder of ReHuNa and a speaker at innumerable events, most of her energies had been centered on building practical experiments in poor areas, inspired by the health reform movement. Over the course of several decades, she helped build a maternity ward that sought to implement the "humanization" approach. In the 1990s, the hospital—that served mainly poor people dependent on the public health system in a small town in an agricultural region of central Brazil—gained national renown. Hundreds of visitors and medical and nursing interns, some from other countries, helped disseminate this approach.

These are not the only career routes that might lead one to institutional activism. One activist we interviewed worked for decades within government, as part of the health movement, and for sure, there are many other possible trajectories. Different experiences gave activists different kinds of skills. The three feminist activists we interviewed had skills and experiences in articulating feminist ideas in contentious environments. One of them described her work in the government as largely related to promoting women's health policies throughout the vast Ministry of Health and with other government agencies. Another mentioned the work she did trying to build dialogue with feminist organizations outside the state. Vilela brought with her a different kind of resource. Her deep knowledge of health care practice gave her many ideas about how to design procedures and training programs, and write manuals and policy documents. She also brought with her a network of other people with practical experience: She hired a large number of consultants who, like her, had been working in the health profession trying to promote alternative approaches.

The Art of Institutional Activism

This chapter does not intend to provide a conclusive theory of institutional activism. Our intention is much more an invitation to study a phenomenon that often has been invisible in social movement theory. Still, the social movement literature provides important theoretical and methodological tools that allow us to take some steps in that direction, but we need to invest more systematically in understanding how activism works inside the bureaucracy. Latin America, and Brazil in particular, provides a rich terrain for this investigation. At various territorial levels, and in a diversity of institutional environments and policy areas, activists have occupied positions within the state. How can we define this kind of activism more precisely? What are the differences between the practices of a state official inserted in social movement networks and those of an ordinary bureaucrat or of one whose ties are to other kinds of networks (such as political parties, families, or economic interest groups)? What kinds of public policies result when social movement activists become policy-makers? These are the kinds of questions that Brazilian scholars are beginning to explore and which are likely of interest to other Latin American scholars as well.

We hope to move forward in the construction of conceptual tools that allow us to identify, name, and evaluate the richness and complexity of institutional activism. Our discussion here helps us think about two aspects of the phenomenon: what kind of work institutional activists do and what difference it makes that these actors are connected to social movement networks.

The work involved in institutional activism is characterized by political and operational constraints and involves a great deal of creative problem-solving around micro-issues on a day-to-day basis. Action in bureaucracies is limited by red tape on the one hand, and by the commands of higher officials on the other. Institutional activists are likely to have more flexibility when their projects coincide with those of their superiors, a situation that is likely to fluctuate over time, depending on broader political and party dynamics. Synchrony of projects creates, for the institutional activist, an opportunity to advance her goals. Indeed, it is often such synchrony that allows for activists to get appointed to a particular job in the first place. Working in understaffed and underfunded policy agencies is much more difficult than working in more efficient ones, yet the Brazilian experience suggests that it is precisely these agencies that are more likely to give jobs to people from social movements, since such organizations are more likely to need their expertise. The Brazilian Ministry of Health had few permanent employees and depended greatly on the work of consultants and subcontracted personnel who rarely stayed for very long in one place. This uninstitutionalized character gave activists some flexibility, but it also made it difficult to get projects implemented on a large scale. They usually had to content themselves to making incremental changes, and to trying to maximize the effects of small actions, such as a well-placed word in a decree or a training manual.

Links to social movement networks influence this incremental problem-solving work with resources, opportunities, limits, and meanings. We propose two arguments about how the networks that these state officials have built over their previous activist careers affect their work inside government agencies.

First, institutional activists survive the inhospitable terrain of the bureaucracy in part because they use those networks—and the resources they can access through them—to deal with the particular constraints of working within government institutions. Ann Mische's (2009) relational approach to social movements helped us think of how activists mobilize resources through networks. Her framework draws on a Simmellian view of modern social life as constructed through "intersecting social circles" (Mische 2009, p. 22). The projects people define for themselves and the resources they mobilize to pursue those projects are constructed out of life experiences through which they participate in and help build a multiplicity of interconnecting networks. People define future projects by scanning "their typified knowledge from past experiences while confronting an uncertain, multipronged array of future possibilities" (Ibid., 45). Mische encourages us to look at the life experience and career trajectory of activists to better understand the kinds of strategies in which they engage.

If as Abers and von Bülow (2011) propose, social movements can be thought of as networks with filaments creeping into (or even growing out from) the bureaucracy, then institutional activists may be distinguished from other kinds of bureaucrats in that they have access to the resources contained in movement networks (Lin 2002). Our case study identified this kind of network-based resource mobilization in various forms. Activists used their networks politically: to gain political support and to build alliances, to sustain agendas and to mobilize reactions against set-backs. They also used their networks to get work done. They regularly met with people they knew who had experience in the field to help design projects, implement training efforts, write pamphlets, and many other activities. It was common practice for institutional activists to get short-term consulting jobs for people who they had worked with in the past or otherwise knew and trusted through past experience. These connections serve a dual purpose: If on the one hand, they help the institutional activist deal with the challenges of their job, they also offer other network members the chance to influence policy-making.

Second, social movement networks put constraints on the actions of institutional activists that other public officials do not face. The networks that activists belong to can be a source of guidance—instigating insider activists, for example, to maintain radical goals or to defend particular priorities. But when activists are unable to fulfill those expectations, they risk losing access to the precious resources just discussed above. This is particularly true when the policy climate weighs against movement goals, as many feminists understood the situation to be when Dilma Rousseff included religious groups in her political coalition.

These problems are made worse by the fact that social movements like feminism are complex and contradictory. Institutional activists may have loyalties to particular agendas (abortion, natural childbirth, LGBT issues, and so on), but to maintain legitimacy, they may need to be accountable to other groups in the broader movement. But these groups have different understandings of what it means to be a feminist and of what kind of policies "really" advance women's rights. Under these conditions, satisfying everyone is impossible. Institutional activism is, to a certain extent, about figuring out how to navigate all these demands and limitations. Activists must deal not only with the rigidity of the bureaucracy and the changing demands from superiors engaged in government-wide coalition building, but also with the demands of activists on the outside, who are often quick to question the commitments of their colleagues on the inside.

By exploring the micro-strategies of activists involved in making Brazil's women's health policy, we hope to help break open the "black box" of the Latin American state in social movement studies. Although the literature on social movements has largely gone beyond the presumption that the state and movements are inherently antagonistic, few studies have explored the dynamics of relations between movements and bureaucracies. In particular, we need to know more about what activists do when they decide to take up jobs in government. The presence of bureaucrats committed to social movement goals and with close professional connections to social movement networks is not a phenomenon that began in the 2000s when leftist parties such as the Workers Party came to federal office. These practices have a longer history but are largely invisible in a literature that tends to see the state as the object of claims making rather than as a place where activism might actually occur. We hope that by looking at the dynamics of that activism, we have shed some light not only on the intricacies of state-movement relations, but also on the day-to-day challenges of working toward transformative goals in any kind of highly institutionalized, politically contentious environment.

References

Abers, Rebecca Neaera, 2000. *Inventing local democracy: grassroots politics in Brazil.* Boulder: Lynne Rienner.

Abers, Rebecca Neaera, Serafim, Lizandra and Tatagiba Luciana, 2014. "Repertoires of state-society interaction in a heterogeneous state: the experience under Lula." In: Fabio de Castro, Kees Koonings and Marianne Wiesebron, eds. *Brazil of Lula: A country in transformation.* London: Palgrave.

Abers, Rebecca Neaera and Keck, Margaret E., 2013. *Practical authority: agency and institutional change in Brazilian water politics.* New York: Oxford University Press.

Abers, Rebecca Neaera and von Bülow, Marisa, 2011. "Movimentos sociais na teoria e na prática: como estudar o ativismo através da fronteira entre estado e sociedade?" *Sociologias*, 13(28), pp. 52–84.

Alonso, Angela, 2009. "As teorias dos movimentos sociais: um balanço do debate." *Lua Nova*, 76, pp. 49–86.

Alonso, Angela, Costa, Valeriano and Maciel, Débora, 2007. "Identidade e estratégia na formação do movimento ambientalista Brasileiro." *Novos estudos-CEBRAP* (79), pp. 151–67.

Alvarez, Sonia E., 1990. *Engendering democracy in Brazil. Women's movement in transition politics.* Princeton: Princeton University Press.

———, 1998. "A 'globalização' dos feminismos Latino-Americanos: tendências dos anos 90 e desafios para o novo milênio." In: Sonia E. Alvarez, Evelina

Dagnino and Arturo Escobar, eds. *Cultura e política nos movimentos sociais Latino-americanos: novas leituras.* Belo Horizonte: UFMG, pp. 383–426.

Alvarez, Sonia E. and Escobar, Arturo eds, 1992. *The making of social movements in Latin America. Identity, strategy, and democracy.* Oxford: Westview Press.

Arnson, Cynthia J. and Perales, José Raúl, 2007. *The 'new left' and democratic governance in Latin America.* Washington D.C.: Woodrow Wilson Center.

Banaszak, Lee Ann, 2005. "Inside and outside the state: movement insider status, tactics, and public policy achievements." In: David S. Meyer, Valerie Jenness and Helen M. Ingram, eds. *Routing the opposition: social movements, public policy, and democracy.* Minneapolis: University of Minnesota Press, pp. 149–77.

———, 2010. *The women's movement inside and outside the state.* New York: Cambridge University Press.

Banaszak, Lee Ann, Beckwith, Karen and Rucht, Dieter eds, 2003. *Women's movements facing the reconfigured state.* New York: Cambridge University Press.

Berk, Gerald, and Galvan, Dennis, 2009. "How People experience and change institutions: a field guide to creative syncretism." *Theory and Society,* 38(6), pp. 543–80.

Bevir, Mark, and Richards, David, 2009. "Decentering policy networks: a theoretical agenda." *Public Administration,* 87(1), pp. 3–14.

Blikstad, Karin Deleuze, 2012. *O agir coletivo nas interfaces da sociedade civil e do sistema político. O caso da atuação do movimento de moradia de são Paulo sobre a política pública de habitação.* Unicamp, Dissertação de Mestrado, 2012.

Boschi, Renato and Valadares, Licia, 1983. "Problemas teóricos na análise de movimentos sociais; comunidade, ação coletiva e o papel do Estado." *Espaço & Debates,* 3(8), pp. 42–60.

Cannon, Barry and Peadar, Kirby, 2012. *Civil society and the state in left-led Latin America.* London: Zed Books.

Cardoso, Ruth, 1983. "Movimentos sociais: balanço crítico." In: SORJ and Maria Herminia T. Almeida, eds. *Sociedade e política no Brasil pós-64, B.* São Paulo: Brasiliense.

———, 1987. "Movimentos sociais na América Latina." *Revista Brasileira de Ciências Sociais,* 03(1), pp. 27–37.

Chappell, Louise, 2003. *Gendering government: feminist engagement with the state in Australia and Canada.* Toronto: UBC Press.

Cohen, Jean L., and Arato, Andrew, 1992. *Civil society and political theory.* Cambridge: MIT Press.

Coit, Katharine, 1978. "Local action, not citizen participation." In: William K. Tabb and Larry Sawyers, eds. *Marxism and the metropolis: new perspectives in urban political economy.* New York: Oxford University Press.

Correa, Sonia, 1993. "PAISM. Uma história sem fim." *Revista Brasileira de Estudos Populacionais, Campinas,* 10(1/2), pp. 3–12

Costa, Ana Maria. n.d. "Política de saúde integral da mulher direitos sexuais e reprodutivos." In: Lígia Giovanella, Sarah Escorel, Lenaura de Vasconcelos Costa Lobato, José Carvalho de Noronha and Antonio Ivo de Carvalho, eds. *Políticas e sistema de saúde no Brasil*, 2nd edition. Fiocruz, CEBES, [online] Available at: <http://www.abem-educmed.org.br/pdf/politicas_sistema.pdf> [Accessed on 7 June 2013].

———, 1992. PAISM: uma política de assistência integral à saúde da mulher a ser resgatada. Comissão de Cidadania e Reprodução, São Paulo [online] Available at: <http://www.ccr.org.br/pesquisas-dossies-detalhe.asp?cod=28>.

———, 2009. "Participação social na conquista das políticas de saúde para mulheres no Brasil." *Ciência e Saúde Coletiva*, 14(4), pp. 1073–1083.

Dagnino, Evelina, Olvera, Alberto J. and Panfichi, Aldo, 2006. "Para uma Outra Leitura da Disputa pela Construção Democrática na América Latina." In: Evelina Dagnino, Alberto J. Olvera and Aldo Panfichi, eds. *A disputa pela construção democrática na América Latina*. São Paulo: Paz e Terra, pp. 13–92.

D'Araújo, Maria Celina ed., 2007. *Governo Lula: contornos sociais e políticos da elite no poder*. Rio de Janeiro: CPDOC.

Davis, Diane, 1999. "The power of distance: re-theorizing social movements in Latin America." *Theory and Society*, 28, pp. 585–638.

Departamento de Ações Programáticas, in press, 2013. "Teste rápido de gravidez na atenção básica: guia técnico." 1ª edição, Série A. Normas e Manuais Técnicos. *Série Direitos Sexuais e Direitos Reprodutivos*. Ministério de Meio Ambiente: Brasília–DF.

Diani, Mario, 1992. "The concept of social movement." *The Sociological Review*, 40, pp. 1–25.

Diani, Mario and McAdam, Doug ed., 2003. *Social movements and networks: relational approaches to collective action*. Oxford: Oxford University Press.

Doimo, Ana Maria, 1995. *A vez e a voz do popular: movimentos sociais e participação política no Brasil pós-70*. Rio de Janeiro: Relume-Dumará.

Dowbor, Monica, 2012. *Arte da institucionalização: estratégias de mobilização dos sanitaristas (1974–2006)*. Tese de doutorado: Universidade de São Paulo.

Dowding, Keith, 2008. "Model or metaphor? A critical review of the policy network approach." *Political Studies*, 43(1), pp. 136–58.

Eisenstein, Hester, 1990. "Femocrats, official feminism, and the uses of power." In: Sophie Watson ed. *Playing the state: Australian feminist interventions*. Philadelphia: Temple University Press, pp. 87–103.

Emirbayer, Mustafa, and Mische, Ann, 1998. "What is agency?" *American Journal of Sociology*, 103(4), pp. 962–1023.

Feltran, Gabriel de Santis, 2006. "Deslocamentos—trajetorias individuais, relações entre sociedade civil e estado no Brasil." In: Evelina Dagnino, Alberto J. Olvera and Aldo Panfichi, eds. *A disputa pela construção democrática na América Latina*. São Paulo: Paz e Terra, pp. 371–416.

Folha de São Paulo, 2012. "Governo estuda adotar medidas de redução de danos para aborto ilegal," June 6, 2012. [online] Available at: <http://www1.folha.

uol.com.br/fsp/cotidiano/47248-governo-estuda-adotar-medidas-de-reducao-de-danos-para-aborto-ilegal.shtml> [Accessed on 15 March 2013].

Foweraker, Joe, 1995. *Theorizing social movements.* London: Pluto Press.

Gittell, Marilyn, 1983. "The consequences of mandating citizen participation." *Policy Studies Review*, 3(1), pp. 90–95.

Giugni, Marco G., and Passy, Florence, 1998. "Contentious politics in complex societies: new social movements between conflict and cooperation." In: Marco G. Giugni, Doug McAdam and Charles Tilly, eds. *From contention to democracy.* Lanham: Rowman & Littlefield, pp. 81–107.

Gohn, Maria da Glória, 2000. *Teoria dos movimentos sociais. Paradigmas clássicos e contemporâneos.* São Paulo: Edições Loyola.

Goldstone, Jack A., 2003. "Bridging institutionalized and noninstitutionalized politics." In: Jack A. Goldstone, ed. *States, parties, and social movements*, New York: Cambridge University Press, pp. 1–24.

Grattet, Ryken, 2005. "The policy nexus: professional networks and the formulation and adoption of workers' compensation reforms." In: David S. Meyer, Valerie Jenness and Helen M. Ingram, eds. *Routing the opposition: social movements, public policy, and democracy.* Minneapolis: University of Minnesota Press, pp. 177–206.

Gurza Lavalle, Adrian, 2003. "Sem pena nem glória. O debate da sociedade civil nos anos 1990." *Novos Estudos Cebrap*, 66, pp. 91–109.

Haas, Peter M., 1992. "Introduction: epistemic communities and international policy coordination." *International Organization*, 46(1), pp. 1–35.

Hellman, J.A., 1992. "The study of new social movements in Latin América and the question of autonomy." In: Arturo Escobar and Sonia Alvarez, eds. *The making of social movements in Latin American. Identity, strategy and democracy.* Boulder: Westview Press, pp. 52–61.

Ingram, Mrill and Ingram, Helen M., 2005. "Creating credible edibles: the organic agriculture movement and the emergence of US federal organic standards." In: David S. Meyer, Valerie Jenness and Helen M. Ingram, eds. *Routing the opposition: social movements, public policy, and democracy.* Minneapolis: University of Minnesota Press, pp. 121–48.

Jenkins, J. Craig and Perrow, Charles, 1977. "Insurgency of the powerless: farm worker movements (1946–1972)." *American Sociological Review*, 42(2), pp. 249–68.

Jenkins-Smith, Hank C. and Sabatier, Paul, 1993. *Policy change and learning: an advocacy coalition approach.* Boulder: Westview Press.

Katzenstein, Mary Fainsod, 1999. *Faithful and fearless: moving feminist protest inside the church and military.* Princeton: Princeton University Press.

Kowarick, Lucio, 1987. "Movimentos urbanos no Brasil contemporâneo: uma análise da literatura." *Revista Brasileira de Ciências Sociais*, 3(1), pp. 38–50.

Lavalle, Adrian Gurza, 2003. "Sem pena nem glória: o debate sobre a sociedade civil nos anos 1990." *Novos Estudos*, 66, pp. 91–109.

Lin, Nan. 2002. *Social capital: a theory of social structure and action*. Cambridge: Cambridge University Press.

Losekann, Cristiana, 2009. A presença das organizações ambientalistas da sociedade civil no Governo Lula (2003–2007) e as tensões com os setores econômicos. Universidade Federal do Rio Grande do Sul, Tese de Doutorado, 2009.

Marris, Peter and Rein, Martin, 1967[1982]. *Dilemmas of social reform*. Chicago, University of Chicago Press.

McAdam, Doug and Tarrow, Sidney, 2010. "Ballots and barricades: on the reciprocal relationship between elections and social movements." *Perspectives on Politics*, 8(02), pp. 529–42.

Meyer, David S., 2005. "Introduction. Social movements and public policy: eggs, chicken, and theory." In: David S. Meyer, Valerie Jenness and Helen M. Ingram, eds. *Routing the opposition: social movements, public policy, and democracy*. Minneapolis: University of Minnesota Press, pp. 1–26.

Meyer, David S. and Tarrow, Sidney G., 1998. *The social movement society: contentious politics for a new century*. Lanham: Rowman & Littlefield.

Ministério da Saúde, Secretaria de Gestão Estratégica e Participativa, 2010. "Saúde da mulher: um diálogo aberto e participativo." Brasília, Distrito Federal," [online] Available at: <http://portal.saude.gov.br/portal/arquivos/pdf/saude_da_mulher_um_dialogo_aberto_part.pdf>.

Mische, Ann, 2009. *Partisan publics: communication and contention across Brazilian youth activist networks*. Princeton: Princeton University Press.

Negretto, Gabriel L., 2004. "Policy making by decree in Latin America: The cases of Brazil and Argentina." *Comparative Political Studies*, 37(5), pp. 531–62.

Osis, Maria José Martins Duarte, 1998. "PAISM: um marco na abordagem da saúde reprodutiva no Brasil." *Caderno Saúde Pública*, 14 (Supl. 1), pp. 25–32.

Pereira, Carlos, Power, Timothy J. and Rennó, Lucio, 2008. "Agenda power, executive decree authority, and the mixed results of reform in the Brazilian congress." *Legislative Studies Quarterly*, 34, pp. 5–34.

Piven, Frances Fox, 1970. "Whom does the advocacy planner serve?" *Social Policy*, 1 (May–June), pp. 32–36.

Piven, Frances Fox and Cloward, Richard, 1977. *Poor people's movements: why they succeed, how they fail*. New York: Vintage Books.

Rich, Jessica A.J., 2013. "Grassroots bureaucracy: intergovernmental relations and popular mobilization in Brazil's AIDS policy sector." *Latin American Politics and Society*, 55(2), pp. 1–25.

Rhodes, R.A.W., 1997. *Understanding governance: policy networks, governance, reflexivity, and accountability*. Buckingham: Open University Press.

Santoro, Wayne A., and McGuire, Gail M., 1997. "Social movement insiders: the impact of institutional activists on affirmative action and comparable worth policies." *Social Problems*, 44, pp. 503–19.

Sawer, Marian. 1990. *Sisters in suits: women and public policy in Australia*. Sydney: Allen and Unwin.

Selznick, Philip, 1949. *TVA and the grass roots: a study in the sociology of formal organization.* Berkeley: University of California Press.

Silva, Marcelo Kunrath, 2010. "De volta aos movimentos sociais?–Reflexões a partir da literatura brasileira recente." *Revista Ciências Sociais Unisinos,* 46, pp. 2–9.

Silva, Marcelo Kunrath and de Lima Oliveira, Gerson, 2011. "A face oculta(da) dos movimentos sociais: trânsito institucional e intersecção Estado-Movimento—uma análise do movimento de economia solidária no Rio Grande do Sul." *Sociologias,* 13(28), pp. 86–125.

Tarrow, Sidney, 1994. *Power in movement: social movements, collective action and politics.* Cambridge, Cambridge University Press.

Tatagiba, Luciana, 2009. "Relação entre movimentos sociais e instituições políticas no cenário brasileiro recente. Reflexões em torno de uma agenda preliminar de pesquisa." In: Sonia E. Alvarez, Gianpaolo Baiocchi, Agustín Laó-Montes, Jeffrey W. Rubin and Millie Thayer, eds. (forthcoming). *Interrogating the civil society agenda: social movements, civil society and democratic innovation.*

———, 2011. "Relação entre movimentos sociais e instituições políticas na cidade de São Paulo. O caso do movimento de moradia." In: Lucio Kowarick and Eduardo Marques, eds. *SÃO PAULO Miradas Cruzadas: Sociedad, política y cultura.* Quito: Olacchi.

Tatagiba, Luciana and Blikstad, Karin, 2011. "Como se fosse uma eleição para vereador: dinâmicas participativas e disputas partidárias na cidade de São Paulo." *Lua Nova,* 84, pp. 175–217.

Tatagiba, Luciana, Zagatto Paterniani, Stella and Trindade, Thiago, 2012. "Aparecido. Ocupar, reivindicar, participar: sobre o repertório de ação do movimento de moradia de São Paulo." *Opin. Publica,* 18(2), pp. 399–426.

Thatcher, Mark, 1998. "The development of policy network analyses from modest origins to overarching frameworks." *Journal of Theoretical Politics,* 10(4) (October 1), pp. 389–416.

Tilly, Charles, 1978. *From mobilization to revolution.* Reading, Addison-Wesley.

Weyland, Kurt, Madrid, Raul and Hunter, Wendy, 2010. *Left governments in Latin America: successes and shortcomings.* New York: Cambridge University Press.

PART II
The Politics and Economics
of Protests

Chapter 5

The Role of Threats in Popular Mobilization in Central America

Paul D. Almeida

Introduction

Hostile political and economic conditions often drive some of the largest and most extensive popular mobilization campaigns in the global South. Examples abound of unfavorable circumstances stimulating collective action from protests against brutal state repression to a variety of anti-austerity protests (Almeida 2008; Silva 2009; Rossi 2013; Tavera Fenollosa in this volume), including increasing food and electricity prices associated with the withdrawal of state subsidies. Given the abundance of research on the *positive incentives* in the political environment driving collective action in the form of opportunities (Tarrow 2011; McAdam 1999; Meyer 2004), this study seeks to build on the revived interest in the role of threat or the *negative* conditions in generating popular collective action (Goldstone and Tilly, 2001; Van Dyke and Soule 2002; Almeida 2003; Reese, Giedritis and Vega 2005; McVeigh 2009; Snow and Soule 2009; Dixon and Martin 2012; Dodson 2015).

As more scholarly attention over the past decade has focused on various forms of threat, a more precise classification of types of threats will assist in our shared understanding of the influence of negative incentives on collective action. Such an exercise also contributes to striking a balance in a field that has long emphasized the role of political opportunities in facilitating social movement activity (Jasper 2011). Because of the heavy emphasis on opportunities in previous research, I largely focus on threats in this chapter while acknowledging that in complex political environments various forms of both opportunity and threat may activate episodes of joint action. Below, I provide a conceptual typology of three forms of threat as scholars have previously developed for political opportunities. The typology is then applied to cases of mass collective action in Central America over the past century. I conclude with suggestions on future lines of inquiry that may further advance our understanding of the role of threats in generating large scale social movement-type activities.

I analyze cases from Central America because much collective action in this world region is driven by *negative* incentives, providing dozens of exemplary social struggles characterized by threat-induced mobilization. State repression, fiscal and economic crises, and environmental destruction provided the incentives for some of the largest acts of collective resistance in the region. From the 1950s to the 1980s, military repression drove the most dramatic acts of defiance in Guatemala, El Salvador, and Nicaragua (Booth 1991; Brockett 2005). From the 1990s to the 2000s, economic liberalization measures associated with the foreign debt crisis motivated the largest protest campaigns in all six Central American nations (Almeida 2014). In the 2010s, in addition to neoliberal economic policies, environmental harms appear to be creating conditions for dozens of mass struggles throughout the region.

These negative conditions are more precisely defined below as the threats of 1) state repression, 2) state-attributed economic problems, and 3) environmental harms. Subaltern groups must also obtain organizational resources and assets in order to sustain collective action in the face of mounting threats. In the following sections I offer a conceptual framework for understanding threat-induced contention and apply this multi-dimensional perspective to popular mobilization in Central America. The chapter aims to increase our understanding of the conditions in which specific forms of threat eventuate in collective action.

Three Forms of Threat

Charles Tilly made the original distinction between opportunities and threats in the late 1970s as two primary and independent forces driving collective action. He defined opportunities as "the extent to which other groups, including governments, are vulnerable to new claims which would, if successful, *enhance* the contender's realization of its interests" (Tilly 1978, p. 133). As a distinct and independent catalyst for mobilization, Tilly defined threats as the "extent to which other groups are threatening to make claims which would, if successful, *reduce* the contender's realization of its interests" (Tilly 1978, p. 133). It is largely the costs of inaction that motivates threatened groups to join collectively to defend their interests (Tilly 1978; Goldstone and Tilly 2001).

Tilly also contended that a "given amount of *threat tends to generate more collective action* than the 'same' amount of opportunity" (Tilly 1978, pp. 134–35). Hence, if threats are predicted to produce more collective action than opportunity, social movement scholars should be especially interested in carefully defining types of threats as analysts have previously dissected the core dimensions of political opportunity (McAdam 1996; Tarrow 2011). Social movement scholarship in the 1980s and 1990s largely focused on mobilization generated by political opportunities (Jasper 2011), submerging Tilly's original contribution (McAdam 1999, pp. x–xi). In the 2000s, a growing number of students of social movements began to incorporate threat models into their empirical research. Three core forms of threat found in this recent research include: 1) State Repression, 2) State-Attributed Economic Problems, and 3) Environmental Harms. By classifying threats into this typology we can better appreciate under what conditions particular forms of threat may launch collective action campaigns.[1]

Repressive Threats

State repression involves acts by government and government-linked agents that attempt to suppress dissent within a population. Such state actions vary from soft repression of stigma and ridicule (Marx-Ferree 2005), to intimidation, arrests, martial law, torture, mass killings, and genocide (Davenport 2010; Maher 2010; Einwohner and Maher 2011). The literature on the relationship between repression and protest is abundant and complex, with cases of state repression suppressing collective action to situations in which governmental coercion clearly escalates the level of resistance (Johnston 2011; Earl 2011). The most influential contributions to these studies focus on the contexts and conditions in which repression either heightens popular protest or pacifies it (Brockett 2005). The repressive threat is to human physical safety and well-being, and the sooner the threat is removed via collective action the better off the populace will be from state coercion.

Repressive threats also tend to radicalize collective action relative to other forms of threat (Almeida 2007; Alimi 2009). That is, state repressive actions over a long period of time may lead to more radical forms of collective action such as disruptive and even violent tactics and revolutionary appeals to overthrow the regime (Goodwin 2001). The coercive political structure radicalizes the *orientation* of collective action (Walder 2009). Nonetheless, as we move into the twenty-first century we are witnessing more nonviolent challenges to acts of state repression as states enhance and upgrade their control of policing within their territorial boundaries (Goodwin 2001; Schock 2005; Nepstad 2011). This trend can be observed in the Arab Spring mobilizations of 2011–2012 (although Libya and Syria escalated into armed rebellion) as well as the nonviolent resistance to the 2009 military coup in Honduras (Sosa 2014).

Before repressive threats activate social movement-type campaigns, would-be activist groups must attain a certain level of organizational capacity, usually a mixture of formal and informal social structures that can be appropriated for mobilization purposes (McCarthy 1996; McAdam 2003; Edwards and McCarthy 2004). Organizations provide a collective vehicle to sustain opposition for excluded social groups (Oxhorn 2003). Collective mobilization often first

---

1   In my original classification scheme in earlier work, I included the threats of state-attributed economic problems, erosion of rights, and state repression (Almeida 2003). This scheme was conceptualized to explain social movement dynamics in authoritarian and semi-authoritarian contexts. In this chapter I incorporate the threat of the erosion of rights within state repression. I have also added the threat of environmental harms in this chapter, an emerging threat that appears to be initiating mass mobilization throughout the developing world. The present classification system addresses social movements in a greater variety of political settings, including relatively more democratic political environments.

emerges from already existing organizations and institutions such as religious venues, social clubs, labor-based associations, and other civic groups (McAdam 2003). Inside of organizational boundaries mutual awareness of grievances and solidarity relations are enhanced (Gould 1995). Influential allies (Tarrow 2011) provide another pathway to achieve a sufficient level of organizational capacity in the face of authoritarian regimes and the onslaught of repressive threats.[2] In Latin America, the Catholic Church has provided such valuable outside assistance to marginalized urban and rural groups by organizing them into cooperatives and other collectivities (Smith 1991; Loveman 1998). In summary, pre-existing networks and organizations are critical in determining if repressive threats will both escalate and radicalize collective action.

State-Attributed Economic Problems

A second major form of threat involves state-attributed economic problems. When economic problems are viewed by the populace as rooted in state policy and actions, the probability of collective action increases. Groups assess that they will be economically worse off if they fail to collectively mobilize (Goldstone and Tilly 2001). Particular economic grievances that are often blamed on the state include land distribution, mass unemployment, price inflation, and neoliberal economic policies.

Land related issues from share cropping to distorted concentrations of land ownership have fueled rural mass movements throughout the developing world (Paige 1975; Scott 1976; Wolford 2010). Peasant and small farmer movements often target the state and particular state agencies (for example, institutes of agrarian reform and ministries of agriculture) to resolve such conflicts as the ultimate authority in legalizing the distribution of property. Mass unemployment also stimulates large-scale mobilization, as recent examples in Greece, Occupy Wall Street, and the unemployed workers' movement (*piquetero*) in Argentina (Rossi 2015) provide vivid testimony in the early twenty-first century. Such collective actions target the government for unemployment relief and the creation of job programs. Finally, rapid increases in prices and austerity policies also generate protest campaigns calling on the state to rescind the policy or provide subsidies on basic consumer goods (Walton and Seddon 1994; Almeida 2014).

Environmental Threats

Environmental threats are harms to ecosystems and human health that may instigate campaigns of collective action (Johnson and Frickel 2011; Arce 2014).

---

2   Much of the political process literature identifies influential and external allies as a core political opportunity (McAdam 1996; Tarrow 2011). I prefer to identify allies as a critical resource that may be used by excluded social groups to mobilize in the face of threats or political opportunities.

One of the largest grassroots movements in the United States in the 1980s and 1990s was over the distribution of toxins, hazardous waste, and pollution (Szasz 1994; Edwards 1995). As mining, manufacturing, and industrialization spread around the globe in an uneven fashion in the late twentieth century, so too has environmental pollution and threats of resource depletion of forests, waterways, and native cultural practices. In response, a variety of new ecologically-oriented movements have arisen to reduce the threat of environmental damage to people and their sources of livelihood. In Latin America, these struggles range from anti-mining conflicts to pesticide poisoning and the implementation of transgenic crops, among a multitude of other ecological hazards (Modonesi 2012, p. 258).

All three threats of repression, state-attributed economic problems, and environmental harms have produced large scale social movement activity in Central America. However, prolonged repressive threats are most likely to produce radicalized collective action (especially under authoritarian regimes). Economic and environmental threats usually result in more pacific forms of protest (though at times highly disruptive). In the next section, I apply these forms of threat and demonstrate the decisive roles they played in major episodes of popular contention in Costa Rica, El Salvador, Guatemala, Honduras, Nicaragua, and Panama.

Repressive Threats and Revolution in Central America

Under repressive military regimes such as Guatemala, El Salvador, and Nicaragua in the 1970s, or Panama under General Noriega in the 1980s, and Honduras following the 2009 military coup, scholars need to explain the origins of resistance movements operating in these hostile political environments. Movements likely do not spring up spontaneously overnight under authoritarian regimes, the costs are too high. One avenue for explaining the rise of opposition to authoritarian regimes and repressive threats is found in periods of political liberalization *prior* to the transition to a more exclusive government. Political liberalization periods allow for the formation of organizations (that is, labor unions, civic associations, student groups, agricultural cooperatives) and experience in nonviolent collective action (Almeida 2003).

In Guatemala, early rebel groups battling the military government in the 1960s and 1970s had organizational roots in the labor and student movements in the liberalization period between 1944 and 1954. The Salvadoran insurgents that formed the Frente Farabundo Martí para la Liberación Nacional (Farabundo Martí National Liberation Front) (FMLN) in 1980 and took on the repressive military regime were organizational heirs of the student, teacher, labor, and peasant associations that spread across the national territory during the political liberalization in the 1960s that included legalization of civil society associations and competitive local and parliamentary elections (Almeida 2008; Martín Álvarez and Cortina Orero 2014). The sustained mobilizations against the military coup in Honduras from 2009 to 2011 by the Frente Nacional de Resistencia Popular

(FNRP) also benefited from the growth of civil associations during the democratic transition in the decades prior to the overthrow of President Manuel Zelaya (Almeida 2014).

Throughout Central America, following Vatican II in the early 1960s, the Catholic Church as an external ally played an indispensable role organizing the subaltern classes in El Salvador, Guatemala, Honduras, and Nicaragua in rural cooperatives, urban Christian base communities, and several other initiatives (Brockett 1991). These church-sponsored organizational assets and skills on how to work and cooperate collectively carried over into more radical mobilization against repressive military regimes in the 1970s and 1980s (Inclán and Almeida 2013).

Much of the radicalization of collective action into revolutionary struggles in twentieth-century Central America can be directly linked to repressive threats. Once a sufficient organizational infrastructure is attained by civil society groups, repressive threats will likely stimulate anti-regime mobilizations. A popular insurrection took place in El Salvador in 1932 attempting to overthrow the newly installed Maximiliano Hernández Martínez dictatorship—one of the largest acts of rebellion during the Great Depression in Latin America (Ching 2013). The 1932 indigenous-peasant-worker uprising in El Salvador came on the heels of the government cracking down on protests over a two-year period, including enacting states of emergency and repressing demonstrations with mass arrests and killings (Gould and Lauria Santiago 2008). Down to the local level, in a geographical analysis of the revolt, municipalities experiencing repressive threats in the two years prior to the revolt were found to be much more likely to participate in the rebellion (Almeida 2007).

The strongest revolutionary movements erupting in Guatemala in the 1970s also emerged out of extreme governmental repression in the highlands against indigenous peasant organizing and rural cooperatives (Vela Castañeda 2012). Elsewhere in Central America, revolutionary movements surfaced in the 1970s in Honduras, Nicaragua, and El Salvador in direct response to repressive threats against the organized opposition by military governments (Goodwin 2001; Wood 2003; Viterna 2013). In El Salvador, radical popular organizations in the 1970s commonly named themselves after the dates of government massacres or the names of martyrs killed by state repressive actions—etching repressive threats deep into the identities of the participants in the resistance movement (Almeida 2008). There are upper limits of repressive threats inducing mass mobilization (Johnston 2011). When repressive acts reach genocidal levels, they will likely bring down the level of mass participation. The ethnocidal crackdown on the 1932 rebellion in El Salvador (known as *la matanza*), and the killing of tens of thousands of people by security forces in both El Salvador and Guatemala in the early 1980s wiped out *mass participation* in the revolts (Brockett 2005; Vela Castañeda 2014).

Organizational Capacity beyond Repressive Threats

The organizational basis of social movement organizing in Central America has shifted from the authoritarian era of the mid-to-late twentieth century to neoliberal democracies in the twenty-first century (Lehouq 2012). Some scholars believed we would observe less street politics with democratization in Latin America because of greater institutional access and state sanctioned channels to resolve grievances. However, it appears the opposite is occurring with greater levels of popular contention in the contemporary democratic period with the massive waves of anti-neoliberal protests in Argentina, Bolivia, Ecuador, and other large-scale campaigns in nearly every Latin American country in the past two decades. Arce and Bellinger (2007) have empirically demonstrated this relationship in their cross-national time series study of Latin America between 1970 and 2000. They find levels of collective protest especially high in democracies undergoing economic liberalization measures. The particular economic and environmental threats driving popular mobilization in contemporary Central America are outlined below. First, it is critical to discuss a few of the social networks and organizations that make these rounds of collective action even viable. Democracy and neoliberalism are two distinct processes occurring simultaneously that shape the organizational dynamics in contemporary civil society in Mesoamerica.

Democracy allows more space to mobilize with relatively less state repression. Democratic regimes also bestow more rights to organizations operating within their national territories such as legal recognition and freedom to assemble. This organizational infrastructure acts as a crucial platform for subaltern groups to launch collective action campaigns. A variety of new social movements and nongovernmental organizations have taken advantage of this political opening. In Guatemala, dozens of indigenous rights groups and NGOs have emerged on the political scene since the 1990s (Brett 2008). In El Salvador and Nicaragua, a wide array of NGOs has also flourished whose missions range from rural health to women's rights collectives. While the day-to-day activities of NGOs may revolve around serving the immediate material needs of marginalized communities, NGOs may also be activated for particular social movement campaigns such as consumer rights issues in Nicaragua, anti-water privatization in El Salvador, or against electricity price hikes in Guatemala (Almeida 2014).

Democratic transitions also encourage the formation of political parties to participate in competitive elections at the local and national levels of government. The organizational structures of oppositional political parties are often not exclusively used to mobilize voter turnout in election cycles, but also to partner with social movements in protest campaigns (Keck 1992). For example, between 2004 and 2007, the Partido de Acción Ciudadana (PAC) in Costa Rica used its party resources to support protest against the Central American Free Trade Agreement (CAFTA). In Guatemala, the Alternativa Nueva Nación (ANN), Unidad Revolucionaria Nacional Guatemalteca (URNG-MAIZ), and the Frente Democrático Nueva Guatemala (FDNG) oppositional parties have participated in major protest campaigns in the late 1990s and 2000s. Similar actions have been carried out by the Unificación Democrática (UD) and Libertad y Refundación (LIBRE) in Honduras, the FMLN in El Salvador, the Frente Sandinista de Liberación Nacional (FSLN) in Nicaragua, and the Frente Amplio por Democracia (FAD) in Panama. In short, democracy facilitates the participation of traditional organizations such as labor unions, student associations, and rural cooperatives in protest campaigns, but also encourages the growth of newer collectivities such as new social movements, NGOs, and oppositional political parties. These newer organizational structures (NGOs, new social movements, and oppositional political parties) play crucial organizational roles in the neoliberal period with the weakening of rural cooperative and labor unions. Nonetheless, some form of state-attributed economic or environment threat usually serves as the incentive structure to motivate the above organizations and networks into collective action.

Threats of State-Attributed Economic Problems and Protest Campaigns

In the twentieth century, land distribution, mass unemployment, and price inflation provided the state-attributed economic threats in Central America producing the greatest level of mass mobilization. In the late twentieth and early twenty-first centuries, neoliberal economic policies act as the most pressing state-attributed economic problem inducing large-scale protest campaigns.

Land Access Issues

For much of the past century, large majorities lived in the Central American countryside laboring on family farms and/or migrating as a semi-proletarian class to large agricultural estates cultivating coffee, bananas, sugar cane, and cotton (Bulmer-Thomas 1987). Highly concentrated land distribution served as the catalyst to organizing in the countryside throughout the region by the mid-twentieth century, resulting in some cases in revolutionary mobilization and in others in substantial agrarian reform programs (Brockett 1998). The high concentration of United Fruit Company lands in Guatemala led to the agrarian reform program in Guatemala in the early 1950s (with high levels of peasant participation) before it was reversed in a US-sponsored military coup in 1954. Grievances for rural mobilization in the early 1970s continued in Guatemala because of the scarcity of land in the highlands for subsistence pushing the migration of indigenous Mayan groups to lowland plantations in the expanding agro-export industries, heightening class conflicts (Paige 1983). Similar high concentrations of United Fruit Company lands in Honduras lead to a major general strike in 1954 and subsequent land reform and state-sponsored rural cooperative programs (Argueta 1995).

The failure to enact agrarian reform in the 1970s resulted in the radicalization of land-starved peasant organizations such as the Federación Cristiana de Campesinos Salvadoreños (FECCAS) and the Unión de Trabajadores del Campo (UTC) in El

Salvador and the creation of the pro-Sandinista Asociación de Trabajadores del Campo (ATC) in Nicaragua (Enríquez 1991). Inequitable access to land also led small famers and peasants to mobilize successfully for agrarian reform and the colonization of frontier lands in Honduras, Panama, and Costa Rica in the 1960s and 1970s (Cordero Ulate 2011). Particularly intense conflicts and collective rural organizing over unequal land distribution continue in the 2000s in Guatemala and the Aguán Valley of Honduras. In all of the above rural struggles, the state serves as the central target for claims as it retains the ultimate authority in adjudicating the distribution of land and property within its administrative boundaries.

Price Inflation and Unemployment

Consumer inflation and mass unemployment act as two additional state-attributed economic problems mobilizing large numbers of people throughout Central America in the twentieth century. The historic tenants' strikes over exorbitant housing rent prices in Panama served as some of the largest protest campaigns in the 1920s and 1930s, organized by leftist political parties. The crisis of unemployment led to mass marches of jobless workers in El Salvador and Costa Rica in the early 1930s in the midst of the worldwide economic depression. Double digit inflation on basic consumer goods (food, clothing, and transportation) led to the more prominent urban mobilizations by students, women's groups, labor unions, and community associations in the mid-1970s in Costa Rica, El Salvador, and Guatemala.

Neoliberal Policies

An entirely new set of state-attributed economic threats entered the political and social landscape of the region at the end of the twentieth century linked directly to the foreign debt crisis. After extensive external borrowing for state infrastructure development and modernization programs in the 1960s and 1970s, during a period marked by rapid economic growth, all six Central American nations found themselves in extreme debt by the early 1980s as world commodity prices dropped precipitously for agricultural exports (Almeida 2014). By the mid-1980s, each nation faced at least a $2 billion external debt. In order to manage the repayment of loans and prevent future defaults, the International Monetary Fund (IMF) and World Bank stepped in to renegotiate the outstanding debts owed to foreign governments and banks in the global North. The IMF and World Bank began making structural adjustment agreements with individual nations in Central America, which involved restructuring debt payments in exchange for neoliberal reforms to national economic structures (Robinson 2003; Spalding 2014). These structural adjustment agreements resulted in a series of measures that were perceived as state-attributed economic threats to the subaltern classes in the region and galvanized the most extensive campaigns of popular mobilization in the past three decades (Almeida 2014).

Every country in the region with the exception of Nicaragua experienced massive austerity protest in the region in the 1980s.[3] Costa Rica erupted with protests over electricity price hikes related to an IMF agreement in 1983, and the small farmers' movement was active for most of the decade over agricultural subsidy cuts (Edelman 1999). Between 1983 and 1986, Panamanian citizens unleashed a series of protest campaigns against the first and second structural adjustment agreements signed by the Noriega-controlled government and the IMF and World Bank leading to price increases, wage freezes, and labor flexibility laws. Labor unions, teachers' associations, and students also participated in protest campaigns in Guatemala and El Salvador in the mid-1980s against economic stabilization measures that brought down the standard of living for working-class majorities.

By the 1990s, as the foreign debt crisis continued to accelerate, a new round of structural adjustment was implemented. In this decade, privatization of the public sector and infrastructure began to produce massive campaigns of resistance. In the early 1990s, the largest sustained protest campaigns since the 1970s rocked Honduras and Nicaragua over privatization and currency devaluation imposed by newly elected neoliberal governments (Robinson 2003; Sosa 2013). In both countries the protests were headed by urban labor unions (often in the public sector) with substantial participation of rural labor unions and cooperatives. The anti-neoliberal protests continued in Nicaragua throughout the 1990s with heavy participation by the public university students organizing several disruptive campaigns against the cutting back of the budget for higher education (Almeida and Walker 2007). By 1995, Costa Rican teachers, universities, students, and labor unions fought a major campaign against the government's third major structural adjustment accord with the IMF and World Bank (PAE III). The 1995 austerity measures in Costa Rica included augmenting the retirement age for public educators, subsidy cuts on basic consumption goods, and a series of privatizations (Almeida and Walker 2007). In 1995 and 1998, respectively, Panama followed the regional trend with the unleashing of protest campaigns against labor flexibility laws and water privatization. Each of the above campaigns reached massive levels of civil society involvement, with the participation of between 50,000 and 150,000 people in the individual campaigns.

The momentum for popular mobilization seemed to be on the upswing in the early 2000s, as even larger and more disruptive campaigns occurred against economic liberalization and privatization in Costa Rica, El Salvador, Guatemala, Honduras, and Panama (Spalding 2014). In Costa Rica, the new millennium commenced with a three-week protest campaign in March–April of 2000 against telecommunications and energy privatization. Students, public sector unions,

---

3 Nicaragua experienced austerity-type protests in 1988 and 1989 under the first Sandinista government. Strikes by school teachers and other urban unions were held against wage freezes connected to the government's budget deficit caused by the US embargo and counter-revolutionary attacks on its borders (Stahler-Sholk 1995).

and community groups erected hundreds of barricades along the nation's major transportation corridors until the government repealed the privatization legislation. A few years later, a similar coalition of groups mobilized between 2003 and 2007 against the Central American Free Trade Agreement (CAFTA), holding general strikes and convoking some of the largest demonstrations in modern Costa Rican history that reached up to 150,000 participants (Raventos 2013). El Salvador also experienced historic mobilizations over the issues of privatization and free trade (Spalding 2014). In 2000 and again in 2002–2003, Salvadoran citizens were under the threat of health care privatization via a plan to outsource services in the Social Security Institute (ISSS) hospitals and clinics. In both rounds, doctors, health care workers, labor unions, students, the women's movement, the FMLN political party, and an impressive coalition of NGOs cohered into a combative campaign to prevent the privatization process, including dozens of mass marches, strikes, and roadblocks around the country. A similar coalition attempted unsuccessfully to prevent the implementation of CAFTA in El Salvador between 2003 and 2007 (Spalding 2007, 2014).

Guatemala, emerging from a civil war peace accord in late 1996, also witnessed major rounds of anti-neoliberal protests in the 2000s. The neoliberal threats of a regressive IMF sales tax mobilized thousands of citizens in 2001 and 2004. After Costa Rica, Guatemala experienced the most disruptive protest against CAFTA between 2004 and 2007, with substantial participation of NGOs, teachers, and indigenous organizations. By the late 2000s, the privatization of the energy sector was leading to multi-sectoral campaigns against consumer electricity prices across the national territory. IMF agreements in Honduras between 1999 and 2008 stimulated several social movement campaigns against a wide variety of austerity and privatization measures (Sosa 2013). The teachers' associations, public sector unions, environmental organizations, students, women's movement, and rural cooperatives created umbrella organizations to attempt to resist the structural adjustment agreements made in a series of letters of intent with the IMF. Most importantly, after nearly a decade of sustained anti-neoliberal mobilizations, these same groups effectively used their inter-organizational linkages and bonds of solidarity to coordinate mass actions against the Honduran military coup between 2009 and 2011 with the formation of the Frente Nacional de Resistencia Popular (FNRP).

Finally, in Panama the restructuring and partial privatization of the Social Security system threatened large portions of the population with loss of access to health care and an increase in retirement age. In 2003 and 2005, two of the largest campaigns in several decades took place to prevent the Social Security system's restructuring along neoliberal lines. A wide coalition of groups formed the Front for the Defense of Social Security (FRENADESSO) to coordinate the two colossal episodes of contention. The FRENADESSO coalition included the most powerful teachers' associations, the militant construction workers' union (SUNTRACS), health care workers, the radical labor confederation CONUSI, and high school and university students. The 2003 campaign involved highway blockades, strikes, and dozens of marches resulting in an accord to halt the privatization process. The 2005 protest campaign drew in even greater numbers of participants from civil society as the new government of Martín Torrijos attempted another restructuring of the Social Security System. In the face of this renewed threat, FRENADESSO coordinated a month-long general strike, the largest in Panamanian history, along with similar protest repertoires of the 2003 campaign of roadblocks, marches, and rallies (Almeida 2014). While the movement had some success in preventing the augmentation of the retirement age, it was unable to block the partial privatization of Social Security funds.

Sustained attention is given above on the anti-neoliberal campaigns in Central America because of their extremely high levels of mobilization and citizen participation. The combination of democratic space with the state-attributed economic threats of neoliberalism appears particularly explosive. Multiple groups and large sectors of the population at times are threatened by the loss of access to vital public services and utilities via privatization and the removal of state subsidies. These particular economic threats mobilize the largest numbers of people in the twenty-first century in the region (more than other alternative grievances or threats). Only repressive threats earlier in the twentieth century and the corresponding revolutionary movements they shaped challenged governments to the degree of recent anti-neoliberal protest campaigns. In El Salvador, Nicaragua, and Costa Rica, the anti-neoliberal sentiment has been converted into electoral mobilization and success for left-of-center political parties at the local and national levels of government.

Environmental Threats and Collective Action

In the 2010s, Central American governments learned in part to moderate the level of aggressiveness in the implementation of free market reforms in the face of two decades of mass opposition (Spalding 2014), while left-oriented governments came to executive power in Nicaragua in 2007 and in El Salvador in 2009 (and a moderate left-of-center government in Costa Rica in 2014). However, important anti-neoliberal campaigns continued in Guatemala, Honduras, and Panama between 2010 and 2015. A newer trend of *environmental threats* began inducing episodes of collective action throughout the region over the past 10 years. The environmental threats activating the largest campaigns in contemporary Central America include mega-projects of dams, deforestation, and mining.

Throughout Central America dozens of battles are being waged against hydroelectric dam and mining projects. The campaigns at times draw attention of national and international level groups such as political parties and NGOs, but the battles usually occur at the community level with the participation of the local population directly under the ecological threat of dam construction or mineral exploration/extraction. For example in El Salvador, Cartagena Cruz (2015) has documented 65 environmental struggles in the country between 1992 and 2013 and found that 48 of the battles (74 percent) impacted a single locality.

In Guatemala, a series of mobilizations have taken place against gold and silver mining and other mega-development projects in the western departments of Huehuetenango, San Marcos, Quiche, Quetzaltenango, Tononicapán, and Sololá with high densities of rural Mayan inhabitants. The residents in these regions have held popular consultations over approval of mining operations within their respective municipalities and have voted them down in nearly all cases by large majorities. In Costa Rica, one of the largest social conflicts after CAFTA was over open pit gold mining in Las Crucitas in northern Alajuela province near the Nicaraguan border. Several mass marches, *caminatas*, and demonstrations were held between 2007 and 2010, leading to a successful court ruling against open-pit mining and leading to the closure of operations. The perceived environmental threat of cyanide contamination from extraction activities drove the anti-mining coalition of university students, environmentalists, and local community members into the multi-sectoral alliance that resulted in a movement favorable outcome. Another successful Costa Rican environmental struggle involving the Teribe people took place between 2004 and 2013 to prevent the Diquís hydroelectric dam project in the village of Térraba in the province of Puntarenas (Cordero Ulate 2013). Under the environmental threat of dam construction and displacement, the local community formed the *Frente de Defensa Indígena de Térraba*. The movement escalated its tactics to the point of occupying the local high school for several days until governmental negotiators recognized local indigenous authorities as the legitimate representatives of the community. The indigenous opposition to the dam led to a local victory in 2011 (Ibid.).

In Panama between 2011 and 2012, massive protests occurred in the indigenous lands of the Ngobe-Bugle people against mining concessions and hydroelectric dam construction. The protests were national in scope and highly conflictual with the blocking of the Pan-American highway for several days and the deaths of indigenous activists (and the injury of dozens of others). The Ngobe-Bugle people attained an unprecedented level of solidarity with outside groups, such as banana workers, students, teachers, and labor unions manning barricades, holding work stoppages, and mobilizing demonstrations against the newly imposed environmental threats to the indigenous *comarcas*. By March 2012, the movement was able to change government law and ban mining contracts on indigenous lands and mandate local consultation on any future dam projects.

In Honduras, some of the more successful rural movements in recent years involve battles against the environmental threats of deforestation, mining, and hydroelectric dams. In the early 2000s, a loose coalition of several municipalities formed the Movimiento Ambientalista de Olancho (MAO). MAO carried out two national marches (*caminatas*) across the Honduran territory in 2003 and 2004 (called the "March for Life") to raise national and international awareness about deforestation and clear-cutting. At the local level in Olancho, multiple communities have held roadblocks, tree-hugging sessions, and demonstrations at city halls to prevent clear-cutting in their respective municipalities (Sosa and Tinoco 2007). The coalition has also participated in movements against environmental destruction associated with the construction of hydroelectric dams and gold mining. MAO also acts as integral ally to the Frente Nacional de Resistencia Popular (FNRP) against the military coup that has more recently formed the LIBRE political party. In the western region of the country, the indigenous movement organization, the Civic Council of Indigenous and Popular Organizations of Honduras (COPINH), mobilized multiple groups in the early and mid-2000s to halt the construction of the Tigre dam project (and community displacement) on the Lempa River dividing Honduras and El Salvador.

Conclusion: Threats, Collective Action, and Future Lines of Inquiry

While favorable political environments such as regime liberalization, democratization, and sympathetic state policies may in part explain particular phases of struggle and the emergence of specific social movements, such political contexts do not adequately account for the kinds of mass mobilizations and revolutionary struggles experienced in Central America over the past century. This chapter shows that many of the largest and most historic struggles and movements for social change and economic redistribution in the region were also shaped by various forms of threat such as governmental repression, state attributed economic problems, or environmental hazards. At the same time, these threats likely would not have activated collective action if some favorable context (that is, some level of political opportunity) did not exist in the recent past or present to build the organizational foundations and social network ties necessary for mobilization.

Scholars and activists should examine more precisely the timing of threats and when they act as a catalyst for mobilization. State repressive threats seem to escalate collective action when the target groups are already organized with pre-existing associations such as in El Salvador in the early 1930s and 1970s or in Nicaragua in the 1970s. This is a crucial dimension often under-emphasized in studies of the repression-protest dynamics. Organizations and pre-existing networks are critical factors shaping the unfolding of popular reactions to state-sponsored repression, especially in terms of a movement's ability to sustain mobilization. Repressive threats also maintain a qualitative difference in relation to other forms of threat in terms of radicalizing collective action. It is under repressive state actions of extreme human rights abuses and mass killings that movements begin to call for a complete restructuring of the state and society using more radical methods of struggle, even if the movement originated from an economic or environmental threat.

In terms of environmental threats, much more attention needs to be given not only to the level of mobilization potential in the community, but also to the transnational activist networks operating in the vicinity of the locality facing ecological harms (Keck and Sikkink 1998; von Bülow 2011), such as Rose Spalding's (2013) work on the transnational and domestic alliances attempting to prevent gold mining activities in northern El Salvador. As environmental health and ecological rights become institutionalized in world society (Longhofer and Schofer 2010), many local activists groups may be able to connect to international nongovernmental organizations (INGOS) working on environmental issues to reduce local level ecological hazards (Bob 2005), especially as global resource scarcities drive transnational extraction industries into the region.

Neoliberal policy-making appears to be the most salient state-attributed economic threat in the past three decades in Central America, and likely the most important contemporary threat in terms of large-scale collective action (most of the emerging environmental conflicts remain contained to particular local regions even with transnational solidarity). Several history-making protest campaigns against economic liberalization were described above. Many of these episodes of popular mobilizations against privatization, free trade, and economic restructuring were unprecedented for their size, duration, cross-sectoral participation, and outcomes. Nonetheless, analysts need to better understand why particular types of neoliberal measures seem to push higher mobilization levels than others. One promising path would be to carefully trace the neoliberalization process of particular countries and examine earlier experiences with neoliberal economic threats in terms of public opinion and forms of mobilization. Did earlier privatization measures pass through with societal approval? Was civil society consulted before the implementation of the measure? Was the measure passed by presidential decree or legislative approval? Did services improve and prices go down after the privatization process in the early years of neoliberalism? Did the opposition to the neoliberal measure effectively frame the issue as to why it may be a threat to large sectors of the population? Did the opposition mobilize multiple and diverse groups or were protests contained only in the sector most directly affected by the privatization such as public sector employees in the institute being sold? Reconstructing these societal experiences with neoliberalism in the past, will likely shed light onto why and when particular neoliberal policy threats lead to notable protest campaigns of opposition as well as when they suppress mass action.

Also, in terms of advancing our knowledge of threat and collective action in general, scholars need to continue to define concepts and causal relationships more precisely. This chapter provided three specific forms of threat and a variety of cases in which they acted as the primary stimulants to collective action. Much work needs to be carried out on the relationships between various forms of threat, organizations, social networks, and political opportunities. Developing more well-defined political environments based on particular constellations of threat, opportunity, and pre-existing social ties and organizations will assist in understanding the likelihood of mobilization erupting and the forms it takes.

References

Alimi, Eitan, 2009. "Mobilizing under the gun: theorizing political opportunity structure in highly repressive setting," *Mobilization*, 14(2), pp. 219–37.

Almeida, Paul, 2003. "Opportunity organizations and threat induced contention: protest waves in authoritarian settings." *American Journal of Sociology*, 109(2), pp. 345–400.

———, 2007. "Organizational expansion, liberalization reversals and radicalized collective action." *Research in Political Sociology*, 15, pp. 57–99.

———, 2008. *Waves of protest: popular struggle in El Salvador, 1925–2005*. University of Minnesota Press.

———, 2014. *Mobilizing democracy: globalization and citizen protest*. Baltimore: Johns Hopkins University Press.

Almeida, Paul and Johnston, Hank, 2006. "Neoliberal globalization and popular movements in Latin America." In: Hank Johnston and Paul Almeida, eds. *Latin American social movements: globalization, democratization, and transnational networks*. Lanham: Rowman & Littlefield, pp. 3–18.

Almeida, Paul D. and Walker, Erica, 2007. "El avance de la globalización neoliberal: una comparación de tres campañas de movimientos populares en Centroamérica." *Revista Centroamericana de Ciencias Sociales*, 4(1), pp. 51–76.

Arce, Moisés and Bellinger, Jr. Paul T., 2007. "Low-intensity democracy revisited: the effects of economic liberalization on political activity in Latin America." *World Politics*, 60(1), pp. 97–121.

Arce, Moises. 2014. *Resource extraction and protest in Peru*. Pittsburgh: University of Pittsburgh Press.

Argueta, Mario. 1995. *La gran huelga bananera: 69 días que conmovieron a Honduras*. Tegucigalpa: Editorial Universitaria.

Bob, Clifford, 2005. *The marketing of rebellion: insurgents, media, and international activism*. New York: Cambridge University Press.

Booth, John, 1991. "Socioeconomic and political roots of national revolts in Central America." *Latin American Research Review*, 26(1), pp. 33–73.

Brett, Roddy, 2008. *Social movements, indigenous politics and democratization in Guatemala, 1985–1996*. Leiden: Brill.

Brockett, Charles D., 1991. "The structure of political opportunities and peasant mobilization in Central America." *Comparative Politics*, 23(3), pp. 253–74.

———, 1998. *Land, power, and poverty: agrarian transformation and political conflict in Central America*. Boulder, CO: Westview Press.

———, 2005. *Political Movements and Violence in Central America*. Cambridge: Cambridge University Press.

Bulmer-Thomas, Victor, 1987. *The political economy of Central America since 1920*. Cambridge: Cambridge University Press.

Cartagena Cruz, Rafael, 2014. "Environmental conflicts and social movements in post-war El Salvador." *Handbook of social movements across Latin America.* New York: Springer.

Ching, Erik. 2013. *Authoritarian El Salvador politics and the origins of the military regimes, 1880–1940.* Notre Dame: University of Notre Dame Press.

Cordero Ulate, Allen, 2011. *Los Movimientos campesinos costarricenses: vistos a través de tres casos de asentamientos del IDA.* San José: FLACSO.

———. 2013. "El movimiento social indígena en Térraba, Costa Rica. La lucha contra el Proyecto Diquís." Paper presented at the Latin American Studies Association (LASA) Meetings in Washington D.C. May 31.

Davenport, Christian, 2010. *State repression and the domestic democratic peace.* Cambridge: Cambridge University Press.

Dixon, Marc and Martin, Andrew W, 2012. "We can't win this on our own: unions, firms, and mobilization of external allies in labor disputes." *American Sociological Review,* 77, pp. 946–69.

Dodson, Kyle. 2015. "Globalization and protest expansion." *Social Problems* 62, pp. 15–39.

Earl, Jennifer, 2011. "Political repression: iron fists, velvet gloves, and diffuse control," *Annual Review of Sociology,* 37, pp. 261–84.

Edelman, Marc, 1999. *Peasants against globalization.* Stanford: Stanford University Press.

Edwards, Bob, 1995. "With liberty and environmental justice for all: the emergence and the challenge grassroots environmentalism in the USA." In: Bron Taylor ed. *Ecological resistance movements: the global emergence of radical and popular environmentalism.* Albany: SUNY Press, pp. 35–55.

Edwards, Bob and McCarthy, John D., 2004. "Resources and social movement mobilization." In: D. Snow, S. Soule and H. Kriesi, eds. *The Blackwell companion to social movements.* Oxford: Blackwell, pp. 116–52.

Einwohner, Rachel L. and Maher, Thomas V., 2011. "Threat assessments and collective-action emergence: death camp and ghetto resistance during the holocaust." *Mobilization,* 16, pp. 127–46.

Enríquez, Laura, 1991. *Harvesting change: labor and agrarian reform in Nicaragua, 1979–1990.* Chapel Hill: University of North Carolina Press.

Goldstone, Jack and Tilly, Charles, 2001. "Threat (and opportunity): popular action and state response in the dynamic of contentious action." In: R. Aminzade, J. Goldstone, D. McAdam, E. Perry, W. Sewell, S. Tarrow and C. Tilly, eds. *Silence and voice in the study of contentious politics.* Cambridge: Cambridge University Press, pp. 179–94.

Goodwin, Jeff, 2001. *No other way out: states and revolutionary movements, 1945–1991.* Cambridge. Cambridge University Press.

Gould, Jeffrey and Lauria-Santiago, Aldo A., 2008. *To rise in darkness: revolution, repression, and memory in El Salvador, 1920–1932.* Durham: Duke University Press.

Gould, Roger, 1995. *Insurgent identities: class, community, and protest in Paris from 1848 to the commune.* Chicago: University of Chicago Press.

Inclán, María and Almeida, Paul, 2013. "Indigenous peoples and revolutionary movements in Mesoamerica." In: Donna Lee Van Cott, José Antonio Lucero and Dale Turner, eds. *The Oxford handbook on indigenous politics.* Oxford: Oxford University Press.

Jasper, James, 2011. "Introduction: from political opportunity structures to strategic action." In: J. Goodwin and J. Jasper, eds. *Contention in context: political opportunities and the emergence of protest.* Stanford: Stanford University Press, pp. 23–74.

Johnson, Erik W. and Frickel, Scott, 2011. "Ecological threat and the founding of US national environmental movement organizations, 1962–1998." *Social Problems*, 58(3), pp. 305–29.

Johnston, Hank, 2011. *States and social movements.* Cambridge: Polity Press.

Keck, Margaret, 1992. *The workers' party and democratization in Brazil.* New Haven: Yale University Press.

Keck, Margaret and Sikkink, Kathryn, 1998. *Activists beyond borders: advocacy networks in international politics.* Ithaca: Cornell University Press.

Lehuoucq, Fabrice, 2012. *The politics of modern Central America.* New York: Cambridge University Press.

Longhofer, Wesley and Schofer, Evan, 2010. "National and global origins of environmental association." *American Sociological Review*, 75, pp. 505–33.

Loveman, Mara, 1998. "High risk collective action: defending human rights in Chile, Uruguay, and Argentina." *American Journal of Sociology*, 104(2), pp. 477–525.

Maher, Thomas V., 2010. "Threat, resistance, and mobilization: the cases of Auschwitz, Sobibór, and Treblinka." *American Sociological Review*, 75(2), pp. 252–72.

Marx Ferree, Myra, 2005. "Soft repression: ridicule, stigma and silencing in gender-based movements." In: Christian Davenport, Hank Johnston and Carol Mueller, eds. *Repression and mobilization.* Minneapolis: University of Minnesota Press, pp. 138–55.

Martín Álvarez, Alberto and Cortina Orero, Eudald, 2014. "The genesis and internal dynamics of El Salvador's People's Revolutionary Army, 1970–1976." *Journal of Latin American Studies*, (July), pp. 1–27.

McAdam, Doug, 1996. "Conceptual origins, current problems, future directions." In: D. McAdam, J.D. McCarthy, and M. Zald, eds. *Comparative perspectives on social movements: political opportunities, mobilizing structures, and cultural framings.* Cambridge: Cambridge University Press, pp. 23–40.

———, 1999 [1982]. *Political process and the development of black insurgency.* 2nd ed. Chicago: University of Chicago Press.

———, 2003. "Beyond structural analysis: toward a more dynamic understanding of social movements." In: Mario Diani and Doug McAdam, eds. *Social movement analysis: the network perspective.* Oxford: Oxford University Press, pp. 281–99.

McCarthy, John, 1996. "Constraints and opportunities in adopting, adapting, and inventing." In: D. McAdam, J.D. McCarthy and M. Zald, eds. *Comparative perspectives on social movements: political opportunities, mobilizing structures, and cultural framings.* Cambridge: Cambridge University Press, pp. 141–51.

McVeigh, Rory, 2009. *The rise of the Ku Klux Klan: right-wing movements and national politics.* Minneapolis: University of Minnesota Press.

Meyer, David, 2004. "Protest and opportunities." *Annual Review of Sociology*, 30, pp. 125–45.

Modonesi, Massimo, 2012. "Entre desmovilización y removilización. Consideraciones sobre el estado de las luchas populares en el marco de los llamados gobiernos progresistas latinoamericanos durante 2011," *Anuario del Conflicto Social, 2012*, Barcelona: Observatorio del Conflicto Social, pp. 252–61.

Nepstad, Sharon Erickson, 2011. *Nonviolent revolutions: civil resistance in the late twentieth century.* New York: Oxford University Press.

Oxhorn, Philip, 2003. "Social inequality, civil society, and the limits of citizenship in Latin America." In: S. Eckstein and T. Wickham-Crowley, eds. *What justice? Whose justice? Fighting for fairness in Latin America.* Berkeley: University of California Press, pp. 35–63.

Paige, Jeffrey, 1975. *Agrarian revolution: social movements and export agriculture in the underdeveloped world.* New York: Free Press.

———, 1983. "Social theory and peasant revolution in Vietnam and Guatemala." *Theory and Society*, 12(6), pp. 699–737.

Raventos, Ciska, 2013. "'My heart says no': political experiences of the struggle against CAFTA-DR in Costa Rica." In: J. Burrell and E. Moodie, eds. *Central America in the new millennium: living transition and reimagining democracy.* New York: Berghahn Books, pp. 80–95.

Reese, Ellen, Giedritis, Vincent and Vega, Eric, 2005. "Mobilization and threat: campaigns against welfare privatization in four cities." *Sociological Focus*, 38(4), pp. 287–307.

Robinson, William, 2003. *Transnational conflicts: Central America, social change, and globalization.* London: Verso.

Rossi, Federico M., 2013. "Juggling multiple agendas: the struggle of trade unions against national, continental, and international neoliberalism in Argentina." In: E. Silva, ed. *Transnational activism and national movements in Latin America: bridging the divide.* New York: Routledge, pp. 141–60.

———, 2015. "Beyond clientelism: the piquetero movement and the state in Argentina." In: P. Almeida and A. Cordero, eds. *Handbook of social movements across Latin America.* New York: Springer.

Schock, Kurt, 2005. *Unarmed insurrections: people power movements in nondemocracies.* Minneapolis: University of Minnesota Press.

Scott, James, 1976. *The moral economy of the peasant: rebellion and subsistence in southeast Asia*. New Haven: Yale University Press.

Silva, Eduardo, 2009. *Challenges to neoliberalism in Latin America*. Cambridge: Cambridge University Press.

Smith, Christian, 1991. *The emergence of liberation theology: radical religion and social movement theory*. Chicago: University of Chicago Press.

Snow, David and Soule, Sarah, 2009. *A primer on social movements*. New York: W.W. Norton.

Sosa, Eugenio and Tinoco, Marco, 2007. *Optaron por la vida: el movimiento ambientalista de olancho*. Tegucigalpa: Editorial Guaymuras.

Sosa, Eugenio. 2013. *Dinámica de la protesta social en Honduras*. Tegucigalpa: Editorial Guaymuras.

_____, 2014. "Honduras: Entre criminalidad, enfrentamiento mediático, protesta social y resultados electorales cuestionados." *Revista de Ciencia Política* 34, pp. 203–19.

Spalding, Rose, 2007. "Civil society engagement in free trade negotiations: CAFTA Opposition Movements in El Salvador." *Latin American Politics and Society*, 49(4), pp. 85–114.

_____, 2013. "Transnational activism and national action: El Salvador's anti-mining movement." In: E. Silva ed. *Transnational activism and national movements in Latin America: bridging the divide*. New York: Routledge, pp. 23–55.

_____, 2014. *Contesting trade in Central America: market reform and resistance*. Austin: University of Texas Press. [online] Available at: <http://utpress.utexas. edu/index.php/books/spacon#sthash.GJxtK7YJ.pdf.>

Stahler-Scholk, Richard, 1995. "The dog that didn't bark: labor autonomy and economic adjustment in Nicaragua under the Sandinista and UNO governments." *Comparative Politics*, 28(1), pp. 77–101.

Szasz, Andrew, 1994. *Ecopopulism: toxic waste and the movement for environmental justice*. Minneapolis: University of Minnesota Press.

Tarrow, Sidney, 2011. *Power in movement: social movements and contentious politics*. Cambridge: Cambridge University Press.

Tilly, Charles, 1978. *From mobilization to revolution*. Reading: Addison-Wesley.

Van Dyke, Nella and Soule, Sarah, 2002. "Structural social change and the mobilizing effect of threat: explaining levels of patriot and militia organizing in the United States." *Social Problems*, 49(4), pp. 497–520.

Vela Castañeda, Manolo, 2012. *Guatemala, la infinita historiade las resistencias*. Guatemala City: La Secretaría de la Paz de la Presidencia de la República de Guatemala.

_____, 2014. *Los pelotones de la muerte: la construcción de los perpetradores del genocidio guatemalteco*. Mexico City: Colegio de México.Viterna, Jocelyn, 2013. *Women in war: the micro-processes of mobilization in El Salvador*. Oxford: Oxford University Press.

von Bülow, Marisa, 2011. *Building transnational networks: civil society and the politics of trade in the Americas*. Cambridge: Cambridge University Press.

Walder, Andrew, 2009. "Political sociology and social movements." *Annual Review of Sociology*, 35, pp. 393–412.

Walton, John and Seddon, David eds, 1994. *Free markets and food riots: the politics of global adjustment*. Oxford: Blackwell.

Wolford, Wendy, 2010. *This land is ours now: social mobilization and the meanings of land in Brazil*. Durham: Duke University Press.

Wood, Elisabeth Jean, 2003. *Insurgent collective action and civil war in El Salvador*. Cambridge: Cambridge University Press.

Chapter 6

Eventful Temporality and the Unintended Outcomes of Mexico's Earthquake Victims Movement[1]

Ligia Tavera Fenollosa

Introduction

The first decade of this century witnessed a renewed interest in the outcomes of social movements. However, despite the dramatic increase in the number of publications on the consequences of social movements (McCammon et al. 2001, 2008; Stearns and Almeida 2004; Whittier 2004; McVeigh, Neblett and Shafiq 2006; Meyer 2006; Olzak and Ryo 2007; Kolb 2007; Almeida 2008; Gupta 2009; Staggenborg and Lecomte 2009; Zemlinskaya 2009; Giugni and Yamasaki 2009), most existing work focuses on intended and anticipated consequences of movements (Giugni 1998; Giugni and Bosi 2012). Therefore, we still know little about the unintended outcomes and if there are patterns in their occurrences that can inform social movement theory.

The principle of unintended consequences notes the possibility and occurrence of unanticipated, perhaps even, untoward, consequences from actions directed to other ends (F.C.G. 1993, p. 83). Within the study of movement outcomes, unintended effects refer to protest movement consequences that do not bear on movement claims (Tilly 1999, p. 269). The importance of this range of effects was already underscored by leading theorists in the field in the late 1990s (Tilly 1999, p. 268). More recently, in a state-of-the-art piece, Giugni and Bosi (2012, p. 23) concluded that "movements often have the greatest effect not by meeting their stated goals, but by bringing about other, unintended outcomes." Although claims of the importance of the unintended effects of social movements have been made, to identify the potential changes that movements can provoke unintentionally and to study them systematically are still major research tasks.

In this chapter I address such a task, and propose a conceptual scheme for analyzing the unintended outcomes of social movements. Arguments are based upon an empirical analysis of the earthquake victims movement in Mexico City,

1   I would like to thank the editors of this volume Federico Rossi and Marisa von Bülow, as well as Hank Johnston, Margaret Keck, Jacinta Palerm, and an anonymous reviewer for their many helpful comments on earlier drafts.

which was instrumental in Mexico's political transition. The movement, considered "a stellar moment in the history of social movements at the international level" (Haber 1997, p. 355), was very successful in meeting its stated goals. Its effects, however, far surpassed the explicit demands made by activists. Even though the movement had disaster relief as its immediate objective and was not explicitly concerned with either cultural or political change, it contributed to the democratic re-evaluation of citizenry and government in Mexico City.

There are some puzzling aspects about the earthquake victims movement and its unintended consequences that challenge current research on movement outcomes. Whereas existing research typically sees movement outcomes as the result of their actions, the unintended effects of the earthquake victims movement suggest that in order to better understand the movement's far-ranging impacts, we need to distance ourselves from a movement-centered perspective. Instead of an analysis that focuses on a movement's strategic choices I propose to analyze movement outcomes from an eventful perspective (Sewell 1996, 2005, 2009), and think of social movements as historical events.

I begin by assessing the existing social movement literature on movement outcomes and showing how, by following William Gamson's (1990/1975) path-breaking analysis of movement outcomes too closely, researchers have overlooked the consequences movements can provoke unintentionally. I then identify key areas in which further theoretical development will advance current knowledge, and draw upon William Sewell's eventful sociology to outline a theoretical model for the study of the unintended outcomes of social movements. Building on this theoretical proposition and complementing it with Jeffrey Alexander's theory of the symbolic code of civil society, I examine the 1985 earthquake victims movement and its impact on the democratic re-evaluation of citizenry and government of Mexico City. The evidence indicates that an eventful conception of social movements can help us better understand their unintended outcomes.

The Study of Movement Outcomes

Studies of social movements stem from the belief that movements represent an important force for social change. Thus, after devoting decades to understanding the mix of factors that give rise to a movement, research on movement outcomes has lately burgeoned.[2] Although policy and legislative effects still form the bulk of existing work (Giugni 2004; Giugni and Bosi 2012), inquiries on the consequences of movement actions have expanded to other arenas such as the cultural (Earl 2000, 2004), organizational (Cress and Snow 2000; Amenta and Caren 2004), and

---

2   In contrast, researchers focusing on non-democratic countries have long considered the study of the consequences of social movements an attractive and relevant topic. See, for example: Foweraker 1989; Foweraker and Craig 1990; Mainwaring 1987, 1989; Mainwaring and Viola 1984; Escobar and Alvarez 1992; Alvarez et al.1998.

biographical (McAdam 1989; Van Dyke, McAdam and Wilhelm 2000; Giugni 2004, 2008). At the same time, research on movement outcomes has become more complex so that distinctions between direct (Cress and Snow 2000; Burstein and Linton 2002; Uba 2009), indirect (McAdam and Su 2002; Amenta, Caren and Olasky 2005), conditional (Bosi and Uba 2009), and joint effects (Giugni 2007; Giugni and Yamasaki 2009) as well as internal and external consequences of social movements (Kriesi, Koopmans, Duyvendak and Giugni 1995; Earl 2000; Amenta, Caren and Olasky 2005; Giugni and Bosi 2012) are now common. Nevertheless, the unanticipated and unintended consequences of movements remain largely unaddressed (but see Deng 1997; Giugni 2004; Holzer 2008). Various reasons account for this situation.

For one thing, the tendency to focus on the political outcomes of social movements and, more narrowly, on their impacts upon public policy and legislation, has contributed to the pre-eminence of the intended (direct or indirect) effects of social movements within research on movement outcomes and therefore few studies have addressed their broader cultural and institutional effects (Giugni 2004, p. xx). Other reasons for this focus might be related to the fact that most of the perspectives on social movement outcomes have been developed by examining social movements that operated in consolidated democracies. Although scholars have encouraged expansion to other geographical areas (Giugni 1998, 2008; Burstein and Linton 2002; Uba 2009) research on the effects of social movements has focused on the United States and European contexts. Interestingly, studies of the unintended political outcomes of social movements have been to date limited to non-democratic states[3] (but see Holzer 2008). And finally, the overwhelming influence of Gamson's (1975, 1990) path-breaking analysis of the political effects of social movements leads researchers to define movement outcomes in terms of success or failure, and to focus on their direct impacts, overlooking the indirect and unintended consequences produced by movements.

Gamson's The Strategy of Social Protest

Research on movement outcomes has been deeply influenced by William Gamson's *The Strategy of Social Protest*. This book, published in 1975, has been considered "the most systematic attempt to isolate the effects of organized social movements" (McAdam, McCarthy and Zald 1988, p. 727). It provided a theoretical perspective on movement outcomes that emphasized the salience for research of two interrelated aspects: the conceptualization of movement outcomes in terms of success, and an emphasis on a movement's strategic decisions and organization as the explanatory variables.

Equating the outcomes of social movements to their success gave researchers a sharp analytical starting focus when the field of social movement research was

---

3   See, for example, Deng's (1997) research on the unintended outcomes of the 1989 Chinese student movement.

just getting established. However, the definition of movement outcomes in terms of the successful accomplishment of its intended purposes has been criticized by a number of authors (Piven and Cloward 1977; Amenta and Young 1999; Giugni 1999; Rucht 1999; Tilly 1999; Snow, Soule and Kriesi 2004; Snow and Soule 2009, Chapter 6). Some have argued that this conceptualization is problematic because it presupposes that challenging groups are homogeneous entities, assumes that success is equally assessed by all participants and overemphasizes the intention of movement participants in producing changes (Giugni 1999, p. xx–xxi). Others have noted that such a definition presumes that success or failure is absolute rather than relative to a certain area or goal (Rucht 1999, p. 205), whereas still others have observed that to define movement outcomes in terms of the successful achievement of a movement's demands obscures the possibility for movements to produce collective goods for their constituents (Amenta and Young 1999, p. 25). From a different viewpoint, theorists working from the new social movements perspective have already noted that it is not sufficient to assess movement success by documenting changes in policies and/or changes in legislation as scholars studying movement consequences have tended to, but also by examining the transformations wrought in the public perception of social issues, in collective self-definitions, and in the meanings that shape everyday life (Troyer and Markle 1983; Melucci 1985).

Whereas to date there seems to be a general agreement that social movements outcomes should not be reduced to the simple terms of "success" (Bosi and Uba 2009, p. 410), the emphasis on movement strategic decisions still pervades much of the studies on movement outcomes which continue to be anchored in the actions/impact relationship (for an earlier critique, see Goldstone 1980).

Whether focusing on the mechanisms that mediate between movements and outcomes or dealing with their more direct effects, research on movement outcomes has directed its attention to movement choices and actions for the explanation of their consequences. Following Gamson, scholars have found that a movement impact is influenced by strategic choices regarding organizational forms (Mirowsky and Ross 1981; Staggenborg 1988; McCarthy and Zald 2002; McVeigh, Welch and Bjarnason 2003; Andrews 2004; King, Cornwall and Dahlin 2005), the nature and/or scope of goals (Steedly and Foley 1979; Mirowsky and Ross 1981), the use of violent and/or disruptive tactics (Schumaker 1975; Piven and Cloward 1977, 1979; Mueller 1978; Gurr 1980; Gamson 1990; McAdam and Su 2002; Uba 2009, but see Soule et al. 1999; McCammon et al. 2001; King, Bentele and Soule 2007), and framing processes (Cress and Snow 2000; McVeigh et al. 2003 McCammon et al. 2008, McCammon 2009).

Other authors have proposed a "political mediation model" (Amenta, Carruthers and Zylan 1992) and have argued that movement outcomes—defined also in Gamson's terms of recognition and benefits for supporters—are mediated by political conditions such as the political system and the party system (Ibid.); movement-party relationships (Tarrow 1989); the openness of the policy-making system (Eisinger 1973; Tarrow 1983; Kitschelt 1986), alliances to other groups

(Steedly and Foley 1979), "outside support" and/or tolerance of political elites (Jenkins and Perrow 1977), and institutional life and political circumstances (Piven and Cloward 1979).

Despite the incorporation of the political context to the analysis of movement outcomes, scholars doing research from this perspective also focus on movements' strategic decisions. In a recent review, Amenta et al. (2010) concluded that scholars doing research within this domain had "developed more complex theoretical ideas about the conditions under which influence occurs" (2010, p. 299). He continues that their complexity lies in the specification of the "interactions between aspects of movements *and their actions* and other political actors and political contexts, often deploying concepts from political science and political sociology" (2010, pp. 299–300, emphasis added). In short, studies have either aimed at establishing an empirical relationship between movement activity and a given outcome, or have strove to identify and measure whatever mix of mechanisms appears to mediate the activity/outcome relationship (McAdam and Su 2002, p. 700).

Preferences for arguments that rely on movement strategic choices might well be linked to the fact that "these are things that challenging groups can control" and that therefore this kind of argument "has immediate relevance for practice" (Gamson 1990, p. 1058 quoted in Buechler 2004, p. 56). However, such a position obscures the range of potential effects movements can trigger. Although it is possible that unintended outcomes of movements bear on the subsequent strategic decisions of movement leaders (Deng 1997), my research on the earthquake victims movement suggests that the unintended effects of movements are best understood by decoupling strategic decisions from impact, and by adopting an *eventful perspective* on social movements.

New Pathways to the Study of Movement Outcomes

Recently, researchers have called for the adoption of a comparative and historical perspective in the study of the political consequences of social movements (Amenta et al. 2010), and have made the argument that historical analyses are "the best way to examine the influences of movements that go beyond a quick response" (2010, p. 300). To analyze movement outcomes, scholars have combined historical analyses with large N-quantitative and formal qualitative analyses (Amenta, Caren and Olasky 2005; Amenta 2006; Chen 2007), as well as small-N analyses with quantitative analyses (Banaszak 1996; Giugni 2004). Qualitative comparative analysis and fuzzy set applications have also been applied to the study of the political consequences of movements (Amenta, Caren and Olasky 2005; McCammon et al. 2008) and to the outcomes of homeless mobilizations (Cress and Snow 2000). In this chapter, I draw from a different branch of historical analysis to examine the unintended effects of movements. I look, in particular, at William Sewell's eventful sociology.

According to Sewell (2005), historical sociology as represented in the works of Immanuel Wallerstein, Charles Tilly, and Theda Skocpol has not taken temporality seriously. In his view, the temporality that has animated historical sociology has been either "teleological" or "experimental," and events have correspondingly been conceptualized either as "markers on the road to the inevitable future," as "effects, never causes of change," or as "artificially interchangeable units" (Sewell 2005, Chapter 3). Against these "a-historical perspectives," Sewell calls for an eventful concept of temporality. An eventful notion of temporality sees the course of history "as determined by a succession of largely contingent events" (Sewell 2005, p. 83). Hence, eventful temporality differs sharply from teleological and experimental temporality on the matter of contingency. An eventful concept of temporality implies that contingency "characterizes not only the surface but the core or the depths of social relations" (Ibid., 102). It implies that social processes are inherently contingent, discontinuous, and open-ended. This assumption means that nothing in social life is ultimately immune to change. Therefore, "… a theoretically robust conception of event is a necessary component of any adequate theory of social change" (Ibid., 227).

What makes historical events so important to theorize is that "they reshape history, imparting an unforeseen direction to social development and altering the nature of the causal nexus in which social interactions take place" (Ibid., 227). Building on the work of anthropologist Marshall Sahlins (1985, 1991), Sewell defines historical events in an expressly loose way as "a sequence of occurrences that is recognized as notable by contemporaries" and that "results in a durable transformation of structures" (Sewell 2005, p. 228). From an eventful perspective, events and structures are mutually dependent categories, and not opposing terms. In fact, it is the structured character of social life what makes the event not only an interesting and problematic category, but also what makes possible the recognition of the event as event (Ibid., 199).

Sewell believes that societies should be conceptualized as the sites of a multitude of overlapping and interlocking relatively autonomous structures. It is precisely the existence of a multiplicity of structures that makes the transposition of meanings and interests from one structural location to another structural location possible. Therefore, a plural rather than a singular conception of structure is "crucial for a plausible theory of events" (Ibid., 209).

Cultural structures, defined both as systems of symbols and meanings and as spheres of practical activity, lie at the core of Sewell's eventful sociology. Events bring about historical changes "in part by transforming the very cultural categories that shape and constrain human action." Moreover, it is the contravention of culturally defined categories that distinguishes events from other occurrences; "events can be distinguished from uneventful happenings only to the extent that they violate the (categorical) expectations generated by cultural structures" (Ibid., 199). Change is brought about by "the necessary but risky application of existing cultural categories to novel circumstances, the action of culturally marking things in the world that, at least occasionally, transforms the meanings of the cultural markers and thereby reorients the possibilities of human social action" (Ibid., 219).

The transformative power of events lies in the violation of categorical expectations as much as on the interested action of agents. Events transform the meanings and relations of cultural categories not only because "the world fails to conform to categorical expectations" but also, "because actors bend categories to their own ends in the course of action" (Ibid., 203–04). It is the use of cultural categories by "acting subjects in their personal projects" that makes cultural change a risky endeavor.

The eventful conception of temporality assumes that social relations are not only contingent, as noted above, but also that they are characterized by path dependency and by temporal heterogeneity. Events are path dependent, which means that "what has happened at an earlier point in time will affect the possible outcomes of a sequence of events occurring at a later point in time" (Ibid., 100). Temporal heterogeneity refers to the importance of historical contextualization for understanding or explaining social practices. We cannot know what an act or utterance means and what its consequences might be without knowing the logics that characterize the world in which the action takes place (Ibid., 10).

Temporal heterogeneity implies causal heterogeneity or the idea that "the consequences of a given act are not intrinsic in the act but will depend on the nature of the social world within which it takes place" (Ibid., 172). One significant characteristic of historical events is that "they always combine social processes with very different temporalities—relatively gradual or long-run social trends, more volatile swings of public opinion, punctual accidental happenings, medium-run political strategies … which are brought together in specific ways, at specific places and times, in a particular sequence" (Ibid., 9).

Sewell's eventful sociology calls for rethinking events as a theoretical category, which I argue can serve as a template for analyzing the unintended outcomes of social movements.

An Eventful Conception of Social Movements

Following Sewell, I propose to think of social movements as historical events, that is, as sequences of occurrences which result in cultural/political/social change. This proposal implies not that all movements result in changes, but rather, that all movements have the potential of becoming historical events, *regardless of their stated goals*. Sequences of occurrences begin with a rupture of some kind, that is, "a surprising break with routine," a "disruption of cultural categories," and/or a "breakdown of expectations." Social movements, I argue, are one type of rupture. They introduce the possibility of change while pointing to the contingent character of social life. They bring into social life new conceptions of what really exists, of what is desirable, and of what is possible. They are, literally, significant.

However, because most ruptures are "neutralized" and "reabsorbed" through various means, a single, isolated rupture rarely has a transformative effect (Sewell

1996, pp. 843–44). Ruptures bring about change, only through sequences of interrelated ruptures. Thus, a social movement only becomes a historical event when it touches off a chain of occurrences that durably transform previous structures, practices and/or relations.

Social movements can lead to a chain of occurrences with long lasting effects that go beyond a movement's stated goals when their emergence challenges cultural categories. Therefore, the unintended consequences of social movements are recognizable only within the terms provided by a cultural structure. This implies that symbolic interpretation lies at the core of the unintended outcomes of social movements. However, in order for social movements to have unintended outcomes, this transgression or rupture needs to be taken up, expanded, or amplified by other actors.

Social movements are more likely to have unintended outcomes when they violate cultural categories and when their transgression of cultural categories can be transposed from one structural location to another structural location. Therefore, while cultural structures are central to an eventful perspective on movement outcomes, so are cultural practices, in particular those oriented to the creative cultural action of meaning importation across structures.

Although I find myself inspired by Sewell's (1996, 2005, 2009) eventful sociology, I believe that explaining the unintended outcomes of social movements from such a perspective requires us to push it farther and inquire into the cultural codes that a) make repair of the initial rupture difficult, b) facilitate the transposition of ruptures across structures, and c) make novel articulations possible. I consider Jeffrey Alexander's work on the symbolic premises of civil society to be particularly useful for such a task. I will develop these points in my analysis of the movement.

The 1985 Earthquake

At 7:19 on the morning of September 19, 1985, the most severe earthquake in Mexico's modern history shook its capital, Mexico City, and a large section of the country. The earthquake measured 8.1 on the Richter scale and reached levels VIII and IX in the Mercalli scale (US Department of Commerce, National Geophysical Data Center, 1990). The devastation it caused in Mexico City's central area, was without precedent. Of Mexico City's population of 18 million, at least an estimated 10,000 people were killed and 50,000 injured,[4] and property damage amounted to $5 billion—which represented a full 2 percent of the 1985 GNP (US Department of Commerce, 1990). The impact of the earthquake was so devastating, both

---

4   There is a lot of variance regarding the earthquake's death toll. However, most observers agree that not less than 10,000 people lost their lives (*El Universal*, 26 September 1985, p. 1).

physically and psychologically, that in the days following the disaster, an average of 5,000 people left the city every 24 hours (Aguilar Zinzer et al. 1985, p. 32).

The earthquake struck off in the midst of one of the country's worst economic crises characterized by increasing unemployment, declining investments, unprecedented capital flight, galloping inflation, decreasing production, and a difficult debt-related financial situation. Politically, it occurred in a situation of unrest defined by the electoral retreat of the ruling PRI party, especially in several northern states, urban areas, and Mexico City, and by powerful opposition forces and multiple expressions of collective dissent by large sectors of the middle class, urban poor, organized workers, and the peasantry (Haber 1992, p. 104).

Furthermore, the earthquake was marked by a series of contingent and unexpected events that accidentally disclosed, in the most dramatic way, the corruption, negligence, and violation of human rights by Mexican authorities. Fallen buildings revealed that construction materials had not always meet requirements, and that in order to maximize profits, shoddy work methods and materials had been used in the construction of public hospitals, schools, and apartment complexes. The earthquake also brought to light the violation of human rights within Mexico's system of justice when presumably tortured corpses appeared among the debris of the Mexico City Attorney General's Office (Monsiváis 1986, p. 9), as well as the existence of illegal garment factories revealing the "monstrous collusion among inspectors, labor authorities, and unions in the garment industry" (Carrillo 1990, ftn2, p. 233).

From the clear exhibition of the government's corrupt practices arose sharp criticisms from national as well as international observers. The image of the Mexican government as a corrupt one was so pervading, that some international organisms and NGOs refused to use official channels and directly donated their aid to earthquake victims organizations, universities, local NGOs, and local parishes (Serna 1995). Indeed, the earthquake destruction was not perceived as being only, or even mainly, the consequence of a natural disaster, but the result of governmental corruption and wrongdoing.

The Earthquake Victims Movement

Mexicans could not recall an earthquake so violent; neither could they recall an instance where social mobilization, organization, and solidarity in response to a disaster reached the levels attained after the 1985 earthquakes. Almost every sector of Mexican society contributed to earthquake victim relief. Such a massive mobilization and organization led observers to describe the initial social response to the Mexico City earthquake as a "movement of solidarity" (Monsiváis 1988).

In sharp contrast with the social response to the emergency, the government's relief efforts were belated, poorly managed, and insensitive. Its initial reaction was mainly aimed at controlling the situation and putting a halt to the massive social response to the disaster, which was clearly taking place outside governmental channels. Thus, President de la Madrid ordered the implementation of the DN-

III plan, a national disaster plan keyed to the Mexican Army. Although disaster studies have documented that the involvement of the military in emergency situations is not only common, but also very helpful (Anderson 1968, pp. 5–6), its implementation in the case of Mexico City raised sharp criticism and contributed little to the relief of earthquake victims (Aguilar Zinzer 1985, p. 113; Poniatowska 1988, pp. 32–3).

Manifestations of solidarity, which often substituted for governmental action, were accompanied by a wide variety of mobilizations by those directly affected by the earthquake. On September 23, dwellers of a government-sponsored housing project destroyed by the earthquake gathered at the president's residence to denounce corrupt practices by local authorities. That same day, in another section of the city, residents of another government sponsored housing project rallied at the offices of the agency in charge of administering the buildings they lived in. The next day, earthquake victims organized yet another demonstration at the official residence against the army surrounding their houses, and on September 26 neighbors from Tepito and from Tlatelolco—two of the most devastated neighborhoods—protested outside congress demanding the investigation and punishment of those responsible for the collapse of their buildings and houses.

Such uncoordinated mobilizations came together on September 27 when more than 30,000 people from 10 affected neighborhoods marched with their mouths covered, as a "sign of respect" for the thousands of people killed by the earthquake, to "manifest their grief, and anger, as well as their dignity"; to denounce abuses by local authorities, owners of the *vecindades*[5] and technical experts; and to demand the expropriation of the *vecindades* they lived in, soft housing credits, the reconnection of services (electricity, water), as well as the direct deliverance of international relief (Serna 1995, pp. 63–4).

In the six weeks following the earthquake, victims took to the streets on 25 occasions to request the reconstruction of their houses, to demand the expropriation of land for rebuilding purposes, to ask for their participation in the government's reconstruction program, and for other disaster-related purposes. In addition to the marches and demonstrations, and with the continuous and generous national and international support, earthquake victims refused to go to the shelters set up by the government, and remained on the streets, usually close to where their houses had once been, and set up their own, independent shelters.

In early October, 28 organizations of earthquake victims, that had either been created after the disaster or had been transformed from pre-existing neighborhood associations, united to create the *Coordinadora Única de Damnificados* or Sole Coordinating Committee of Earthquake Victims (CUD). The CUD actively participated in the reconstruction program and successfully negotiated with the government the construction or renovation of 43,000 houses, benefiting more than 200,000 people (Herrasti 1993, p. 20).

---

5   Poor people in downtown Mexico City tend to live in vecindades, which are one- or two-storey severely run-down apartment complexes arranged around a central patio.

As shown here, the earthquake victims movement was not explicitly concerned with political change. Although some of its leaders occasionally criticized the lack of a democratically elected, and therefore more accountable, government for the Federal District of Mexico City (more on this shortly), the movement did not press for political reform. It did not seek the extension of full political rights for the residents of Mexico City, nor did it demand the introduction of a more democratic political structure for the city. Instead, the movement oriented its actions to expropriating land for reconstruction purposes, securing cheap housing for the thousands of earthquake victims, and, more generally, successfully negotiating the reconstruction program with the government (CUD 1986).

Due to the post disaster situation, and in sharp contrast with its interaction with social movements in the eve of the earthquake when repression against urban popular organizations peaked (Hernández 1987), de la Madrid's administration was highly responsive to the movement's requests. By rapidly responding to the movement's most fundamental demand for the expropriation of the buildings damaged by the earthquake, the government pre-empted any possible direct political challenge from the movement.[6] Although earthquake victims would still have to fight for the satisfaction of their claims, the expropriation allowed them to remain in their neighborhoods, which was one of their main demands (CUD 1986). As a result, the movement limited its discourse and practice to disaster related issues.

According to Gamson's definition, the earthquake victims movement was extremely successful. Its outcomes, however, were not limited to its recognition as a valid representative of the earthquake victims' interests and to the new and important benefits it gained for its members. The movement had also significant, and less well known, unintended consequences, which went beyond both the leaders' claims and the system's responsiveness. Its consequences reached the political arena where it was implicated in the processes of democratization in Mexico City.

Mexico City's Government

Like other capital cities in federal states, Mexico City is the locale of federal powers. As such, it is not politically incorporated to any particular state, but is formally constituted as a federal district (D.F.). At the time of the earthquake, the D.F. had no locally elected legislative body to represent its millions of residents, and none of its local authorities were chosen by direct popular election. Instead, it was governed by a presidentially appointed mayor or chief of the Federal District

---

6 Surprisingly, on October 11, 1985, President de la Madrid took a radical step and expropriated 5,563 buildings in benefit of earthquake victims. Although the list of expropriated buildings contained numerous mistakes and was later modified, it clearly satisfied a basic demand of the earthquake victims movement.

Department (DDF), the administrative body in charge of the city's management. Besides appointing the mayor, the president also had the privilege of appointing or confirming the heads of the 16 administrative territories into which the city is subdivided. This had not always been the case. Before 1928 residents could elect some municipal officials, but since the reform of 1928 the administrative structure in Mexico City offered no opportunity for local participation (Meyer 1987).

The overall importance of the Federal District made the democratization of its government central to prospects for democracy at the national level, and was an ongoing demand of opposition parties since the mid-1960s (Raquel Hérnandez de Arce 2004). However, prior to 1985, PRI governments had been very successful in deflecting any discussion of granting full citizenship to the residents of the Federal District and opening its government to electoral competition.

During the 1982 presidential electoral campaign the issue of introducing more democratic structures into Mexico City's government had been, once more, a matter of open discussion (*Proceso*, May 14, 1982). In the midst of generalized pressure from political parties to reform existing political arrangements (*Cámara de Diputados* 1983, p. 40), the official party's (PRI) presidential candidate and future President Miguel de la Madrid (1982–1988) had vaguely addressed the problem of citizen participation in local government. As part of his campaign on "integral democracy," de la Madrid had expressed the need to "establish specific coordination and collaboration goals and tasks between citizens and government to build true instances of democratic action in all levels, from the National Congress to the local level" (de la Madrid 1982a, p. 158).[7] A couple of months later, in his inaugural speech, the newly elected president had committed himself to convening: "… a public debate to examine the state of the process of political reform, the function and integration of the Republic's Senate, citizen participation in the government of the Federal District, and the reform of the judiciary" (de la Madrid 1982b, p. m7). Nevertheless, for the first three years of his term, de la Madrid's government took no public action regarding democratic reform, and the president's announcement proved to be empty rhetoric.

Instead, in December 1983, when a series of reforms to the Organic Law for the Federal District was examined in the Chamber of Deputies, the official position actually limited the reforms to administrative changes—the creation of various agencies within the DDF—and further increased presidential powers. From 1983 onwards, not only the mayor was to be appointed by the president, but also his closest collaborators within the DDF (*Cámara de Diputados* 1983). The opinion of a member of one of Mexico's most important opposition parties of the time, the *Partido Socialista Unificado de México*, Mexico's Unified Socialist

---

7 Until 1988 when elections for the Assembly of Representatives of the Federal District were held for the first time, citizen representation was channeled through a pyramid of neighborhood organizations or *comités de manzana*. Because of their administrative character, and though formally a participatory structure, this system did not permit political representation of the citizens of Mexico City.

Party (PSUM), nicely illustrates the position regarding political reform in Mexico City before the emergence of the earthquake victims movement:

> In place of facts that substantiate words pronounced in public, we find ourselves with the opposite fact of a set of reforms that will not modify the structure of government in this city, but, on the contrary, will validate it, consolidate it, and perpetuate it (*Cámara de Diputados* 1983, p. 41).[8]

Furthermore, if public consultations about political reform for the D.F. were, despite the official discourse and the pressure from opposition parties, quite remote in 1983, two years later the official party's electoral recoil in Mexico City made the discussion even more unlikely. The results of the elections for the national legislature of July 1985 were particularly distressing for the PRI in the D.F., where it obtained its lowest support. Whereas in rural districts it still managed to attain 79.5 percent of the votes, in Mexico City the official party gained only 42.6 percent of the total vote, almost 6 points less than in 1982 (Molinar 1991, p. 144).

In 1985 few would have expected a public discussion, let alone a political reform, regarding D.F. citizens' right to elect their local authorities. Despite continuous pressure from opposition parties, and although President de la Madrid had expressed on several occasions his intent to convoke a public debate on citizen participation in the government of the Federal District, the democratization of Mexico City was simply not part of the government's agenda. Surprisingly, on November 1, 1985, just two months after the September earthquake, Mexico City Mayor Ramón Aguirre unexpectedly announced before the chamber of deputies President de la Madrid's willingness to hold public hearings on citizen participation in local government. In explaining the reasons for the government's sudden shift, after almost 60 years of denying Mexico City residents the right to elect their local authorities, the mayor said:

> The way in which Mexico City's society has responded to various very critical circumstances [referring to the earthquake] indicates that the foundations of an extraordinary civic maturity have been laid out. Therefore, the conditions are ripe for the analysis, dialogue, and presentation of alternatives regarding the transcendental issue of citizen participation in local government (*Cámara de Diputados* 1985, p. 22).

---

8   Mexico's Unified Socialist Party (PSUM) was one of Mexico's most important opposition parties. In the early 1980s the PSUM won several elections at the local level, the first political party to win an election during the PRI regime. *Coalición Obrera, Campesina y Estudiantil del Istmo* (COCEI).

The Earthquake Victims Movement and the Political Reform of the D.F.

Public hearings on the political reform of the D.F. took place seven months after Aguirre's announcement. During six sessions, representatives of all political parties discussed various alternatives for citizen participation in Mexico City's government. Debate centered on the feasibility of transforming the D.F. into a state, the creation of a local congress for the city, and the direct election of the Mexico City mayor (*Secretaría de Gobernación* 1986).

Due to their relatively strong electoral presence in the capital city, and given the importance of the Federal District within national politics, opposition parties had a keen interest in the direct election of local authorities. Therefore, at the public hearings (left-wing) party representatives actively signified the earthquake victims movement as a historical event that called for public reconsideration of the right of Mexico City's residents to elect their local authorities.

At the first public hearing for example, Deputy Alma Flores from the Worker's Revolutionary Party (PRT) stated:

> During the earthquake of September the limited legitimacy of the government of the Federal District was obvious for the most part of the residents of Mexico City. In the face of the tragedy it was the organized population that in an autonomous and democratic way took charge of the most urgent tasks. Mexico City residents demonstrated, once more, their civic and political maturity, their solidarity, and above all their capacity to collectively solve their problems without any imposition ... the ample participation of the people as well as the continued activities of the earthquake victims movement not only succeeded in overcoming bureaucratic tightness and nonsense, they also generated the conditions for discussing if the basic political rights of the residents of Mexico City would be restored or not (*Secretaría de Gobernación* 1986, p. 35).

In a similar way, in her speech at the third public hearing, Beatriz Gallardo of the Worker's Socialist Party (PST) argued that:

> The September earthquake not only physically shook the city, it also shook the obsolete formal structure of citizen organization. The response and solidarity of millions of young people ... surpassed the response of the actual political-administrative structure, demonstrating the [participatory] potential that exists in a society that demands new participation channels that are now being denied to it (*Secretaría de Gobernación* 1986, p. 162–63).

As noted by Arturo Whaley, a representative of Mexico's Unified Socialist Party (PSUM):

> ... these tragic days and weeks discovered for us the organizational skills and the generous spirit of solidarity that exist in Mexico City neighborhoods. The

disaster of September 1985 demonstrated that in spite of urbanization and the loss of our traditional values, community life of the residents of Mexico City is as vigorous and creative as it was in the beginning. To channel such participation means to give enough representation to voters in municipal government (*Secretaría de Gobernación* 1986, p. 191, fourth public hearing).

Deputy Efrain Calvo from the Worker's Revolutionary Party (PRT) dealt with the subject in an extended and paradigmatic way:

During these ill-fated days [that is, the days following the disaster], the erroneous myth of the apathy of the resident of the Federal District fell to pieces. First because of the explosive citizen participation, and later on, when that spontaneous reaction diminished, by the emergence almost out of nowhere of multiple, massive, and autonomous organizations of earthquake victims. These phenomena put a definite end to the existing paternalistic theories about the citizen of Mexico City. The resident of Mexico City is definitely not a child, incapable of self-government, but is an adult that requires and demands self-government. Nothing, absolutely nothing, can substitute the right of the citizens of the Federal District to elect their own way of government and their own governors (*Cámara de Diputados* 1985, p. 82).

On December 28, nearly six months after the public consultations, President de la Madrid sent to Congress his initiative of reform. The initiative did not include the proposals of the opposition or those of the PRI representatives in the Federal District. Instead of suggesting the direct election of the mayor and/or the creation of a local congress, de la Madrid devised the creation of an Assembly of Representatives of the Federal District (*Asamblea de Representantes del Distrito Federal*) with no legislative powers. The new political institution was to be integrated by 66 members; 40 elected through direct vote, and 26 through proportional representation. The Mexico City mayor was still to be appointed by the president. On April 23, 1987, President de la Madrid's initiative was discussed for 12 hours in the Chamber of Deputies. It was approved by the PRI—who had the majority of seats—in the absence of the opposition who left the House of Representatives in protest (*La Jornada*, April 24, 1986). Two days later, the PRI-dominated Senate approved it too.

The creation of the Assembly of Representatives (ARDF) was clearly insufficient to almost all political actors, since it basically kept intact the organization and functioning of the Mexico City government. Nevertheless, the establishment of the ARDF cannot be seen only as another initiative designed to head off demands for a full democratization of the Federal District. This view would ignore the fact that despite its limited impact, the initiative represented a major qualitative change vis-à-vis previous reforms. None of the previous institutional arrangements, which had been introduced since 1929, involved the creation of a new political/representative body implying overt party competition. In contrast, the creation of the ARDF in 1987 finally opened the D.F. to electoral competition. Moreover, from the very beginning, members of the assembly sought to increase turf and "in a short time, the ARDF exceeded its administrative functions, and transformed itself into a political interlocutor of the mayor" (Ballinas and Urrutia 1992). Furthermore, no matter how short the actual reform fell from the democratic ideal, the democratization of the Federal District of Mexico became, from 1985 on, a central part of the political agenda. And, even if limited, it established the framework for subsequent amendments that have led to increased democratization of Mexico City.

The Earthquake Victims Movement as Historical Event

The social response to the 1985 earthquakes so amply highlighted by party representatives during the public hearings, and by journalists and intellectuals in the numerous articles published in Mexico's newspapers and political magazines[9] in the weeks following the earthquakes, is a typical, ordinary response to large-scale emergencies, as numerous studies on post-disaster behavior have documented.[10] Why then was the mobilization and organization of Mexico City residents recognized as a "notable" occurrence? Why was the cultural category "resident of Mexico City" transformed by the movement, and why was its new meaning causally linked to the political reform of Mexico City's government? In other words, why is the earthquake victims movement considered to be a historical event, and why did it initiate a sequence of interrelated ruptures that contributed to the democratization of Mexico City?

Social movements can lead to a chain of occurrences with long lasting effects that go beyond a movement's stated goals when their emergence challenges cultural categories. This in turn depends on the semiotic or symbolic codes of society and implies that the unintended consequences of social movements are recognizable only within the terms provided by a cultural structure. I believe that Jeffrey Alexander's work on the symbolic code of civil society offers some insights as to when, why, and how a social movement can have unintended—political—outcomes.

---

9   See, for example, "La hermosa gente del D. F.," *El Universal*, September 21, 1985. "Solidaridad con mayúsculas," *El Día*, September 30, 1985. "Solidaridad y organización," *La Jornada*, September 23, 1985. "Adelante a pesar de la tragedia," *El Nacional*, September 23, 1985. Manuel Aguilera Gómez. "Ante la tragedia, refrendo de entereza," *Excélsior*, September 25, 1985.

10   Research on the social responses to disasters has amply documented that the kind of response exhibited by Mexico City residents is common in large-scale emergencies that do not result in community annihilation (Miltei, Drabek and Haas 1975, p. 59 cited in Drabek 1986, p. 139; Raphael 1986, p. 232). Such response is known in the disasters literature as the "rise and fall of the post-disaster utopia" (Wolfenstein 1957).

In Alexander's view, civil society is not merely an institutional domain, but also, "a realm of structured, socially established consciousness, a network of understandings that operates beneath and above explicit institutions and the self-conscious interests of elites" (Alexander 1992, p. 290). Such "networks of understandings" form what he calls the symbolic code of civil society. For Alexander, codes have a universal binary structure composed of sets of oppositions at three different levels: motives, relationships, and institutions. Such oppositions although "when presented in their simply binary forms ... appear merely schematic ... reveal the skeletal structures on which social communities build their familiar stories, the rich narrative forms, that guide their everyday, taken-for-granted political life" (Alexander 1992, p. 294). Codes, argues Alexander, are stable and concrete features of civil society and are generally not contested. What is contested is their application. Who's going to be placed in which side of the code?

The placement of a group on the grid of civil culture depends on whether it exhibits or is presumed to exhibit the motives, relationships, and institutional arrangements associated to the positive side of the democratic code, what he calls the "discourse of inclusion." Liberal political scientists have in general defined worthy democratic citizens on the basis of certain qualities considered to be axiomatic of democracy. To be members of the democratic polity, liberal democrats argue, actors must be active rather than passive, autonomous rather than dependent, rational instead of irrational, reasonable and not hysterical, and so on. The relationships they establish should be open, trusting, critical, and honorable, as opposed to secretive, suspicious, deferential, and self-interested (Alexander 1992, pp. 292–95). The symbolic basis of citizen inclusion and exclusion implies that in order to be incorporated into the civic sphere segregated individuals and groups must be construed under the positive side of the democratic code.

In states with an authoritarian past, dominant actors and institutions constantly engage in practices geared towards constructing a semiotic and political field of differences, one that simultaneously legitimizes inclusion and exclusion, since both inclusion and exclusion (or any other distinction such as high and low, the legal and the criminal, and so on) are defined in terms of contrasts with one another. Through its active response to the emergency, its solidarity, and its autonomous organization, the earthquake victims movement not only challenged the meaning of the cultural category "resident of Mexico City" but symbolically relocated Mexico City residents on the positive side of the democratic code.

Opposition parties, as well as the critical press, made use of the symbolic code of civil society to attach the abstract available symbols of the positive side of the democratic code—autonomy, solidarity, public engagement, participation—to the residents of Mexico City. Reflecting on the emergence of the movement, a journalist of the daily *El Universal* wrote:

> Since we are used to not taking into consideration manifestations that come directly from society, the response of our fellow citizens has been surprising to some. We have forged a myth about the supposed indifference of Mexicans

to engage in collective action. We have believed that apathy and individualism dominate our fellow citizen's attitudes. We have seen that this is not the case (*El Universal*, September 23, 1985, p. 4).

In the words of the editors of the influential magazine *Nexos* (1985, p. 12):

It was an eruption of unknown forces that must lastingly modify our conception of urban life and of its institutional reality, of the political system and of the exercise of citizenship, of the social and administrative organization of the Federal District. [W]hat we knew by segments revealed itself in all its totality: the DF is no longer an entity that can be governed through antidemocratic and archaic methods.

The discrepancy between the newly assigned meaning to the cultural category "resident of Mexico City" and existing channels for political participation was further magnified by the government's response to the disaster. The government's failure to provide rapid and appropriate assistance to the earthquake victims certainly brought into question its capacity to manage the city, and the newly asserted competence of Mexicans living in D.F. for participating in the public sphere, was compared to the government's incompetence for dealing with the crisis situation. In addition, the "high moral value of all Mexicans" so openly recognized by mayor Aguirre in his speech before the chamber of deputies, contrasted acutely with the immorality of Mexican authorities unveiled by the disaster. As a result, the government was unable to "neutralize" the initial rupture triggered by the movement.

To sum up, the 1985 earthquake was certainly a transformative event in the history of Mexico City. But how it affected political arrangements, what its specific political consequences were, resulted not simply from its devastating effects, the government loss of control, or from the ample solidarity the event triggered and the organization of earthquake victims in a highly successful movement, but from its violation of the cultural category of "resident of Mexico City" and from the transposition of the newly assigned meaning from one structural location (the cultural realm) to another structural location (the realm of politics). The critical press as well as opposition parties, who had for a long time fought for political reform of the Federal District, played on the symbolic code of civil society in accord with their interests to cast the earthquake victims movement as a concrete instance of the positive side of the code, importing the association between the democratic code and citizenship rights, to their demand for the democratization of Mexico City's government.

Conclusion

Conceptions on temporalities of social life differ between historians and sociologists. Whereas historians have traditionally thought of events as: "highly contingent happenings that could change the very direction of historical development in a given society," sociologists have seen them as the "historical consequences of long-term structural causes" (Sewell 2010). The introduction of an eventful conception of temporality in the study of movement outcomes can help us understand the range of potential changes that movements can provoke unintentionally. My research on the 1985 earthquake victims movement suggests that the unintended effects of movements are best understood: by distancing ourselves from a movement-centered perspective, decoupling movement outcomes from strategic decisions, and defining social movements as historical events.

To consider social movements as historical events is to acknowledge that their unintended outcomes are the result of a combination of a variety of social processes with different temporalities. In other words, an eventful perspective on social movements sees unintended outcomes as determined by a juxtaposition of multiple processes and multiple temporalities. The unintended political effects of the earthquake victims movement combined unexpected occurrences, like a very severe earthquake; punctual happenings, like the (normal) social response to the emergency; and contingent specific occurrences such as the discovery of tortured corpses within judicial institutions or illegal garment workshops; relative gradual and long-term political demands, such as the demand for democratizing Mexico City government on behalf of opposition parties; as well as medium-term processes like the breaking down of the PRI's near complete control of Mexican political life.

In addition, temporal heterogeneity refers to the importance of historical contextualization for understanding the processes by which social movements can produce unintended outcomes. Temporal heterogeneity implies causal heterogeneity or the idea that consequences are not intrinsic in the act but depend on the "nature of the social world within which it takes place" (Sewell 2005, p. 10).

As noted earlier, events transform the meanings and relations of cultural categories because "the world fails to conform to categorical expectations" insomuch as actors bend categories to their own ends (Sewell 2005, p. 204). The response of Mexico City residents to the earthquake did not follow prevailing cultural expectations regarding their (lack of) competence for participating in the public sphere. Through its ample mobilization and organization independently from the official party, the earthquake victims movement unintentionally gave the cultural category of "resident of Mexico City" a new meaning.

However, the recognition by contemporaries of the earthquake victims movement as a noteworthy event that challenged cultural expectations about the residents of the Federal District was not enough for setting up a sequence of occurrences that led to political change. Opposition parties took advantage of this categorical change and bent the cultural category of "resident of Mexico City" to their own ends. It was through the intentional articulation of the newly acquired meaning of the cultural category "resident of Mexico City" to the city's political structure by the media and the opposition that the movement's initial rupture was conducive to democratic reform. This novel articulation was made possible by the symbolic code of civil society.

Results suggest that where residues of a less democratic past persist, as is the case in Mexico and several other Latin American states, movements often have their greatest effects by bringing about unintended outcomes, since channels of more direct impact are closed by the unresponsiveness of political institutions. In such political contexts, to study movement outcomes from an eventful perspective can be especially instructive.

Nevertheless, the unintended political outcomes of the earthquake victims movement also expand prevalent research on the democratizing impact of social movements in other geopolitical contexts. Contrary to the arguments that social movements only promote democracy when they "organize around a wide variety of claims including explicit demands for democracy" (Tilly 1994, p. 22; Maravall 1982, p. 12; Przeworski 1991, p. 61), or when they explicitly aim at affecting citizenship rights and obligations (Giugni 1998, p. xxi), findings suggest that the democratizing impact of social movements need not be determined by their explicit demands for democratic change. They indicate too that the political impact of social movements lies not in the creation of a more democratic political culture, as has often been argued, but rather in their challenge to the symbolic premises upon which exclusion is based. Findings also suggest that movement effects are not only mediated by the structural characteristics of the political context as proposed by the political mediation model (Amenta, Carruthers and Zylan 1992, p. 308–10), but depend on its symbolic underpinnings. More generally, results take issue with work that sharply distinguishes between political and cultural consequences of social movements and steer a middle course between those who emphasize changes in political institutions and public policies and those who stress transformations in the cultural realm.

My analysis indicates that introducing an eventful perspective on social movements to the study of movement outcomes can help us better understand their unintended outcomes. Such an approach calls into question excessively movement-centered research that views social movement effects as a result of the strategic decisions of movements, and focuses instead on the cultural conditions and political processes through which interested non-movement actors assign movements potentially disruptive meanings that set off interlocking sequences of occurrences that durably transform structures. To examine other mechanisms and conditions by and in which social movements can become historical events is an area that promises to further our understanding of how social movements can be crucial actors in processes of change.

References

Aguilar Zinser, Adolfo, 1985. "El temblor de la República y sus réplicas." In: A. Aguilar Zinser, C. Morales and R. Peña, eds. *Sociedad política y cambio social: el terremoto del 19 de septiembre de 1985.* México, D.F.: Editorial Grijalbo.

Alexander, Jeffrey, 1992. "Citizen and enemy as symbolic classification: on the polarizing discourse of civil society." In: M. Lamont and M. Fournier, eds. *Cultivating differences. Symbolic boundaries and the making of inequality.* Chicago: University of Chicago Press, pp. 289–308.

Almeida, Paul, 2008. "The sequencing of success: organizing templates and neoliberal policy outcomes." *Mobilization*, 13, pp. 165–87.

Alvarez, Sonia, Dagnino, Evelina and Escobar, Arturo eds, 1998. *Cultures of politics. Politics of cultures*, Colorado: Westview Press.

Amenta, Edwin, 2006. *When movements matter.* Princeton: Princeton University Press.

Amenta, Edwin, Carruthers, G. Bruce and Zylan, Yvonne, 1992. "A hero for the aged? The Towsend movement, the political mediation model, and US old-age policy, 1934–1950." *American Journal of Sociology*, 98, pp. 308–39.

Amenta, Edwin and Young, Michael, 1999. "Making an Impact: Conceptual and Methodological Implications of the Collective Goods Criterion." In: M. Giugni, D. McAdam, and Ch. Tilly, eds. *How social movements matter.* Minneapolis: University of Minnesota Press, pp. 22–41.

Amenta, Edwin and Caren Neal, 2007/2004. "The legislative, organizational, and beneficiary consequences of state-oriented challengers." In: D. Snow, S. Soule and H. Kriesi, eds. *The Blackwell companion to social movements.* Malden: Blackwell Publishing.

Amenta, Edwin, Caren Neal and Olasky, Sheera Joy, 2005. "Age for leisure? Political mediation and the impact of the pension movement on US old-age policy." *American Sociological Review*, 70, pp. 516–38.

Amenta, Edwin, Caren, Neal, Chiarello, Elizabeth and Su, Yang, 2010. "The political consequences of social movements." *Annual Review of Sociology*, 36, pp. 28–307.

Anderson, Jon W. 1968. "Cultural adaptation to threatened disaster." *Human Organization* 27, pp. 298–307.

Andrews, Kenneth, 2004. *Freedom is a constant struggle: the Mississippi civil rights movement and its legacy.* Chicago: University of Chicago Press.

Ballinas, Victor and Urrutia, Alonso, 1992. "Hacia la democratización del distrito federal." *Perfil de la Jornada. La Jornada*, March 3.

Banaszak, Lee Ann, 1996. *Why movements succeed or fail: opportunity, culture and the struggle for woman suffrage.* Princeton: Princeton University Press.

Beetham, David, 1991. *The legitimation of power.* Palgrave: Macmillan.

Bosi, Lorenzo and Uba, Katrin, 2009. "Introduction: The Outcomes of Social Movements." *Mobilization*, 14, pp. 409–15.

Buechler, Steven, 2007/2004. "The strange career of strain and breakdown theories of collective action." In: D. Snow, S. Soule and H. Kriesi, eds. *The Blackwell companion to social movements*. Malden: Blackwell Publishing.

Burstein, Paul and Linton, April, 2002. "The impact of political parties, interest groups, and social movement organizations on public policy: some recent evidence and theoretical concerns." *Social Forces*, 81, pp. 381–408.

Cámara de Diputados, 1983. *Debate y legislación sobre el distrito federal*. México: Cámara de Diputados. Periodo Ordinario de Sesiones. LII Legislatura.

———, 1985. *Comparecencia del jefe del departamento del distrito federal Ramón Aguirre Velázquez ante la LII legislatura*. México: Cámara de Diputados. LII Legislatura.

Carrillo, Teresa, 1990. "Women and independent unionism in the garment industry." In: J. Foweraker and A.L. Craig *Popular movements and political change in Mexico*. Boulder, Colo.: Lynne Rienner.

Cazés, Daniel, 1995. *Volver a nacer memorial del 85*. México, D.F.: Ediciones La Jornada.

CEPAL, 1985. *Daños causados por el movimiento telúrico en México y sus repercusiones sobre la economía del país*. México: Naciones Unidas.

Chen, Anthony, 2007. "The party of Lincoln and the politics of state fair employment practices legislation in the north, 1945–1964." *American Journal of Sociology*, pp. 1713–774.

CME, 1985. *Comisión metropolitana de emergencia*. Informe. México.

Convenio de Concertación Democrática, 1986. "Convenio de concertación democrática para la reconstrucción de la vivienda del programa nacional de renovación popular." *Revista Mexicana de Sociología*, 2 (Abril–Junio).

———, 1986b. "Convenio de concertación celebrado por la secretaría de desarrollo urbano y ecología para la reconstrucción de la unidad habitacional de Tlatelolco y para la vivienda en el distrito federal." *Revista Mexicana de Sociología*, 2 (Abril–Junio).

Coo, Jorge, 1986. "Después de la caída." In: Adolfo A. Zinser, Cesáreo Morales and Rodolfo Peña, eds. *Aún tiembla: sociedad política y cambio social: el terremoto del 19 de septiembre de 1985*. México, D.F.: Editorial Grijalbo.

Cress, Daniel and Snow, David, 2000. "The outcomes of homeless mobilization: the influence of organization, disruption, political mediation, and framing." *American Journal of Sociology*, 104, pp. 1063–104.

CUD, 1986. "Pliego petitorio de demandas presentado por la coordinadora única de damnificados al presidente de la república." *Revista Mexicana de Sociología*, 86, pp. 293–97.

De la Madrid, Miguel, 1982a. *Nacionalismo revolucionario. Siete tesis fundamentales de campaña*. México: PRI, Secretaría de Información y Propaganda.

———, 1982b. "Inaugural Speech." Mexico City Domestic Service in Spanish 1701 GMT.

Deng, Fang, 1997. "Information gaps and unintended consequences of social movements: the 1989 Chinese student movement." *American Journal of Sociology*, 102, pp. 1085–112.

Drabek, Thomas, 1979. "Communication: key to disaster management." *Insight*, 3 (July 3–4).

———, 1986. *Human system responses to disaster: an inventory of sociological findings*. Colorado: The University of Denver.

Drabek, Thomas, Key, William, Erickson, Patricia and Crowe, Juanita, 1975. "The impact of disaster on kin relationships." *Journal of Marriage and the Family*, 37 (August), pp. 481–94.

Dudasik, Stephen, 1980. "Victimization in natural disaster." *Disasters* 4(3), pp. 329–38.

Earl, Jennifer, 2000. "Methods, movements, and outcomes." *Research in Social Movements, Conflicts and Change*, 22, pp. 9–13.

———, 2007/2004. "The cultural consequences of social movements." In: D. Snow, S. Soule and H. Kriesi, eds. *The Blackwell companion to social movements*. Malden: Blackwell Publishing.

Eisinger, Peter, 1973. "The conditions of protest behavior in American cities." *The American Political Science Review*, 67, pp. 11–28.

Escobar, Arturo and Alvarez, Sonia, 1992. *The making of social movements in Latin America: identity, strategy, and democracy*. Colorado: Westview Press.

F.C.G., 1993. "Unintended Consequences" *American Journal of Economics and Sociology*, 52, pp. 83–84.

Foweraker, Joe, 1989. "Los movimientos populares y la transformación del sistema político Mexicano." *Revista Mexicana de Sociología*, 4, pp. 93–113.

———, 1993. *Popular mobilization in Mexico. The teachers movement, 1977–87*. Cambridge: Cambridge University Press.

Foweraker, Joe and Craig, Ann L. eds, 1990. *Popular movements and political changes in Mexico*. Boulder: Lynne Rienner.

Gamson, William, 1990/1975. *The strategy of social protest*. Dorsey: Homewood.

Giugni, Marco, 1995. "Outcomes of new social movements." In: R. Kriesi, Koopmans, J.W. Duyvendak and M. Giugni, eds. *New social movements in Western Europe*. Minneapolis: University of Minnesota Press.

———, 1998. "Was it worth the effort? The outcomes and consequences of social movements." *Annual Review of Sociology*, 98, pp. 371–93.

———, 1999. "How social movements matter: past research, present problems, future developments." In: M. Giugni, D. McAdam, and Ch. Tilly eds. *How social movements matter*. Minneapolis: University of Minnesota Press, pp. xiii–xxxiii.

———, 1999. *How social movements matter*. Minneapolis: University of Minnesota Press.

———, 2007/2004. "The cultural consequences of social movements." In: D. Snow, S. Soule and H. Kriesi, eds. *The Blackwell companion to social movements*. Malden: Blackwell Publishing.

————, 2007. "Useless protest? A time series analysis of the policy outcomes of ecology, antinuclear, and peace movements in the United States, 1975–1995." *Mobilization*, 12, pp. 101–16.

————, 2008. "Political, biographical, and personal consequences of social movements." *Sociology Compass*, 2, pp. 1582–600.

Giugni, Marco, McAdam, Doug and Tilly, Charles, eds, 1998. *From contention to democracy*. Colorado: Rowman & Littlefield.

Giugni, Marco and Bosi, Lorenzo, 2012. "The study of the consequences of armed groups: lessons from the social movement literature." *Mobilization*, 17, pp. 85–98.

Giugni, Marco and Yamasaki, Sakura, 2009. "The policy impact of social movements: a replication through qualitative comparative analysis." *Mobilization*, 14, pp. 467–84.

Goldstone, Jack, 1980. "The weakness of organization: a new look at Gamson's 'The Strategy of Social Protest.'" *American Journal of Sociology*, 85, pp. 1017–42.

Gupta, Devashree, 2009. "The power of incremental outcomes: how small victories and defeats affect social movement organizations." *Mobilization*, 14, pp. 417–32.

Gurr, Ted, 1980. "On the outcomes of violent conflict." In: T. Gurr, ed. *Handbook of Political Conflict*. California: Sage, pp. 101–30.

Haber, Paul, 1992. *Collective dissent in Mexico: The politics of contemporary urban popular movements*. Ph.D. Thesis Department of Sociology, Columbia University.

Hernández, Ricardo, 1987. *La coordinadora nacional del movimiento urbano popular, CONAMUP: su historia 1980–86*. México: Equipo Pueblo.

Herrasti, Emilia, 1993. "Espacios y actores sociales de la autogestión urbana en la ciudad de México." In: R. Coulomb and E. Duhau, ed. *Dinámica urbana y procesos sociopolíticos*. Mexico: Observatorio de la ciudad de México -Universidad Autónoma Metropolitana.

Holzer, Elizabeth, 2008. "Borrowing from the Women's Movement 'for reasons of public security': a study of social movement outcomes and judicial activism in the European Union." *Mobilization*, 13, pp. 25–44.

Jenkins, Craig and Perrow, Charles, 1977. "Insurgency of the powerless." *American Sociological Review*, 42, pp. 249–68.

King, Brayden, Bentele, Keith and Soule, Sarah, 2007. "Protest and policymaking: explaining fluctuation in congressional attention to rights issues, 1960–1986." *Social Forces*, 86, pp. 137–63.

King, Brayden, Cornwall, Marie and Dahlin, Eric, 2005. "Winning woman suffrage one step at a time: social movements and the logic of the legislative process." *Social Forces*, 83, pp. 1211–34.

Kitschelt, Herbert, 1986. "Political opportunity structures and political protest: antinuclear movements in four democracies." *British Journal of Political Science*, 16, pp. 57–95.

Kolb, Felix, 2007. *Protest and opportunities: the political outcomes of social movements.* Frankfurt: Campus Verlag.

Koopmans, Ruud and Statham, Paul, 1999. "Ethnic and civic conceptions of nationhood and the differential success of the extreme right in Germany and Italy." In: M. Giugni, D. McAdam and Ch. Tilly, eds. *How social movements matter.* Minneapolis: University of Minnesota Press, pp. 225–51.

Kriesi, Hanspeter, Koopmans, Ruth, Duyvendak, Willem and Giugni, Marco. 1995. *New social movements in western europe: a comparative analysis.* Minneapolis: University of Minnesota Press.

Kriesi, Hanspeter and Wisler, Dominique, 1999. "The impact of social movements on political institutions: a comparison of the introduction of direct legislation in Switzerland and the United States." In: M. Giugni, D. McAdam and Ch. Tilly, eds. *How social movements matter.* Minneapolis: University of Minnesota Press, pp. 42–65.

López Portillo, José, 1975/1921. *Elevación y caída de porfirio díaz.* México: Editorial Porrúa.

Mainwaring, Scott, 1987. "Urban popular movements, identity and democratization in Brazil." *Comparative Political Studies,* 20, pp. 131–59.

———, 1989. "Grass roots popular movements, and the struggle for democracy: Nova Iguacu." In: A. Stepan, ed. *Democratizing Brazil.* Princeton: Princeton University Press, pp. 168–204.

Mainwaring, Scott and Viola, Eduardo, 1984. "New social movements, political culture, and democracy: Brazil and Argentina in the 1980s." *Telos,* 61, pp. 17–52.

Maravall, José, 1982. *The transition to democracy in Spain.* New York: St. Martin's Press.

McAdam, Doug, 1983. "Tactical innovation and the pace of insurgency." *American Sociological Review,* 48, pp. 735–54.

———, 1989. "The biographical consequences of activism." *American Sociological Review,* 54, pp. 744–60.

———, 1996. "The framing function of movement tactics: strategic dramaturgy in the American civil rights movement." In: D. McAdam, J.D. McCarthy, and M. Zald, eds. *Comparative perspectives on social movements.* New York: Cambridge University Press, pp. 338–55.

———, 1999. "The biographical impact of activism." In: M. Giugni, D, McAdam and Ch. Tilly, eds. *How social movements matter.* Minneapolis: University of Minnesota Press, pp. 119–46.

McAdam, Doug, McCarthy, John and Zald, Mayer, 1988. "Social movements." In: N. Smelser, ed. *Handbook of sociology.* California: Sage, pp. 695–737.

McAdam, Doug and Su, Yang, 2002. "The war at home: anti-war protests and congressional voting, 1965 to 1973." *American Sociological Review,* 67, pp. 696–721.

McCammon, Holly, Campbell, Karen, Granberg, Ellen and Mowery, Christine, 2001. "How movements win: gendered opportunity structures and US women's suffrage movements, 1866 to 1919." *American Sociological Review*, 66, pp. 49–70.

McCammon, Holly. 2009. "Beyond frame resonance: the argumentative structure and persuasive capacity of twentieth-century US women's jury-rights frames." *Mobilization*, 14, pp. 45–64.

McCammon, Holly, Chaudhuri, Sommma, Hewitt, Lyndi, Muse, Courtney, Newman, Harmony, Smith, Carrie Lee and Terrell, Teresa, 2008. "Becoming full citizens: the US women's jury rights campaigns, the pace of reform, and strategic adaptation." *American Journal of Sociology*, 113, pp. 1104–147.

McCarthy John and Zald, Mayer, 2002. "The enduring vitality of the resource mobilization theory of social movements." In: J.H. Turner, ed. *Handbook of sociological theory*. New York: Kluwer Academic/Plenum, pp. 533–65.

McVeigh, Rory, Neblett, Carl and Shafiq Sarah, 2006. "Explaining social movement outcomes: multiorganizational fields and hate crime reporting." *Mobilization*, 11, pp. 23–49.

McVeigh, Rory, Welch, Michael and Bjarnason, Thoroddur, 2003. "Hate crime reporting as a successful social movement outcome." *American Sociological Review*, 68, pp. 843–67.

Melucci, Alberto, 1985. "The symbolic challenge of contemporary movements." *Social Research*, 52, pp. 789–816.

Meyer, David. 2006. "Claiming credit: stories of movement influence as outcomes."*Mobilization*, 11, pp. 281–98.

Meyer, Lorenzo, 1987. "Sistema de gobierno y evolución política hasta 1940." In: D.D.F and El Colegio de México, eds. *El atlas de la Ciudad de México*. México: El Colegio de México, pp. 373–75.

Mirowsky, John and Ross, Catherine, 1981. "Protest group success: the impact of group characteristics, social control, and context." *Sociological Focus*, 14, pp. 177–92.

Molinar, Juan, 1991. *El tiempo de la legitimidad: elecciones, autoritarismo y democracia en México*. México: Cal y Arena.

Monsiváis, Carlos, 1988. *Entrada Libre: Crónicas de la Sociedad que se Organiza*. México: Era.

———, 1986. "El día del derrumbe y las semanas de la comunidad (de noticieros y de crónicas)." *Cuadernos Políticos*, 45, pp. 11–24.

———, 1985. "Organizaciones populares y resistencia a su acción." *Proceso*, 21 de octubre, 468, pp. 18–27.

Mueller, Carol, 1978. "Riot violence and protest outcomes." *Journal of Political and Military Sociology*, 6, pp. 49–63.

Olzak, Susan and Ryo, Emily, 2007. "Organizational diversity, vitality and outcomes in the civil rights movement." *Social Forces*, 85, pp. 1561–591.

Piven, Frances and Cloward, Richard, 1977. *Poor people's movements: why they succeed and how they fail*. New York: Phanteon.

———, 1979. "Electoral instability, civil disorder, and relief crises." *American Political Science Review*, 73, p.1012–1019.

Poniatowska, Elena. 1988. *Nada, Nadie, Las voces del temblor.* Mexico: Ediciones Era.

Przeworski, Adam, 1991. *Democracy and the market.* Cambridge: Cambridge University Press.

Quarantelli E.L. and Dynes, Russell, 1977. "Response to social crisis and disaster." *Annual Review of Sociology*, 3, pp. 23–49.

Raquel Hernández de Arce, Regina María, 2004. *El distrito federal. Su definición político–administrativa y territorial. Una visión de conjunto*, PhD dissertation, Departamento de Historia Contemporánea, Universidad del País Vasco, Leioa, 2003, p. 420.

Rucht, Dieter, 1999. "The impact of environmental movements in western societies." In: M. Giugni, D. McAdam and C. Tilly, eds. *How social movements matter.* Minneapolis: University of Minnesota Press, pp. 204–24.

Sahlins, Marshall, 1985. *Islands of history.* Chicago: University of Chicago Press.

———, 1991. "The return of the event, again: with reflections on the beginnings of the great Fijian war of 1843 to 1855 between the kingdoms of Bau and Rewa." In: A. Biersack, ed. *Clio in Oceania: toward a historical anthropology.* Washington, D.C.: Smithsonian Institution Press, pp. 37–100.

Schumaker, Paul, 1975. "Policy responsiveness to protest groups demands." *Journal of Politics*, 37, pp. 488–521.

Secretaría de Gobernación, 1986. *Renovación política electoral–audiencias públicas de consulta.* Vol. 1 & 2, México: Secretaría de Gobernación.

Serna, Leslíe. ed., 1995. *¡Aquí nos quedaremos! Testimonios de la coordinadora única de damnificados.* México: Unión de Vecinos y Damnificados 19 de Septiembre, A.C./Universidad Latinoamericana.

Sewell, William, 1996. "Historical events as transformations of structures: inventing revolution at the bastille." *Theory and Society*, 25, pp. 841–81.

———, 2005. *Logics of history.* Chicago: University of Chicago Press.

———, 2009. "Economic crisis as transformative events," [online] Available at: <http://www.youtube.com/watch?v=iSo4ZK_2GEQ>.

Sewell, William, 2010. "Trois temporalités: vers une sociologie événementielle" in M. Bessin, C. Bidart, and M. Grossetti, eds. *Bifurcations: les sciences sociales face aux ruptures et à l'événement.* Paris: Éditions La Découverte.

Snow, David and Benford, Robert, 1988. "Ideology, frame resonance, and participant mobilization." In: B. Klandermans, H. Kriesi and S. Tarrow, eds. *From structure to action: comparing social movement research across cultures. international social movement research, 1.* Greenwich: JAI Press, pp. 197–217.

Snow, David and Soule, Sarah, 2009. *A primer on social movements*, New York: W.W. Norton & Company.

Snow, David, Soule, Sarah and Kriesi, Hanspeter, 2007/2004. "Mapping the terrain." In: D. Snow, S. Soule and H. Kriesi, eds. *The Blackwell companion to social movements.* Oxford: Blackwell.

Staggenborg, Suzanne, 1988. "Consequences of professionalization and formalization in the pro-choice movement." *American Sociological Review*, 53, pp. 585–606.

Staggenborg, Suzanne and Lecomte Josée, 2009. "Social movement campaigns: mobilization and outcomes in the Montreal women's movement community." *Mobilization*, 14, pp. 163–80.

Stearns, Linda. and Almeida, Paul, 2004. "The formation of state actor–social movement coalitions and favorable policy outcomes." *Social Problems*, 51, pp. 478–504.

Steedly, Homer and Foley, John, 1979. "The success of protest groups: multivariate analyses." *Social Science Research*, 8, pp. 1–15.

Tarrow, Sidney, 1983. "Struggling to reform: social movements and policy change during cycles of protest." Western Societies Program. Occasional Paper, 15. Ithaca: Cornell University.

———, 1989. *Democracy and disorder: protest and politics in Italy 1965–1975*. Oxford: Clarendon.

Tilly, Charles, 1994. "Social movements as historically specific clusters of political performances." *Berkeley Journal of Sociology*, 38, pp. 1–30.

———, 1999. "From interactions to outcomes in social movements." In: M. Giugni, D. McAdam and Ch. Tilly, eds. *How social movements matter*. Minneapolis: University of Minnesota Press, pp. 253–70.

Troyer, Ronald and Markle, Gerald, 1983. *Cigarettes: the battle over smoking*. New Jersey: Rutgers University Press.

Uba, Katrin, 2009. "The contextual dependence of movement outcomes: a simplified meta-analysis." *Mobilization*, 14, pp. 433–48.

US Department of Commerce, 1990. *The earthquake in Mexico City, Mexico September 1985*. Colorado: National Oceanic and Atmospheric Administration, National Geophysical Data Centre.

Van Dyke, Nella, McAdam, Doug and Wilhelm, Brenda, 2000. "Gendered outcomes: gender differences in the biographical consequences of activism." *Mobilization*, 5, pp. 161–77.

Whittier, Nancy, 2004. "The consequences of social movements for each other." In: D. Snow, S. Soule and H. Kriesi, eds. *The Blackwell companion to social movements*. Oxford: Blackwell.

Zemlinskaya, Yulia, 2009. "Cultural context and social movement outcomes: conscientious objection and draft resistance movement organizations in Israel." *Mobilization*, 14, pp. 449–66.

PART III
Brokerage and Coalition Formation

Chapter 7

Institutionalized Brokers and Collective Actors: Different Types, Similar Challenges

Adrian Gurza Lavalle and Marisa von Bülow

Introduction[1]

Brokers are key actors in collective action. As the literature on brokerage has argued, the very existence of collective action depends on the ability to intermediate among different types of actors. In spite of this broad consensus, however, we still know little about how the roles and impacts of brokers vary through time, in different contexts, and according to features of the brokers themselves. This chapter contributes to better understanding of this variation by focusing on an important but understudied type of broker, which we call "institutionalized brokers."

Institutionalized brokers are organizations formally empowered by a more or less bounded group of collective actors to fulfill specific and predetermined intermediation roles. They are "institutionalized" to the extent that they entail the transferring of resources and authority from other actors, and thus, increase non-voluntaristic relationships among them.[2] They perform brokerage roles that could not be achieved by organizations individually. At the same time, they depend on the material and symbolic support of their founders to fulfill such roles. They differ, thus, from the temporary and circumstantial roles played by informal brokers, who are less likely to be accountable to those impacted by their actions. However, the specific organizational design and the tasks performed by institutionalized brokers may vary substantially. Based on our previous work on social networks of civil

1   The authors' names appear in alphabetical order, having both contributed equally to this chapter. Various institutions supported the authors while they were writing this chapter. Marisa von Bülow thanks the funding of Project RS130002, Milenio Scientific Initiative of the Chilean Ministry of Economy, and the Fondecyt Project 1130897 of the Chilean National Commission of Scientific and Technological Investigation. Adrian Gurza Lavalle thanks the Institute for European Studies and the Centre for the Study of Democratic Institutions, both from University of British Columbia, as well as the grant #2012/18439-6 of the São Paulo Research Foundation (FAPESP). The authors thank Rebecca Abers, Federico Rossi, Margaret Keck, and an anonymous reviewer for comments on a previous version of this text.

2   For a thoughtful analysis of the non-voluntaristic component of association, see Warren 2004.

society organizations in Brazil and Mexico, we develop a typology of civil society "institutionalized brokers" to systematically analyze these differences.

We also argue that institutionalizing brokerage is a dynamic process that poses challenges to both brokers and intermediated actors. As Stovel and Shaw (2012) argued in their recent overview of the literature, there is virtually no research on how acts of brokerage shape subsequent relationships, and the dilemmas associated with brokerage are rarely addressed in theoretical debates. Our analysis seeks to fill these gaps. The decision to create specialized organizations to fulfill intermediation roles among civil society organizations and between them and external actors is neither automatic, easy, nor without costs. It entails trade-offs between the concentration of resources and authority on the one hand, and between the autonomy, diversity, and economy of resources on the other. From the point of view of brokers, playing intermediation roles requires continuous and intense negotiations with those who support them and to whom they have to be accountable.

In spite of these challenges, the institutionalization of brokerage has become an increasingly relevant phenomenon, especially in contexts of enlarged civil-society organizational ecologies such as the ones we find in Brazil, Mexico, and elsewhere in post transition Latin America.[3] Borrowing from organizational sociology and from our own previous work on civil society, we define these organizational ecologies as diversified populations of civil society organizations that create specialized organizational forms to cope with their interdependence within shared environments (Hannan and Freeman 1989; Hannan, Pólos and Carrol 2007; Gurza Lavalle and Bueno 2011; 2010).

We do not argue, however, that the institutionalization of brokerage is a new phenomenon. Various types of intermediation organizations have existed for a long time, presented in the literature under different names. In fact, their roots can be traced back to the nineteenth century, to the North American women's federations studied by Skocpol (1992), or the umbrella associations of Mexican artisans analyzed by Forment (2003, pp. 108–9). In the twentieth century, Morris (1981) discusses the key translator and coordinator tasks performed by "movement centers" for the civil rights movement in the United States. In Latin America, the neocorporatism literature focused on structures of interest intermediation between class actors and the state arguing in favor of the institutionalization of class brokers because of its effectiveness (Schmitter 1974; 1971; Malloy 1977).

In spite of these precedents, we found surprisingly few attempts to specify the differences among organizations that act as intermediaries, their roles, their internal

---

3   The literature on mobilization in Latin America points to the greater heterogeneity of civil society associations after transitions to democracy. For instance, Avritzer (1992) argues that, in parallel to democratization processes, there were two important changes in patterns of collective action in the region: the rupture with a homogenizing pattern of action (made possible because of an important decrease in the relevance of labor organizations), and the increase in number and variety of civil associations.

governance practices, and the challenges they face. We draw on these and on more recent efforts to develop a new typology of institutionalized brokers, differentiating among (1) *peak associations*, (2) *associational hubs*, and (3) *multisectoral bodies*, according to the brokerage roles they play and their internal governance.

The empirical examples analyzed in this chapter shed light on the increased relevance of institutionalized brokers and the trade-offs faced by both the actors that create them and the brokers themselves. We analyze *associational hubs* by focusing on the process of creation of transnational nodes in the context of free trade agreement mobilizations in the Americas, and specifically in Mexico and Brazil. We then analyze *peak associations* and *multisectoral bodies* by focusing on the role they play within the organizational ecologies of post-transition civil society in Mexico City and São Paulo. In doing so, we bring together results from two separate research projects, which rely on different types of data and ask research questions at different levels of analysis. In both cases, institutionalized brokerage was a consistent thread that remained conceptually underdeveloped in previous publications. This chapter fills this gap and proposes a theoretical framework to better understand this phenomenon.

Varieties of Brokers

During the 1980s, the literature on social movements highlighted the role of intermediary actors in facilitating mobilization processes (Snow, Zurcher and Ekland-Olson 1980; Klandermans and Oegema 1987; Fernandez and McAdam 1988). In the past decade, brokerage received broader attention, as part of a discussion about mechanisms and processes in explanations about contentious politics. Based on the definitions used by social network analysts,[4] McAdam, Tarrow, and Tilly defined brokerage as "the linking of two or more currently unconnected social sites by a unit that mediates their relations with each other and/or with yet another site" (2001, p. 26). Both in their work and in much of the social network analysis literature, this "unit" could be individuals or organizations who play key positive roles by creating new connections and facilitating the flow of resources (Marsden 1982; Gould 1989; Burt 1992, 2005).

Understanding brokerage in this way sheds light on a relational mechanism that helps explain the diffusion of social movements. However, it does not offer a finer-grained analysis of types of brokers or brokerage roles, and is of little help for understanding the institutionalization of intermediation roles. More recently, Mische (2008) called for a broadening of the view of brokers' positions in networks and their roles, arguing that the "existence of completely disconnected clusters is only a limiting case in relation to more commonly occurring partial forms of

---

4   For example, in an article published in 1982, Peter Marsden defined brokerage as a mechanism "by which intermediary actors facilitate transactions between other actors lacking access to or trust in one another" (Marsden 1982, p. 202).

intersection and disjunction" (Mische 2008, p. 48; see also von Bülow 2011). Furthermore, as we explain below, we cannot simply assume that the impacts of brokerage will be positive.

The contemporary literature on social movements in Latin America has recognized the key intermediation roles played by emerging types of organizations. A study carried out by the United Nations Development Program (UNDP) (2011) on social conflict in 17 Latin American countries, between October 2009 and September 2010, highlights the role of "coordinators of social movements." These are defined as "second order organizations that act as a sort of an institutional umbrella bringing together social movements with similar demands" and "whose main function is to enhance coordination with grassroots organizations or with individual actors" (PAPEP/UNDP 2011, p. 158). The study goes on to argue that these organizations generate collective supra-identities on the basis of relatively new dynamics that have not been adequately studied yet (idem). Similarly, in his comparative analysis about "anti-neoliberal contention" in Latin America, Silva (2009, pp. 3–4; 41) argues that one of the necessary conditions for the contentious episodes happening in these countries was the ability of civil society brokers to help form coalitions among anti-neoliberal movements.

Working on conceptual grounds and focusing in Latin America, two recently published typologies of intermediation organizations have offered a more detailed analysis of their roles. Based on the results of a survey of associations carried out in Buenos Aires (Argentina), Santiago (Chile), Lima (Peru), and Caracas (Venezuela), Handlin and Kapiszewski (2009) identify two types of "coordinating associations," that is, "those for which coordinating other associations is a principal function" (Ibid., 231) nodal NGOs and flexible fronts. For both of these types, coordinating other associations is an important activity. However, contrary to the institutionalized brokers on which we focus in this chapter, the organizations cited by Handlin and Kapiszewski are rarely empowered formally to represent other organizations (Ibid., 231–32). Differences between nodal NGOs and flexible fronts are related to their organizational and financial resources, level of internal democracy, and links to other actors (Ibid., 231–45). According to the authors, their increased relevance is related to a historical shift in popular organizing in Latin America, in which networks of community-based associations and NGOs have replaced party-affiliated labor unions as the predominant organizations for popular mobilization (Collier and Handlin 2009b).[5]

The second typology is the one proposed by Gurza Lavalle and Bueno (2011), based on a similar survey of associations carried out in São Paulo (Brazil) and Mexico City (Mexico). These authors argue that there are different types of "third tier" organizations—those that work for other societal actors: coordinating bodies (*articuladoras*) and fora (*fóruns*). Coordinating bodies are among the most central actors within Mexico City and São Paulo's civil society networks.

---

5   The authors refer to a transition from the "Up-Hub" interest regime to the "A-Net" one. See Collier and Handlin 2009.

Besides coordinating common agendas, strategies, and collective action among its members, coordinating bodies aggregate and scale up claims, and represent their members vis-à-vis public authorities and other civil society actors. Fora are less central in the networks and work mainly as civil society spaces for building consensus around specific policies and fostering common basic agendas among its members. These organizations are the result of a process of differentiation and of functional specialization of an enlarged organizational ecology.

We build on these typologies, but we introduce clearer distinctions in order to produce a more comprehensive typology of institutionalized brokerage. We cast a broader net, including institutionalized brokers that are expected to play a wider array of intermediation roles. Furthermore, while the typologies mentioned were developed inductively, to make analytical sense of intermediation organizations found on the field, ours is deductive.

Toward a Typology of Institutionalized Brokers

As shown in Table 7.1, we differentiate among three types of institutionalized brokers: peak associations, associational hubs, and multisectoral bodies. First, we look at how each type defines who is and who is not a part of the organization, or what Diani (forthcoming) has called "the mechanism of boundary definition." These boundaries may be more or less rigidly defined, and participation may be more or less diverse. Second, we look at the different sets of roles these actors are expected to play, following the differentiation proposed in the brokerage ladder presented in Table 7.2. Third, we analyze some interesting correlated features.

The definition of membership boundaries is closely related to different kinds of relationships with members, ranging from formal and often legally stipulated ties, as in the case of affiliation-based relationships common to peak associations, to looser and more informal ties, as in the case of participation in multisectoral bodies. Also, there is variation in the scope of aims institutionalized brokers may seek to achieve. Around which goals do actors cooperate? Greater diversity implies a more limited range of institutional goals and vice-versa: restricted plurality creates room for defining a wider range of goals. In the case of affiliation-based organizations, brokerage roles are performed with institutionally defined members' interests at heart. The same is not necessarily true for other types of institutionalized brokers, created around broader agendas and a more diverse set of participants.

Table 7.1   Three Types of Institutionalized Brokers

Types	Membership Boundaries		Main Brokerage Roles		Correlated Features	
	Formaliza-tion	Plurality	External	Internal	Relation-ship with Members	Definition of Aims
Peak Associa-tions	Boundaries are rigid and normally set by legal rules	Restricted to a specific subset of actors	Coordinator Articulator Representa-tive	Coordinator Articulator Representa-tive	Members tend to be affiliated	Interests of affiliates
Associa-tional Hubs	Boundaries are flexible but defined by explicit rules	Open to a wide range of actors	Translator Coordinator Articulator Representa-tive	Translator Coordinator Articulator Representa-tive	Members tend to be allies (as in campaign or coalitions)	Common goals
Multisecto-ral Bodies	No clear boundaries, although there are loose implicit rules	Open to a wide range of actors	Translator	Translator Coordinator Articulator	Members tend to be participants in common sites	Same policy issues or themes

Table 7.2   The Brokerage Ladder

Type of Brokerage Role	Main Internal Tasks	Main External Tasks
Translator	Information reception, decodification, and diffusion	Information transmission, codification, and diffusion
Coordinator	Division of labor among participants Reception and distribution of resources Reaching out to new poten-tial participants	Definition of shared commitments. Looking for and bargaining of resources Reach-out to relevant actors
Articulator	Promotion of dialogue to build consensus Capacity building Monitoring of negotiations and/or debates	Promotion of dialogue to promote shared discur-sive platforms Following up on legislation, events, and debates
Representative	Consultation about specif-ic decisions Information about outcomes related to representa-tive tasks Harmonization of internal and external agendas	Speaking on behalf of members in committees, councils, public audiences, and/or negotiating tables Vocalization of claims in public sphere

Source: Adapted from von Bülow 2011: 169.

One way to think about the variety of brokerage roles and how these may change through time is in terms of a "brokerage ladder,"[6] ranging from simpler to more complicated internal and external intermediation tasks (see Table 7.2). Perhaps the most common tasks associated with brokerage are those related to the role of "translator." These are similar to Morris' description of activities conducted by the "movement centers" during the civil rights movement, which received and rebroadcast information. By speaking in terms of "translation," however, we emphasize the creative dimension of such task, as brokers often reframe or recodify the information received or emitted. As actors move up the ladder assuming coordinator, articulator, and representative roles, the corresponding tasks require more complex processes of negotiation.

Whether or not brokers perform all of these roles is an empirical matter, but, at a minimum, brokerage arrangements offer a dynamic meeting point where the coordination of joint initiatives occur, where negotiation of common frames takes place (internal brokerage), and where the vocalization of members' claims (external brokerage) can be heard. Neither the roles nor their corresponding tasks are mutually exclusive, but these are more or less important depending on the type of broker, and may be combined in different ways as well. Thus, while greater plurality renders the role of translator more relevant, less formalization may impose limits to the exercise of representational tasks and, more generally, to external brokerage tasks.

Peak associations have clearer membership boundaries and lesser plurality than the other two types. They are typically restricted to a specific subset of actors that have certain characteristics and are usually brought together by affiliation, as in the case of labor federations, and of associations of NGOs that restrict membership to a predefined type of organization. Peak associations are created to play external brokerage roles, mainly representational ones, and in order to do so they perform the same roles internally. Affiliation normally implies some kind of legal status, and peak associations often have documents formally establishing a basic set of institutional commitments. This set of commitments translates to a wide range of programs, as well as to the specification of tasks. Well-known examples in the Mexican and Brazilian contexts, created in the beginning of the 1990s, are, respectively, the Civil Organizations Convergence for Democracy (*Convergencia de Organismos Civiles por la Democracia*—Convergencia) and the Brazilian Association of Non-Governmental Organizations (*Associação Brasileira de Organizações Não-Governamentais*—ABONG).

In both associational hubs and multisectoral bodies, membership boundaries are less rigid, meaning that they are open to the participation of a broad range of actors. Multisectoral bodies bring together organizations and individuals—who may or may not be called "members"—working around the same policy issues or themes. They have no clear boundaries. Participation, in these cases, is not

---

6   Based on our previous work, we borrow loosely from Sherry Arnstein's (1969) idea about the "ladder of participation" (see von Bülow 2011, p. 168).

defined on the basis of a legal or organizational status, but on the basis of thematic affinities among actors, which tend to meet as participants in specific sites or events. Externally, such loose coalitions perform mainly the role of translator. Internally, loose membership of a plurality of actors does not allow for the definition of clear single goals. Examples are the Social Network for a Mexico Free of Addictions (*Red Social por un México Libre de Adicciones*) and the Brazilian Health Forum (*Fórum de Saúde*). These initiatives provide participants with information, a coordination space, and the possibility of developing common positions and actions.

Finally, associational hubs are in an intermediary position between peak associations and multisectoral bodies in terms of the definition of membership rules. They are more flexible than the former but more rigid than the latter. In contrast to multisectoral bodies, they imply stronger ties among actors, which are not only interested in a common issue or theme, but share political views or common understandings to a degree that lead them to become allies in campaigning and coalition building. The public statement of these understandings or political views works as an explicit definition of rules and common goals to join the coalition or campaign. Associational hubs are created to play both internal and external roles, being in fact the type of broker that deals with the widest range of roles. Good examples are the national chapters of the Hemispheric Social Alliance (*Alianza Social Continental*) analyzed in the next section.

It is important to note that the divisions among these three types of institutionalized brokers are less rigid than they may appear to be by looking at Table 7.1. Furthermore, these are not mutually exclusive alternatives for the actors who participate in them. It is possible (and in fact quite common) that the same social movement organization or NGO may participate in more than one of these brokerage types. Finally, we do not argue that one type of institutionalized broker is *a priori* more or less efficient than the others, nor do we assume that one is more democratic than the others (whatever definition of both "efficiency" and "democratic" is adopted). We only point to the fact that there are different levels of formalization of the rules for access, interrelated organizational aims, and other relevant features. Thus, neither "formalization" nor "plurality" is approached from a normative standpoint. Different types of institutionalized brokerage carry with them different brokerage roles, and thus different challenges and trade-offs.

Trade-Offs of Institutionalizing Brokerage

As discussed in the introduction and in the first section of this chapter, the literature on intermediation, from neocorporatism to the recent contributions on brokerage in the social movement literature, has focused mainly on the positive impacts brokers may have on mobilization and claims making. We argue instead that the creation of institutionalized brokers is a political decision that carries with it trade-offs and challenges. As Hannan and Freeman pointed out in their ground-breaking work on organizational ecologies, "because great quantities of organizational resources are used for building organizations and for administrative overhead, rather than for production of collective action, creation of a permanent organization is a costly way of achieving social goals" (Hannan and Freeman 1989, p. 5). Besides its costly nature, once created, organizations develop their own logic and the staff develops vested interests, posing accountability challenges to its founders—a lesson well learned at least since Michels' 1911 work on political parties and the iron law of oligarchy.

Understanding why civil society actors decide (or not) to join forces goes beyond the goals of this chapter. Our focus is on conceptually developing a comprehensive typology to shed light on different institutionalized brokerage initiatives and the trade-offs they entail for actors who decide to participate in them. Internally, actors have to choose between the concentration of power versus a more distributive approach that promotes egalitarian relations but also fragmentation of resources and inefficiency. Without institutionalized brokers, the capacity to play coordination, articulation and representational roles will depend on moral persuasion, which potentially high opportunity costs and the risk of perpetuating internal conflicts.[7] Externally, the efficiency trade-off poses a choice between remaining autonomous but with small chances of being heard, or, if heard, having limited impact or acting through a broker that will interpret actors' needs, reduce diversity, and even subordinate actors' goals to binding decisions.

However, we should not take it for granted that a set of actors belonging to an enlarged organizational ecology will choose the path of institutionalization of brokerage when facing the efficiency trade-off. Institutionalization is not a recipe for success and failures are possible. Moreover, even when the path has been taken, the status of the broker is not written in stone and members can deinstitutionalize brokerage through voice or exit strategies (Hirschman 1970). Hence, brokerage is risky from the point of view of the broker as well. The threat of deinstitutionalization may be carried out not only because of poor performance, but also because the same asymmetry of resources that makes brokerage possible permanently gives rise to suspicion (Stovel and Shaw 2012). Furthermore, challenges to the broker may come from members that might be more powerful and resourceful than the broker itself (Ahrne and Brunsson 2008). As will be shown in the empirical analysis presented in the next sections, the institutionalization of intermediation is indeed a risky undertaking.

---

7 A trade-off examined by Warren (2004) in terms of the difficulties faced by associations that rely entirely in voluntary relationships, with no organizational components to cope with internal conflict. In that case, the only means available is moral persuasion, but it cannot support too much stress.

The Roles of Brokers in Enlarged Organizational Ecologies

Looking at examples of the three types of institutionalized brokers can shed light on the dynamics of brokerage institutionalization, especially with respect to the challenges faced by civil society actors in these initiatives.

First, we present an analysis of associational hubs, through the cases of the Mexican Action Network on Free Trade (*Red Mexicana de Acción Frente al Libre Comercio*—RMALC), and the Brazilian Network for Peoples' Integration (*Rede Brasileira pela Integração dos Povos*—REBRIP). These are "transnational nodes," defined as organizations that are part of transnational coalition-building efforts and that perform brokerage roles within and across national borders. In the second part of this section, we consider cases of peak associations and multisectoral bodies, by analyzing the role of actors within the civil society organizational ecologies of São Paulo and Mexico City. As clarified above, these sections are based on two different research projects and methodologies that show the increasingly relevant role played by institutionalized brokers. While the section on transnational nodes focuses more on the agency of brokers, the section on peak associations and multisectoral bodies emphasizes the impacts of their positions in networks of civil society organizations.

Associational Hubs and Transnational Collective Action

In the past two decades, a very broad and heterogeneous group of civil society organizations from the Americas gradually became aware of the important impacts of trade agreements and regional integration negotiations on various constituencies and public policy arenas. For these actors, rooted in various countries, creating institutionalized brokers that could help generate transnational collective action became a critical task. As a result of the increasing demand for common meeting spaces and coordination, they built a new hemispheric, multiscale, and multisectoral organizational infrastructure. National alliances brought together NGOs, social movement organizations, small business organizations, and faith-based initiatives. These, in turn, met at the transnational scale under the umbrella of a new coalition, the Hemispheric Social Alliance (HSA), created in 1997.[8]

In deciding whether and how to join in multiscale collective action, actors had to make important decisions in two successive steps. First, they had to decide whether to participate in transnational alliance building or to "go it alone." While the former option entailed an enlargement of frames negotiated with other actors (and at least some loss of visibility of specific organizations and claims), the latter risked isolation and, thus, irrelevance. Second, when accepting to be part of this new collaborative setup, actors had to decide about the internal governance of both

---

8   For a more detailed analysis of the process of creation of the Hemispheric Social Alliance and its national chapters, see von Bülow 2010.

national coalitions and of the HSA. Again, this involved a trade-off between creating powerful brokers, on the one hand, and the autonomy of individual members, on the other. As argued above, both are well-known collective action dilemmas and exemplify the trade-offs related to the institutionalization of brokerage.

The result that was negotiated turned out to be neither a set of loosely organized alliances nor a rigid structure, but rather the creation of domestic organizations with flexible membership boundaries, affiliated at the transnational level to the HSA. All participants shared a critical stance toward multilateral trade agreements and an interest in influencing Latin American regional integration processes. The Executive Secretariats of the domestic coalitions performed the four brokerage roles specified in Table 7.2: the role of *translators*, who produce and diffuse information within and across boundaries; *coordinators*, needed to organize the distribution of resources, responsibilities, and information; *articulators*, who bridge across cleavages to bring together actors and negotiate common positions; and the role of *representatives* in international events and meetings. While the first three are intermediating tasks performed internally, the last one entails links to other actors, such as state officials. We call these organizations "transnational nodes," because they exist as part of a broader network that met at the transnational level, in this case, under the banner of the HSA.

We focus on the experiences of two of the 17 organizations that existed in 2013: RMALC and REBRIP.[9] Through the analysis of the institutionalization of brokerage in these different political and societal contexts, we identify similar dilemmas and the various ways in which actors dealt with them.

RMALC was created in 1991 with a life span that was linked initially to that of debates over NAFTA negotiations. In its early years, it was administered by volunteers and temporarily occupied part of the space of the offices of a small labor federation, the Authentic Labor Front (*Frente Auténtico del Trabajo*—FAT). By 2005, the coalition had six paid staff members and occupied a larger portion of the FAT building in Mexico City, on a permanent basis. It started with 42 affiliated organizations. This number grew during the NAFTA debates to over 100, but dwindled afterwards. In 2013, it brought together around 16 civil society organizations.[10]

REBRIP was created several years after RMALC, in the context of the hemispheric negotiations of the FTAA. Instead of creating a new organization, however, the Brazilian actors decided to put a previously existing one in charge of brokerage roles (the Federation of Organisms for Social and Educational Assistance until 2010, and from then on the Unified Workers' Central—CUT), with a very small structure, and with less dependence than RMALC on paid

---

9 For a more complete analysis of mobilizations around free trade agreements, see von Bülow 2010, 2011.

10 For a list of members, see http://www.rmalc.org.mx/integrantes.htm, accessed April 15, 2013.

staff and on external fundraising. In 2013, REBRIP brought together 67 social movement organizations, NGOs, and coalitions of civil society organizations.[11]

In spite of these differences, the members of the two coalitions faced a similar challenge: how to build efficient brokerage organizations that could perform coordination, articulation, translation, and representation tasks without undermining the autonomy of individual members. In both cases many members had their own direct contacts to allies in other countries, and did not depend necessarily on either REBRIP or RMALC to articulate all collective action related to trade or to regional integration. In REBRIP case, however, these direct contacts were used in parallel to the coalition's, while in the RMALC case, direct ties progressively undermined the coalition's brokerage capacity.[12]

In fact, through time, Mexican organizations relied less and less on RMALC for coordination, articulation, and representation. Nevertheless, it remained an important site of knowledge production and diffusion. Since its founding RMALC had been the most important domestic reference for actors looking for a critical analysis of trade agreements and their impacts, one that presented issues in terms that their members could easily understand, and that linked international negotiations to local realities.[13] However, RMALC was largely unable to sustain the other intermediating roles that it had been created to play.

As one of RMALC's members explained, there was a diminished dependence on the coalition as the single gateway to reach out to organizations in other countries: "At first maybe the door was RMALC, but now we have a series of relationships that have been built ... The process has spilled over to other issues, people became specialized, bilateral contacts were made. Now there are other levels of relationship."[14]

The weakening of RMALC´s brokerage roles is related not only to a natural process of diversification of ties, but more fundamentally to what Stovel and Shaw (2012) called the "inevitable dilemma": the ability of brokers to maintain the trust necessary to continue to perform intermediation tasks.[15] It is also directly related to the trade-offs we have identified. As many of RMALC's former participants explained in interviews, the concentration of decision-making power in a few

---

11   For a list of members, see http://www.REBRIP.org.br/conteudo/34/membros, accessed April 15, 2013.

12   This analysis is based on a series of semi-structured interviews undertaken with the staff of RMALC and REBRIP, and with the staff of the organizations that participated in both coalitions. For more details about the field research, see von Bülow 2010.

13   Several of the Mexican interviewees highlighted the important intellectual role of RMALC in knowledge production. Between 1991 and 2003, RMALC published or co-edited 23 publications, besides numerous popular education materials and bulletins (Massicotte 2004, p. 289).

14   Interview with Brisa Maya, CENCOS, Mexico City, August 2005.

15   This issue came up repeatedly in the interviews undertaken with organizations that were participating in RMALC or that had participated in the past. For a more detailed analysis, see von Bülow 2011.

individuals that claimed to speak for all was one of the most important sources of the crisis (von Bülow 2010; 2011). As a result, RMALC has moved from something closer to the associational hub type, in the 1990s, to becoming a multisectoral body in the 2000s, at least in terms of the brokerage roles it is able to perform (see Table 7.1).

In the REBRIP case, the relationship between the coalition's roles and the autonomy of individual members was a matter of explicit and contentious debate. As an internal report produced in 2007 explained, the result of this debate was an innovative organizational design that attempted to strike a balance between efficiency and autonomy:

> Today in the Brazilian Network for Peoples' Integration (REBRIP) we have reached a dynamic that allows us to affirm that we are both a space and a network. We are not [like] the World Social Forum process, since we do adopt clear positions that guide our actions. However, we are also not a rigid structure that limits its members' autonomy. We act with clear positions, but with the limitation of the minimum common denominator possible (REBRIP 2007).

Thus, in the Brazilian case, the coalition maintained a much lower profile than in the Mexican case. As its Coordinating Group recognized, many of its own members were larger (in terms of social base and political capacities) than the coalition, which meant that their positions were not decided primarily within this arena (REBRIP 2007). Paradoxically, this meant that REBRIP was more successful than its Mexican counterpart. As Diani has argued (2003; 2013), brokers are not necessarily leaders, because in heterogeneous settings playing a strong leadership role may hamper chances to act as a mediator between different factions and organizations.

In spite of these efforts at finding an acceptable equilibrium for all, however, REBRIP was not immune to the dilemma mentioned above. Important member-based organizations such as the Unified Labor Central (CUT) or the Landless Workers' Movement (MST) saw REBRIP as an important space for gaining access to knowledge, coordinating actions around specific goals and issues, and debating with actors who they would not necessarily meet otherwise, but not as an arena to build common binding positions. Furthermore, tensions between these large member-based organizations and NGOs arose when there were representation roles to be fulfilled. Thus, even though REBRIP has been able to sustain high levels of participation, its ability to perform institutionalized brokerage roles—most importantly, that of representation—faced important and increasing limitations through time.[16]

When members created direct ties, bypassing organizations such as RMALC, they risked undermining the whole structure of institutionalized brokerage across the local, national, and hemispheric scales. However, when other gateways were

---

16   For a more detailed analysis, see von Bülow 2011.

used in addition to trade coalitions, as in the REBRIP case, multiplication of ties was potentially positive, and did not necessarily reflect a tendency for actors to shy away from this type of institutionalized broker. In these two cases, challenges to the roles played by institutionalized brokers had different impacts.

Peak Associations and Multisectoral Bodies

In post-transition Brazil and Mexico, a wide range of associations devoted to local development, rights advocacy, and social assistance created innovative organizational forms to perform internal and external brokerage roles among them. Within Mexican and Paulista civil societies (more so in the latter), many intermediation organizations successfully performed these brokerage roles.

Native names vary, but all of them are organizations created by organizations: "fora" (*fóruns*), "centers" (*centrales*), "networks," "NGOs" (working for other NGOs), "federations," "coordinators," (*coordenadoras*) and "foundations" (working for associations). Despite different denominations, they hold strong similarities to multisectoral bodies and peak associations.

While fora and networks resemble multisectoral bodies, centers, federations, coordinators, and NGOs and foundations (working for other organizations) are best classified as peak associations according to our typology. In the case of the multisectoral bodies, diverse actors were involved in founding them: advocacy NGOs, service non-profits committed to social assistance, neighborhood associations, and popular movement organizations. In the case of the peak associations, especially from the 1990s on, NGOs were instrumental, although other actors were also involved (see Gurza Lavalle, Houtzager and Castello 2011).

The specific tasks attached to the brokerage roles are different for both types and so are the implications for the efficiency trade-offs. We rely on existing studies in these countries and, above all, on our previous research on Mexico City and São Paulo's civil society networks (Gurza Lavalle, Castello and Bichir 2007, 2008; Gurza Lavalle and Bueno 2011).

In Mexico, new kinds of peak associations began to appear in the social mobilization landscape in the 1970s, when the underserved, urban lower-class movement known as popular urban movement (*Movimiento Urbano Popular*—MUP) was leading protest movements.[17] Besides popular fronts (*frentes populares*), which are broad coalitions of actors campaigning around specific goals—and are thus similar to associational hubs—more stable and long-lasting initiatives around MUP appeared as well. They expressed the strength of MUP actors on the national and metropolitan levels. For example, the National

---

17 These are new not only because they were emergent actors in the 1970s, but in comparison to the peak organizations created by the labor movement in the country early on, in the 1930s, as part of the Mexican state corporatist arrangement that merged corporations into the state party.

Coordinating Committee of the Urban Popular Movement (*Coordinadora Nacional del Movimiento Urbano Popular*—CONAMUP) excelled in the MUP thanks to its capacity to mobilize people and foster unified action among various types of actors nationwide (Ramírez 1988; Isunza 2001, pp. 179–284; Álvarez 2005, p. 158). CONAMUP and most of MUP peak associations declined at the end of the 1980s and beginning of the 1990s (Bolos 1999, p. 166).

In Mexico City, renewed forms of peak associations with varying degrees of bounded memberships emerged from the 1990s on, engaging in democratic transition campaigns, civil society capacity building, and rights advocacy—examples include Convergence, Regional Network for the Migration (*Red Regional para la Migración*), Human Rights Civil Organizations' National Network (*Red Nacional de Organizaciones Civiles de Derechos Humanos*—Red TDT), and Mexican Alliance of Social Organizations (*Alianza Mexicana de Organizaciones Sociales*—AMOS). These peak associations had become among the most central actors within civil society by the mid-2000s (Gurza Lavalle and Bueno 2011). Only a small number of them had a narrow thematic focus, working with drug addiction or with therapeutic or housing communities. Most worked for broad-based causes, such as gender diversity and reproductive rights, civil and human rights, and democratization (or sponsored support groups for children and adolescents, for example). Peak associations working with the more narrow issues were founded mainly by advocacy NGOs, while the latter group was mostly created by service non-profits engaged in social assistance and civil organizations for family or Christian values.

In Brazil, two groups of civil society organizations are classifiable as peak associations, belonging to what has been characterized in the literature as the "new civil society" and the "new unionism." We focus on the first group. The literature has usually portrayed this group as consisting of NGOs that are intensively engaged in networking and in coordinating agenda setting among civil society actors (Casanovas and García 2000, pp. 69–74; Scherer-Warren 1996). The fact that NGOs are highlighted in this literature is not accidental. Not only are advocacy NGOs frequently important actors in their foundation, but also some highly visible and influential peak associations work exclusively for NGOs. In other words, these intermediation organizations express the increased importance of NGOs—for instance, the Brazilian Association of Non-Governmental Organizations (ABONG).

ABONG carries out programs to facilitate alliance building between social actors; foster political reform; increase the policy influence of civil society on such issues as urban policies, social policies, and participation; and represent its members in the passage of the national laws for the third sector. This peak association, with more than 230 affiliated NGOs spread across all Brazilian regions, defines itself as "democratic, pluralist, antiracist, anti-sexist, aggregating organizations engaged in fighting all forms of discrimination and inequality, and committed to the radicalization of democracy and sustainable ways of life."[18] The type of organization allowed in the legally defined affiliation rules and the way pluralism is defined in ABONG's statute clearly restrict membership to associations positioned in the left-wing spectrum of civil society. It is very telling that in the plenary that officially created this peak association, in 1991, the membership of an association engaged in family planning (instead of defending sexual rights) was unanimously rejected (Nogueira 2014, pp. 179–81).[19]

Unlike Mexico City peak associations, in São Paulo a wider spectrum of actors participated in the creation of this type of broker, ranging from neighborhood associations – such as the National Confederation of Dwellers Associations (*Confederação Nacional de Associações de Moradore*—CONAM) – to market related and corporate social responsibility civil society actors – such as the Central Group of Institutes, Foundations, and Firms (*Grupo de Institutos, Fundações e Empresas*—GIFE).

As in Mexico City, by mid-2000s, "new civil society" peak associations based in São Paulo were also among the most central actors. São Paulo's peak associations cluster around common rights and distributive issues, like gender or neighborhood associations claims. They also cluster around ideological affinities, and have a more clear or programmatic characteristics than the ones found in the Mexican capital. Specifically, they are linked to networks of left-wing advocacy NGOs, funding agencies from the third sector, and Catholic religious networks. These networks not only connect different actors and their organizations' brokers, but also represent different and even opposite views of the meaning of collective action. For some, it involves struggling to change social policies, institutions, and values; for others, it involves co-responsibility, entrepreneurship, and joint action with the public sector; and for others it means helping and supporting vulnerable populations. Thus, the main difference between the two cities is that in São Paulo, a broader range of actors—even peripheral ones such as neighborhood associations—has been able to create peak associations.

With respect to the institutionalization of intermediation and the trade-offs involved, there are similarities between brokers from both cities. Membership boundaries are not always formal and clearly stated, but the organizations in both cities do have some degree of bounded memberships. In both cases, they were founded by other organizations who needed to coordinate their actions, to build common agendas, to increase their capacity for aggregating interests, to promote the interests of their founders and to be represented vis-à-vis other civil society and state actors. Interestingly, since they have become specialized in brokerage for their founders, in both contexts they have few relations with other peak associations.

---

18 See self-definition at ww.abong.org.br, (accessed December 10, 213). See also ABONG's Statute, available at http://abong.org.br/quem_somos.php?id=3.

19 Family Well-Being (Bem-Estar Familiar–Bemfam) had its affiliation to ABONG refused (Nogueira 2004, p. 180).

Having central positions in the enlarged organizational ecologies of the Mexican and São Paulo networks implies advantages for obtaining and transmitting information and other material and symbolic resources and allows for influence over a wide set of actors (Gurza Lavalle and Bueno 2011; Gurza Lavalle, Castello and Bichir 2008).[20] Because the centrality of these peak associations grows from their structural position in civil society networks, it does not tell us much about how different associations actually act and use their positional advantages. However, it does show that the institutionalization of intermediation organizations was successful in creating actors well positioned to play the brokerage roles they are supposed to perform.

Success poses questions about the risks of concentrating resources in order to increase internal and external efficiency. One interesting feature of these peak associations is that they seem to diminish those risks by narrowing down the range of interest, values, and opinions that they defend. In other words, strong ideological affinities and shared programmatic understandings of the meaning of collective action entail self-selection of similar actors who are willing to take the path of institutionalization. Because of such affinities and self-selection, peak associations work from a known set of shared substantive preferences. The reduction of diversity also reduces dissent.[21]

Enlarged organizational ecologies pose intermediation challenges not only for actors sharing similar values, which could be addressed by creating peak associations, but for more heterogeneous sets of civil organizations as well. Associations with diverse characteristics, values and interests may need some degree of coordination among themselves. This has generated a plethora of fora in Brazil, which are distinctly multisectoral bodies. They are relatively open spaces, aimed at fostering debate over general policy priorities among actors with different thematic foci but converging interests. Such fora are normally organized around policy areas—for instance, Forum of Health (*Fórum Saúde*), Forum of the Elderly (*Fórum do Idoso*), Forum of HIV/AIDS (*Fórum HIV/AIDS*), Forum of Recycling (*Fórum da Reciclagem*)—and organizational and individual actors interested in that area may participate regardless of specific organizational features and ideology. Thus, unlike the peak associations analyzed above, the same forum can include neighborhood associations, service non-profits committed to social assistance, advocacy NGOs, popular movement organizations, and self-help associations as active members. Such associations may also discuss issues related to specific public policies, even if they hold different substantive understandings about the role of collective action or of the policy at stake.

---

20   Peak associations centrality is the average of centrality measures for this type vis-à-vis the average of the same measures for other types of actors.

21   Of course, it is plausible to assume that deep-shared values might reduce conflicts across different issues, but increase intensity of conflicts within specific praised issues. That is a logical possibility, and in this section we are exploring the implications of features empirically founded.

Fora are founded and supported by civil organizations, and state officials normally participate only occasionally, if at all. These multisectoral bodies do not enforce or monitor compliance with the resolutions they make, but such decisions do function as guidelines for members and supportive nonparticipants. Moreover, fora are extremely heterogeneous and non-selective, and have little relation with each other. These characteristics are relevant, as they express the role of fora as spaces aimed at making deliberation among actors with no substantive shared values possible. In the first half of the 2000s, fora were not among the most central actors within civil society networks in São Paulo, but that does not mean they were on the periphery. They occupied a mid-level centrality position, connecting otherwise unrelated actors but having a secondary place in the networking strategy of almost all actors.

In the Mexican organizational ecology, multisectoral bodies such as fora exist—such as the Forum of Migrations—but they are not as common, and, not surprisingly, one finds little mention of them in the literature (CESCO 2007, p. 34; Álvarez 2000, p. 182; Coloumb and Duhau 1997, p. 176). Under other names, and on a smaller scale, some multisectoral bodies work as facilitators of dialogue among actors concerned with similar issues. An example is the Consortium for Parliamentary Dialogue and Gender Equality (*Consorcio para el Diálogo Parlamentario y la Equidad de Género*), founded by civil society organizations that facilitate communication between feminist movement actors and parliamentarians. The Mexican Coalition for the International Criminal Court (*Coalición Mexicana por la Corte Penal Internacional*) created by civil society organizations and scholars to promote debates and awareness about the International Criminal Court, is another example of such bodies.

São Paulo's fora and, to a much lesser extent, Mexico's multisectoral bodies have some interesting features related to brokerage and to the trade-offs involved in intermediation. They normally do not develop an agenda for going public or acting by themselves, but are sought after by different actors. This is related to their mid-level centrality. They play an important role enhancing network building among their members, sharing information, and allowing deliberation among very different sets of actors. Thus fora are not surprisingly by far the type of actor that both has the fewest ties with their own kind and is connected to the most diverse range of actors within the broader organizational ecology of São Paulo.

These Brazilian and Mexican multisectoral bodies are institutionalized brokers working directly with civil society organizations grouped by thematic affinity, acting as facilitators for dialogue and spaces for meeting and periodical coordination with minimal entrance requirements, pushing forward basic consensus around general priorities and minimal strategies for shaping public agenda and pressing for policy outcomes. In principle, such a diversity of actors should increase the risks of brokerage, but in fact these intermediation organizations lower such risks by reducing the scope and reach of intermediation tasks to be performed. In other words, these kinds of multisectoral bodies help build consensus, but they have little (if any) capacity to act on their own or to enforce compliance.

Final Comments: Institutionalized Brokerage, a Risky Undertaking

In contexts of enlarged organizational ecologies, as those of post transition Latin America, institutionalized forms of brokerage created by civil society organizations have become increasingly common and relevant. Nevertheless, they have received little systematic attention. In the literatures on social networks and social movements, brokerage has been narrowly conceptualized as a relational mechanism producing positive effects for mobilization, triggered by actors occupying specific positions and performing informal roles. However, as we have argued, the impacts of brokerage are contingent. They are neither inherently good nor bad for promoting social mobilization or for defending the interests of brokered actors. Furthermore, brokerage may be and often is institutionalized. Assuming the horizontality of civil society networks, as often happens in the literature on Latin American social movements, is misleading because it leads us to believe that intermediation is a diffuse function of the network itself, hollowing out challenges and efficiency trade-offs of intermediation, as well as the power relations involved.

The institutionalization of brokerage is not, thus, a "spontaneous" or "natural path," but rather a political decision consciously made by actors that have to build consensus on how to face the challenges and trade-offs of intermediation. Indeed, since creating and maintaining intermediation organizations is costly and difficult, we can think of their proliferation as an indicator that civil society has developed substantial density and capacity for action.

In this chapter we developed a typology of institutionalized brokers (peak associations, associational hubs, and multisectoral bodies), based on membership boundaries and some correlated organizational features, as well as on the differentiation between internal and external brokerage roles. In trying to better understand the dynamic process of the institutionalization of brokerage and the dilemmas involved, we analyzed cases of the three types of institutionalized brokers in Mexico and in Brazil.

The analysis of associational hubs confirmed that sustaining brokerage roles over time among heterogeneous sets of actors and between them and outsiders can indeed be a daunting task. Both REBRIP and RMALC shared similar challenges, but the institutionalization of brokerage led to different outcomes. In the RMALC case, the ability to play brokerage roles became increasingly restricted over time, while REBRIP remained able to perform a wider set of intermediation tasks. However, in both cases representation was the most difficult role to sustain over time and the first to be questioned by members. The comparison between these cases of the institutionalization of transnational brokerage shows the importance of thinking dynamically about the ladder of brokerage roles. Actors permanently negotiate and evaluate the powers that brokers have. It also reinforces the importance of distinguishing between leaders and brokers (Diani 2003; 2013), and at examining how internal governance decisions may affect power relations among actors, and thus the consequences of brokerage.

The analysis of peak associations and multisectoral bodies in Mexico City and São Paulo suggests that the risks associated with institutionalized brokerage can be compensated not only at the level of the actor, as shown by REBRIP's internal governance rules, but also at the level of the organizational ecologies within which they operate. In the cases of peak associations, homogeneity among members narrows down the internal diversity of interests, and makes it easier to perform internal and external brokerage roles. But this occurs at the expense of diversity. Because peak associations are more common in São Paulo, our research suggests that the Brazilian enlarged organizational ecologies are occupied by more resourceful actors than in the Mexican cases. As enlarged organizational ecologies increase interdependence with diverse kinds of organizations, coordination occurs in São Paulo by creating multisectoral bodies (fora) that are open to different actors but have no enforcement capacity. Interestingly, the REBRIP case shows that, at the micro level, we may find a similar compensatory effect, because actors can relate differently to the same institutionalized broker, even when there are strong differences in power and resources among members. This poses a crucial question: Who brokers the brokers? The institutionalization of brokerage may foster internal and external intermediation roles at the ecological and organizational levels, but at the micro or intra organizational level, specific members have their own agendas. Thus, a multilevel approach to the study of brokerage will be important in future research efforts.

This chapter contributes to the organizational literature on collective action by shedding light on the potentially important institutionalized brokerage roles played by organizations in enlarged organizational ecologies. It also suggests the relevance of developing a research agenda focused on institutionalized brokerage in collective action. Further empirical analysis of the internal and external intermediation roles played by different types of institutionalized brokers is necessary if we are to fully understand whether and how actors overcome in specific historical contexts the risks of brokerage and the trade-offs involved.

While we need learn more about this phenomenon, institutionalized brokerage is already undergoing deep changes. New informational technologies affect intermediation roles played by institutionalized brokers and the challenges they face. Part of the literature on the Internet has highlighted the increased relevance of "organizationless" collective action, emphasizing the lesser importance of the intermediation roles we talk about in this chapter.[22] Nevertheless, it seems reasonable to assume, as other authors have argued,[23] that organizations are undergoing a process of adaptation to remain relevant. Thus, research on the intermediation roles played by institutionalized brokers in the "digital age" will raise new challenges for the research agenda we proposed in this chapter.

---

22   See, for example, the discussion of networked social movements by Castells (2012).

23   See the discussion of the process of adaptation of organizations to the digital age in Bimber et al. (2012).

References

Ahrne, Goran and Brunsson, Nils, 2008. *Meta-organizations.* Northampton: Edward Elgar Publishing.

Álvarez, Lucía Enríquez, 2005. *Distrito federal: sociedad, economía, política y cultura.* México: CIICH/UNAM.

Álvarez, Lucía and Ziccardi, Alicia, 2000. "Organizaciones sociales." In: Gustavo Garza, ed. *La Ciudad de México en el fin del segundo milenio.* Distrito Federal: El Colegio de México y Gobierno del Distrito Federal, pp. 684–89.

Arnstein, Sherry, 1969. "A ladder of citizen participation." *Journal of the American Planning Association,* 35(4), pp. 216–24.

Avritzer, Leonardo, 1997. "Um desenho institucional para o novo associativismo." *Lua Nova,* 39, pp. 149–74.

Bimber, Bruce, Flanagin, Andrew and Stohl, Cynthia, 2012. *Collective action in organizations: interaction and engagement in an era of technological change.* Cambridge: Cambridge University Press.

Bolos, Silvia, 1999. *Constitución de actores sociales y la política.* México: Universidad Iberoamericana/Plaza and Valdez Editores.

Burt, Ronald S., 1992. *Structural holes: the social structure of competition.* Cambridge: Harvard University Press.

―――, 2005. *Brokerage and closure: an introduction to social capital.* Oxford: Oxford University Press.

Casanovas, Roberto Sainz and Chacón, Oscar Garcia, 2000. *Las ONGs latinoamericanas y los desafíos del desarrollo organizacional.* Bolivia: ICCO/ PROACTIVA/ IDEPRO.

Castells, Manuel, 2012. *Networks of outrage and hope.* Malden: Polity Press.

Collier, Ruth and Handlin, Samuel ed., 2009a. *Reorganizing popular politics: participation and the new interest regime in Latin America.* University Park: University of Pennsylvania University Press.

―――, 2009b. "Introduction: popular representation in the interest arena." In: R. Collier and S. Handlin, ed. *Reorganizing popular politics: participation and the new interest regime in Latin America.* University Park: University of Pennsylvania University Press, pp. 3–31.

Coloumb, René and Duhau, Emilio, 1997. *Dinámica urbana y procesos socio-políticos,* v.II México: Ocim, CENVI, UAM, pp. 139–73.

De la Garza Toledo, Enrique, 1994. "El corporativismo: teoría y transformación," *Revista Iztapalapa,* 34, July–December, pp. 11–28.

Diani, Mario, 2003. "Leaders or brokers?" In: M. Diani and D. McAdam, eds. *Social movements and networks.* Oxford: Oxford University Press, pp. 105–22.

―――, 2013. "Brokerage." In: D. Snow, D. della Porta, B. Klandermans and D. McAdam, eds. *The Wiley-Blackwell encyclopedia of social and political movements.* Malden: Blackwell Publishing.

————, (forthcoming). "Mapping contentious fields in Latin America," In: Rafael Grasa and Salvador Martí, eds. *Polarización y conflictos en América Latina.* Barcelona: Editorial Bellaterra.

Fernández, Roberto M. and McAdam, Doug, 1988. "Social networks and social movements: multiorganizational fields and recruitment to Mississippi freedom summer." *Sociological Forum*, 3(3), pp. 357–82.

Forment, Carlos, 2003. *Democracy in Latin America, 1760–1900: civic selfhood and public life in Mexico and Peru.* Chicago: University of Chicago Press.

Gould, Roger and Fernández, Roberto M., 1989. "Structures of mediation: a formal approach to brokerage in transaction networks." *Sociological Methodology*, 19, pp. 89–126.

Gurza Lavalle, Adrián and Bueno, Natália, 2010. "Civil society organizations in two Latin American metropolises." *Textos para Discussão CEM*, pp. 1–52.

————, 2011. "Waves of change within civil society in Latin America: Mexico City and São Paulo." *Politics & Society*, 39, pp. 415–50.

Gurza Lavalle, Adrián, Castello, Graziela and Bichir, Renata, 2007. "Protagonistas na Sociedade Civil: Redes e Centralidades de Organizações Civis em São Paulo." Dados, *Revista de Ciências Sociais*, 50, 3, pp. 465–98.

————, 2008. "Atores periféricos na sociedade civil: redes e centralidades de organizações em São Paulo." *Revista Brasileira de Ciências Sociais*, 23, pp. 73–96.

Gurza Lavalle, Adrián, Houtzager, Peter and Castello, Graziela, 2012. "A construção política das sociedades civis." In: Adrián Gurza Lavalle, ed. *O Horizonte da política—Questões emergentes e agendas de pesquisa.* São Paulo: UNESP, pp. 185–259.

Handlin, Samuel and Kapiszewski, Diana, 2009. "Three forms of scaling: embeddedness, nodal NGOs, and flexible fronts." In: Ruth Collier and Samuel Handlin, eds. *Reorganizing popular politics: participation and the new interest regime in Latin America.* University Park: University of Pennsylvania University Press, pp. 230–59.

Hannan, Michael and Freeman, John, 1989. *Organizational ecology.* Cambridge: Harvard University Press.

Hannan, Michale, Pólos, Lászlo and Carrol, Glenn, 2007. *Logics of organizations theory: audiences, codes and ecologies.* Princeton: Princeton University Press.

Hirschman, Albert O., 1970. *Exit, voice, and loyalty: responses to decline in firms, organizations, and states.* Cambridge: Harvard University Press.

Isunza, Ernesto, 2001. *Las tramas del alba. Una Visón de las luchas por el reconocimiento en el México contemporáneo (1968–1993).* México: Porrua/ CIESAS.

Klandermans, Bert and Oegema, Dirk, 1987. "Potentials, networks, motivations and barriers: steps towards participation in social movements." *American Sociological Review*, 52, pp. 519–31.

Malloy, James, 1977. *Authoritarianism and corporatism in Latin America.* University of Pittsburg Press.

Marsden, Peter V., 1982. "Brokerage behavior in restricted exchange networks." In: Peter V. Marsden and Nan Lin, eds. *Social structure and network analysis.* Beverly Hills: Sage, pp. 201–18.

Massicotte, Marie-Josée, 2004. "Mexican sociopolitical movements and transnational networking in the context of economic integration in the Americas." Unpublished dissertation. Department of Political Science, York University.

McAdam, Doug, Tarrow, Sidney and Tilly, Charles, 2001. *Dynamics of contention.* Cambridge: Cambridge University Press.

Michels, Robert, [1911] 2001. *Political parties: a sociological study of the oligarchical tendencies of modern democracy.* Kitchener: Batoche Books.

Mische, Ann, 2008. *Partisan Publics: communication and contention across Brazilian youth activist networks.* Princeton: Princeton University Press.

Morris, Aldon, 1981. "Black southern student sit-in movement: an analysis of internal organization." *American Sociological Review*, 46(6), pp. 744–67.

Nogueira, do Amaral Fernando, 2014. *Gestão da relação entre associação e associados: três casos brasileiros.* Sao Paulo, Ph.D. dissertation theses, Fundação Getúlio Vargas, Escola de Administração de Empresas de São Paulo.

PAPEP/UNDP, 2011. *Los conflictos sociales en América Latina.* La Paz: PAPEP/ UNDP and UNIR-Bolivia.

Ramírez, Juan Manuel Saíz, 1988. "Trabajador y/o colono, ¿Una dicotomía en las luchas sociales? (La articulación entre el movimiento urbano popular y el sindicalismo independiente)." In: Jorge Alonso, ed. *Los movimientos sociales en el Valle de México.* v.II. México: Ediciones de la Casa Chata, pp. 21–99.

REBRIP, 2007. *Balanço do período 2005–2007: roteiro para avaliação e debate.* Rio de Janeiro, mimeo.

Scherrer-Warren, Ilse, 1996. *Redes de movimentos sociais.* São Paulo: Ed. Loyola.

Schmitter, Philippe, 1971. *Interest conflict and political change in Brazil.* California: Stanford University Press.

———, 1974. "Still the century of corporatism?" *Review of Politics*, 36, pp. 85–131.

———, 1992. "The consolidation of democracy and representation of social groups." *American Behavioral Scientist*, 35, pp. 422–49.

Silva, Eduardo, 2009. *Challenging neoliberalism in Latin America.* Cambridge: Cambridge University Press.

Skocpol, Theda, 1992. *Protecting soldiers and mothers. The political origins of social policy in the United States.* Cambridge: Harvard University Press.

Snow, David A., Louis A. Zurcher, and Ekland-Olson, Sheldon, 1980. "Social networks and social movements: a microstructural approach to differential recruitment." *American Sociological Review*, 45, pp. 787–801.

Stovel, Katherine and Shaw, Lynette, 2012. "Brokerage." *Annu. Rev. Sociol.*, 38, pp. 139–58.

von Bülow, Marisa, 2010. *Building transnational networks: civil society and the politics of trade in the Americas.* Cambridge: Cambridge University Press.

————, 2011. "Brokers in action: transnational coalitions and trade agreements in the Americas." *Mobilization*, 16(2), pp. 165–80.

Warren, Mark, 2004. "What kind of civil society is best for democracy?" *Portuguese Journal of Social Science*, 3(1), pp. 37–47.

Chapter 8

Domestic Loops and Deleveraging Hooks: Transnational Social Movements and the Politics of Scale Shift

Rose J. Spalding

Introduction

The rise in transnational activism in recent decades has inspired intense analytical deliberation and conceptual innovation among social movement theorists, in a process that is still unfolding. The field of transnational studies explores the difficult terrain of mapping coalition formation and brokerage across borders. It attempts to explain why this complex form of social mobilization emerges, how these linkages operate, and what impacts they have on the social landscape. Much of the research on transnational social movements highlights patterns and dynamics found in the United States and Europe. My work aims to expand the conceptual framework for interpreting social movement transnationalism, drawing on processes unfolding in contemporary Latin America. Situating theory building in the Latin American context permits analytical refinement and conceptual breadth by capturing the dynamics of transnational mobilization beyond the narrow confines of the Global North.

This chapter traces two transnational mobilization processes, the *domestic loop* and the *deleveraging hook*, in which transnationally aligned networks mobilize different kinds of resources, address distinct targets, and operate on different scales. Both are contextualized in terms of Latin American political development, with the domestic loop exploring links that emerge with recent electoral democratization and the shift to the left, and the deleveraging hook examining activist efforts to address the clash between democratic decision-making and externally enforced neoliberal rules. This work offers new insights into the problem of scale, tracing the interplay between activism in the domestic and international arenas and explaining movement reconfiguration as the site of contention migrates across scales.

This study also introduces the concept of *lateral transnationalism* to describe a variant of transnational activism that connects similarly situated activists in neighboring countries around issues of mutual concern. By linking actors at the sub-regional level, this form of mobilization can attenuate the power differentials and cultural distance that frequently undermine the quality of transnational connections. Thorny problems routinely emerge in north-south movement alliances, given the marked resource inequalities and cultural maps those alliances represent. Lateral transnationalism, while not free of localized hierarchies, can sharply reduce these inequalities and build on shared perceptions in a manner that facilitates mutual understanding and promotes collective action.

Finally, the tensions that inhabit north-south alliances also vary, depending on the degree of centralization and top-down control that shapes their operation. Recognizing this variation, this chapter argues for conceptual refinement of the debate about the impact of northern allies on southern movements. It proposes the development of analytical subcategories, two of which (*domesticating INGOs* and *power-node INGOs*) explore strategically cooperative forms of collaboration between northern-based international non-governmental organizations (INGOS) and their southern allies. This analysis calls for further research into the circumstances under which north-south collective action produces beneficial versus detrimental impacts for southern movements.

The chapter's theoretical contributions are four-fold. First, it extends the literature on the problem of scale by exploring the way that domestic political openings intersect with international constraints to shift the site of contention from the domestic to the international sphere. Second, along with others in this volume, this chapter draws on the Latin American context to illustrate the significance of critical political junctures and the interplay between formal and informal politics. Third, it highlights the impact of lateral forms of social movement transnationalism, correcting the tendency in social movement literature to neglect this potentially rich space of exchange and collaboration. Finally, it identifies two sets of conditions under which north-south networks can produce relatively durable and cooperative bonds, advancing a nuanced analysis that challenges the polarized interpretations of these dynamics. This work employs a dynamic approach to the study of movements, which better traces shifting strategic choices as activists respond to changing opportunities and threats.

Transnational Activism Models, Theory and Concepts

The social movement literature identifies transnational activism as an increasingly common form of collective engagement (Keck and Sikkink 1998; Tarrow 2005; della Porta and Tarrow 2005; della Porta et al. 2006; Smith 2008; von Bülow 2010; Smith and Wiest 2012; and Silva 2013). Differentiating among transnational mobilizations by the range of issues they incorporate and their site of activism, Tarrow (2005) locates both domestically oriented (internal) and internationally oriented (external) contention processes under the broad label of transnational activism. Internal transnationality may be manifest in the use of global issue framing to interpret local problems or in the attention that activists give to the role of external pressure as the source of local grievances. With external transnationality, activists shift their energies away from the domestic scale and focus directly on international institutions and processes. External engagement may give rise to transnational coalition formation, in which activists coalesce in broad networks with groups from different countries pursuing similar claims.

Tarrow's conceptual work on transnational activism emphasizes the process of diffusion, defined as the "transfer of claims or forms of contention from one site to another," and upward and downward scale shift, involving "the coordination of collective action at a different level than where it began" (Tarrow 2005, p. 32). Von Bülow's work on the anti-FTAA movement in the Americas (2010) adds a time dimension, moving beyond the distinction between domestic and international expressions of transnationality to highlight the differences between short-lived, intermittent transnational networks and those that persist across time (von Bülow 2010, pp. 25–34).

Focused research on transnational activism has produced a rich conceptual vocabulary exploring the processes that connect activists across scales. In their classic study of transnational activism, *Activists Beyond Borders*, Keck and Sikkink (1998, p. 12) introduced the concept of the boomerang, noting that "[w]hen channels between the state and its domestic actors are blocked, the boomerang pattern of influence characteristic of transnational networks may occur: domestic NGOs bypass their state and directly search out international allies to try to bring pressure on their states from outside." If governments are unresponsive, "international contacts can amplify the demands of domestic groups, pry open space for new issues, and then echo back these demands into the domestic space" (Ibid., 13). This mechanism allows social activists, operating under duress in their local or national setting, to connect with international allies and leverage external resources in pursuit of domestic goals.

This powerful concept gained analytic purchase in Latin America, where non- or weak-democratic governments were often unresponsive to the demands of social movement actors. As the domestic sphere became more responsive to local pressure, new models were developed to explore how transnational coalitions fit into the domestic arena under conditions of greater political openness. Sikkink (2005) expanded on the boomerang framework to model the variation in levels of openness and closure at the domestic and international levels, producing a four-cell matrix to capture this range (Ibid., 156). In her analytical scheme, closure of the domestic level combined with closure at the international scale serve to diminish the chances of activism of either type. Closure at the domestic level, combined with openness at the international, served to catalyze the boomerang pattern, as we have seen, and also to activate the "spiral model," a more dynamic rendition of the boomerang in which initial changes trigger shifting opportunities and threats, which in turn affect subsequent moves in a longer-term sequence.

To these variations, Sikkink added two models in which the domestic opportunity structure was defined as open. In the first, designated as the "insider/ outsider coalition," both the domestic and the international levels provide open structures in which activists can bring claims and find opportunities to advance. In the second, domestic opportunities open up and activists can more effectively assert pressure in that domain, but the international system remains closed, restricting adjustments in spite of transnational coalition demands. This pattern gives rise to a "democratic deficit," in which initiatives agreed to through democratic deliberation at home are thwarted by international processes that impede the exercise of voice and agency. This dynamic serves as a catalyst for "defensive transnationalization," as activists in transnational NGOs, networks, and coalitions rally to circumvent or challenge an unresponsive international structure and pry open space for multiple publics.

Von Bülow (2013, pp. 59–61) builds on Sikkink's framework by noting that, beyond the issue of institutional openness or closure, civil society activism also requires an "arena of deliberation" (Ibid., 58), which is frequently activated by the appearance of threat. Her more fluid treatment of the linkages between domestic and international activism notes that "[a]ctors do not choose to act solely at the domestic or solely at the regional or global scales, but at various movement in time they prioritize different sites of action and are constantly adjusting these priorities" (Ibid.). This observation raises powerful questions, which we are only beginning to address, about the complex dynamics governing scale shift and adjustments in movement priorities.

My work on movement transnationalism and the politics of scale shift, drawing on the Latin American context, identifies two processes that have particular resonance in this region, each with a set of associated subthemes. The first process, conceptualized as the *domestic loop*, focuses on the strategic interactions between local organizations and their transnational allies, as domestic coalitions, responding to expanding political opportunities at home, mobilize internally in order to exercise direct influence in their home context. The second, the *deleveraging hook*, explores the way in which domestic coalitions propel themselves into the international arena, frequently in an attempt to pry open unresponsive institutions and reduce external pressure on their domestic sphere.

The Domestic Loop Model

The domestic loop model maps the intersection between domestic coalition partners and their multilayered, transnational allies as they construct discourse, frames, and strategies to address local problems of international origin. This process generally aligns with Sikkink's discussion of the insider/outsider coalition and with Tarrow's analysis of internalization. The domestic loop concept, however, more fully situates the process in the Latin American context by incorporating an analysis of three recurring themes that arise in this region. First, this framework emphasizes the way in which decentralized segments of a domestic coalition seek out their own particular set of external allies, some operating at the regional level in creative forms of *lateral transnationalism*. Second, this analysis focuses on complex and shifting relations with northern allies and examines the making of diverse kinds of *north-south alliances*. Third, this approach highlights the interconnection between transnationally aligned social movements and domestic political processes where, in the context of electoral opening, space expands for movements to become *politically embedded.*

Lateral transnationalism

Unlike traditional transnational alliances that organized sectors hierarchically and linked them across the national divide at the top, newer networks, developed in an era of more fluid communications, tend to operate in a relatively decentralized fashion, with international connections strewn through different nodal points (Bennett 2005; Cumbers, Routledge and Nativel 2008; Juris and Khasnabish 2013). This new pattern makes brokerage, bricolage, and frame alignment a laborious venture, and one that does not always succeed (Rossi 2013), since no linear, top-down mechanism exists to direct communication flows and ensure compliance. Drawing on the experience of transnationality as described by the activists themselves, the domestic loop framework allows us to analyze the ways in which distinct coalition segments emerge and then are stitched together through bridging and bonding (Putnam 2000) and multi-faceted brokerage processes (von Bülow 2011), often operating at the regional level.

The present study argues for fine-grained analysis of lateral transnationalism, that is, frame construction and resource flows that emerge through exchanges between activists in most similar, and frequently neighboring, countries. Particularly resonant in Latin America are the cross-border alliances, reflecting historical patterns of connection across formal national boundaries. Established geographical linkages among residents in neighboring countries have been reinforced by recent within-region migration, borderland trade and investment flows, and institutional and physical infrastructure development that connect activists in contiguous cross-national spaces. These connective fibers call researchers to pay close attention to informal modes of transnational coordination that arise through linkages within the region, and to extend academic inquiry beyond the formal mechanisms of collective action that typically provide analytical focus.

North-south alliances

In addition to lateral or cross-border connections, transnational networks in Latin America also link up activists from the global north and south. Thick bonds of hemispheric history regularly draw organizational actors from the United States into contact with counterparts in Latin America, particularly in Mexico, Central America, and the Caribbean, where US interventionism had a long and labored past, and where *maquila* sector expansion has activated organized labor networks. European NGOs also became significant, following an increase in development funding by progressive European institutes and foundations concerned with international human rights and global justice initiatives. While participating in these alliances, domestically rooted coalitions in Latin America struggled with the ever-present threat of mission capture and resource dependence that undermine movement autonomy (Edelman 1999; 2008; Thayer 2010; Hochstetler and Keck 2007; Lucero 2013; Wood 2005; Hertel 2006). Greater political openness, easier access to resources (information, funding, full-time professional staff, and so on), and subtle ethnocentrism position northern allies in a directorial role, often to the detriment of "partners" in smaller or less prosperous states.

The resulting tension has provoked dissembling and even rupture in networks that function across the north-south divide (Bob 2005; Andrews 2010).[1] Although the first generation of studies of transnational activism tended to de-emphasize these tensions and play up the synergies emerging in north-south coalitions, a second generation of research has identified persistent conflicts and exposed the pretense of collaboration in top-down relationships that thinly disguised hegemonic practices (Petras 1997; Pearce 2010; Hertel 2006; Thayer 2010). These resource inequalities require Latin American activists, when they can, to exercise an abundance of caution in the selection of northern partners.

The present study calls for a third generation of research, which recognizes the inherent difficulty of north-south collaboration but acknowledges shades of gray. Posing a more nuanced question, this chapter probes the circumstances under which north-south alliances may, on balance, produce long-term, multi-dimensional, and complementary connections that are highly valued by local activists in spite of the predictable problems. It develops the concept of *domesticating INGOs* to analyze a particular subtype of northern ally that is well integrated into domestic networks and facilitates local work while presenting relatively modest disruption. This analysis argues for a fine differentiation of the ways in which INGOs partner with local allies and the varying degrees of agency exercised by domestic activists as they connect transnationally to the north.

Politically embedded movements
Finally, the domestic loop model allows us to explore the ways in which transnationally aligned coalitions insert themselves in the national political arena as electoral democratization unfolds. Drawing on politically embedded campaign analysis, this framework traces the intersection between social movements and the formal political sphere, including activities such as lobbying and electoral campaign work. It explores the ways that domestic networks bring home discourse and framing infused with international learning; synthesize and adapt these messages for local use; and promote their diffusion in the domestic political scene through partisan and electoral mechanisms. This work integrates the study of social movement activism with analysis of formal democratic institutions

---

1 Recognition of the gaps between the Zapatista movement that emerged in Chiapas and its transnationalized expression has generated dynamic discussion about this intersection. Even those who emphasize complementarity, such as Khasnabish (2013), find the process generates a "double movement." Zapatismo, he argues, "can be understood as the political philosophy and practice of the Zapatista movement located physically, culturally, and politically in the far southeast of Mexico. It can also be understood as a new imagination of political struggle and possibility" (73), producing "a northern node in the Zapatista rhizome" (79).

(Goldstone 2003; Roberts 2008), incorporating insights from the democratic consolidation literature about the critical role of civil society. Exploring the interplay of movements, political parties, and the institutions of government, this framework also connects social movement research with the electoral shift to the left that has animated Latin American politics since 2002.

The domestic battle, however, is only part of the contest. As market reform deepened in Latin America, neoliberal disciplines were codified not only in domestic law but also in international agreements, bilateral partnerships, and the development projects of multilateral lenders (Bilal, de Lombaerde and Tussie 2011; Stiglitz and Charlton 2005; Shadlen 2005; Gallagher 2008). Once integrated into the global economy under neoliberal terms, states find it difficult to shift away, even if popular preferences at the domestic level change and a recalibration of political forces leads to a modification of national priorities. Various processes reinforce neoliberal stickiness, including the work and residential patterns it produces and the resistance to change among the sizable coalition of beneficiaries of market reform both inside and outside the country. Neoliberal rules are generally endorsed by powerful constituencies, which include business elites, technocrats, export-oriented labor, and political, legal, and cultural leaders, who gained leverage and resources under economic liberalization. These actors are formidable opponents to change on the domestic scene; they also enjoy institutional backing at the regional or international level. This international architecture produces a second arena in which the region's transnational social movements struggle to advance their claims.

The Deleveraging Hook Model

The second process defined in the chapter, the deleveraging hook, focuses on the shifts made by transnationally aligned domestic movements when they add a second dimension to their work and expand directly into the international arena. The dynamic associated with the deleveraging hook is located in Sikkink's open domestic/closed international category, where the domestic system is capable of responding to organized demands for change from national networks but the international arena resists such inclusion. The deleveraging struggle exposes the challenges of advancing locally affirmed popular preferences in international institutions that are not designed for public access. This analysis draws us to discussion of the democratic deficit and defensive transnationalization that Sikkink associated with this category.

As a movement that has elicited support at the national level moves to confront its adversaries in unfavorable international terrain, new challenges emerge. Horizontal alliances that strengthen the organizational capacity and resources of a resistance network may contribute to success in the domestic loop process but prove feeble in new international territory. Prominent institutions managing global economic affairs are minimally receptive to public input, especially when it challenges the practices that facilitate corporate globalization.

Locating mechanisms with which to advance the claims of domestic coalitions in international venues may require different kinds of coalitions and new forms of strategic knowledge. The deleveraging hook framework explores the efforts of domestic coalitions to reconfigure as they shift their site of contention.

Transnational activists over the last few decades have pushed international institutions to open up, in some cases with observable effects. Jackie Smith (2008) documented the development of the civil society input process at the United Nations, where broad networks of activists gathered to promote a human rights and social justice agenda. Indigenous rights activists have also used this forum to negotiate common positions and advance their agenda (Escárcega 2013). Even international economic institutions began to develop public consultation processes as social movement activists clamored at their gates and their legitimacy fell into question. Fox and Brown (1998) document the development of the inspection panel of the World Bank; Tussie and Tuozzo (2001) extend the analysis to include the Inter-American Development Bank; even the International Monetary Fund (IMF) faced public pressure for transparency and responded by releasing more detailed information (Scholte 2001). International trade negotiations are now routinely encased in civil society consultation processes, including side rooms that offer space onsite to both business representatives and NGO activists during the negotiation rounds (Spalding 2014).

But the space that opened has been modest, with decisions of international financial institutions still largely determined by technocratic officials or the preferences of dominant powers (international banks, G5 countries) (Park and Vetterlein 2010; Copelovitch 2010). Although social movement coalitions had an impact on the derailment of the Multilateral Agreement on Investment (MAI) agenda and the 2005 "burial" of the FTAA at Mar del Plata, the ability of domestic movements to advance their call for relief in the halls of powerful international institutions has been limited.

Still, once mobilized, transnationally linked coalitions have an ability to swivel between scales and insert defensive claims at the regional or international level. Latin American human rights networks have activated this process repeatedly by presenting complaints to the Inter-American Human Rights Commission and lodging cases with the Inter-American Court. As resistance activism crosses scales, these networks seek to add new allies who can help them confront opponents in unfamiliar territory. In the new scenario, different kinds of allies from the global north, including *power-node INGOs*, become critical collaborators. Power-node INGOs, commonly located in global cities, possess strategic knowledge about the political structures and processes that underlie the operations of powerful international institutions. Armed with this information, domestic collaborators can design new strategies to advance their claims. These strategies seek to deleverage international pressure and allow home governments to honor campaign commitments or pursue popular preferences in keeping with the expectations of democratic decision-making. A reconfigured north-south alliance plays a key role in bringing the views of domestic activists to bear on international institutions.

What follows is an analytical case study designed to flesh out the concepts discussed above. It focuses on the anti-mining movement in El Salvador, where a transnationally aligned coalition emerged to oppose the development of gold mining in 2005. Over a several-year period, various movement clusters, each with their own set of transnational allies, forged the *Mesa Nacional Frente a la Minería Metálica* (the Mesa). This coalition was constructed out of an expanding national network that, through a persistent campaign, contributed to the reshaping of public opinion on the mining issue. As the country's experience with electoral democracy lengthened and public approval of market reform weakened, the political tide turned in El Salvador, much as it did elsewhere in Latin America. Faced with the prospect of electoral defeat at the hands of a center-left coalition led by FMLN-candidate Mauricio Funes, the right wing ARENA President Tony Saca attempted a shift to the center and abandoned the party's pro-mining stance. Elected officials began to recalibrate their positions on the mining debate, and a de facto mining moratorium went into effect.

Unable to gain authorization to mine, Canadian and US corporations then took their case to the World Bank's International Centre for Settlement of Investment Disputes (ICSID), claiming "indirect expropriation" and demanding compensation. As the struggle extended into international institutional territory, Mesa leaders cultivated a new set of allies based in Washington, D.C., subsequently extending their network to include Canadian mine-watch organizations. Working to advance the claims of democratic decision-making and community protection against investment guarantees provided during the heyday of neoliberalism, a reconfigured anti-mining coalition struggled to secure El Salvador's release from a legal obligation to approve the mines. These dynamics, while particular to the Salvadoran case in their specificity, are familiar to many social movement activists elsewhere in Latin America, as they search for a way forward into a post-neoliberal era.

Anti-Mining Mobilization in El Salvador

As in much of Latin America, the extractive sector was opened up in El Salvador following a series of market reforms in the 1990s. Actively encouraged by the World Bank, governments across the region rewrote mining regulations and tax regimes to promote new investments (Fox, Onorato and Strongman 1998; Sánchez Albavera, Ortiz and Moussa 2001). El Salvador's new 1996 mining law and 2001 mining code, combined with rising prices for precious metals, attracted the attention of Canadian, US, and Australian gold mining companies (Henríquez 2008; Dougherty 2011). These corporations obtained exploration licenses and quickly identified commercial quantities of gold and silver. In tandem with the mining advance came the mobilization of anti-mining activism.

Movement Transnationalism in the Domestic Loop

The Salvadoran anti-mining movement was complex and multilayered, with diverse segments building transnational alliances at each level. Close analysis of constituent parts reveals the development of four sectors capped by a coordinating mechanism at the top. Established in 2005, the Mesa incorporated local community organizations such as the *Asociación de Desarrollo Económico y Social* (ADES) and the *Comité Ambiental de Cabañas* (CAC), which represented towns located near proposed mine sites. They were joined by human rights and environmental organizations such as the *Fundación de Estudios para la Aplicación del Derecho* (FESPAD) and *Unidad Ecológica Salvadoreña* (UNES), which helped to frame collective understanding about environmental hazards and the right to water. Activist-oriented research centers such as the *Centro de Investigación sobre Inversión y Comercio* (CIECOM) provided a third element. Finally, religion-based social action organizations, such as Cáritas-El Salvador and the Franciscan Justicia, Paz and Ecología, among others, developed into a fourth component of the alliance (Henríquez 2008, p. 29, n. 15). Each of these clusters cultivated a set of external allies, which were sometimes exclusive to that sector and sometimes connected across layers. These transnational alliances facilitated the flow of information, interpretations, inspiration, symbols, and framing, along with funding and technical advice, in a domestic loop process that targeted public consciousness and built pressure on policymakers. What follows is a brief description of the transnational linkages that emerged in each segment.

Community level resistance

Local level activism focused on communities in the "Gold Belt," a swath of land across the northern departments of Chalatenango, Cabañas, and Morazán. These departments had a long history of organizing around land rights and included communities where liberation theology advocates had been active in the 1980s. During the civil war (1980–1992), the military carried out intense campaigns designed to uproot guerrilla strongholds in this region. Many residents were forced to relocate, either as internal refugees or to UN High Commissioner for Refugees (UNHCR) camps across the border in Honduras. This extended refugee experience, especially in Mesa Grande, the largest of the Honduran camps, served as a crucible in which new forms of revolutionary identity, organizational practice, and autonomy were forged (Todd 2010). The collective return of this exiled population to villages in El Salvador between 1986 and the early 1990s, even as the war continued and in the face of military opposition, further crystallized community cohesion and capacity for resistance. Organizations such as *Comité Cristiano Pro Desplazados de El Salvador* (CRIPDES) and the Santa Marta-based ADES, which planned the refugee return from Honduras and resettlement in contested territory, emerged as key representatives of this displaced rural population in the post-war era.

As gold mine exploration work advanced in this region in the early 2000s, these local activists networked internally with other Salvadoran organizations and externally with anti-mining movements in neighboring countries. When asked about how they came to regard mining in adversarial terms, community activists emphasized the impact of personal communication with Honduran activists, particularly those organizing in the Valle de Siria, near the San Martín open pit gold mine (Spalding 2014). Mining in Honduras, which had begun several years previously, produced population displacement and environmental contamination, including a cyanide spill at the San Andrés mine near Santa Rosa de Copán. Mounting evidence of damage triggered major demonstrations in Honduras, including a protest march led by Cardinal Oscar Andrés Rodríguez in March 2002 (Slack 2009, 125–26). The hard experience of similarly situated, trusted counterparts in Honduras encouraged community activists in El Salvador's gold belt to view the advent of mining with increasing alarm. Diffusion processes at the grassroots level contributed to growing community resistance to mine investments.[2]

Tarrow (2005, 101–2) describes three mechanisms through which movement resources diffuse beyond their point of origin: relational mechanisms (built on interpersonal trust), non-relational mechanisms (using the Internet, media), and mediated diffusion, which operates through conscious brokerage and frame-building exercises. The origin stories of community activists in the Salvadoran anti-mining movement focus on the impact of relational mechanisms and mediated diffusion, emphasizing the issue framing offered by Honduran counterparts and formal and informal exchanges at regional resistance gatherings. The preoccupation of Salvadoran community activists with access to land and water and with the painful experience of displacement, encouraged close attention to the stories told by trusted Honduran allies about land loss, water contamination, and illnesses associated with mining. Thick cross-border ties provided information that was adapted and deployed by grassroots organizers in El Salvador.

Rights and justice organizations
In a pattern that has been observed in many environmental and natural resource battles (Slack 2009; Kuecker 2008; Rasch 2012; Hochstetler and Keck 2007, pp. 155–77), Salvadoran grassroots activists at the community level made common cause with rights-oriented and environmentalist NGOs operating at departmental, national, regional, and international scales. Post-war demobilization following the peace accords in 1992 allowed for the proliferation of civil society organizations in El Salvador, often with the support of international funders (MacDonald 1997). Many of these organizations, such as FESPAD and UNES, focused on human rights protection, including social, cultural, economic, and environmental rights.

---

2 Subsequent research on the diffusion model notes that the successful appropriation of discourse and framing in a new site involves more than simple transfer or emulation; complex processes of translation, experimentation, and application are required to allow a transnational frame to acclimate in a new setting (Chabot 2010).

Activists affiliated with these organizations mobilized repeatedly in the post-war period, supporting major protests in opposition to health care privatization and in defense of water rights (Almeida 2008; Haglund 2010).

The collective experience of civil war and dislocation in the 1980s, combined with shared natural disasters and environmental damage associated with hurricanes, drought, and flooding, tended to connect activists across Central America, in part at the behest of international donors who encouraged NGO collaboration (Gass 2002). Exposure to repeated processes of neoliberal regionalism (Spalding 2008), such as the cross-regional infrastructure development project, Plan Puebla-Panamá, and CAFTA, the Central America-wide free trade agreement with the US, provided a common target for resistance mobilization. In 2001, regional activists launched a series of annual gatherings of the *Foro Mesoamericano por la Autodeterminación y Resistencia de los Pueblos* (Foro) to share information and coordinate strategies (Spalding 2007). This collective-action form provided a tool for cross-regional brokerage and frame alignment around an array of social justice issues. Reaching its organizational apogee in 2004, the year that the CAFTA agreement was signed, the annual Foro gathering brought together several thousand activists from across Mesoamerica for several days of discussion and protest marches, rotating the locale systematically to facilitate broader incorporation.

This process of lateral networking encouraged horizontal connections among activists through which frames and information could churn, in a setting where few asymmetries of power would clog the flow. Global, hemispheric, or continental networks, as constructed in the World Social Forum, the European Social Forum, and the Hemispheric Social Alliance, include members that vary widely in resources and stature. That variation readily translates into hierarchies and stratification, as von Bülow (2010) has documented in the hemispheric alliance against the FTAA. Resistance networks that link activists across the north-south divide may experience acute tensions related to resource imbalances (Wood 2005; von Bülow 2009).

An alternative process, less visible but nonetheless significant, emerges under conditions of lateral transnationalism. Unlike the hierarchical interactions that frequently develop in networks that combine large, well-resourced organizations with small, volunteer-based ones, lateral transnationalism tends to link up organizations with relatively modest resource differences and more extensive commonalities. While losing the resource transfers that could come with unequal alliances, the lateral process connects similar activists whose strategic calculations may be more readily shared, fostering authentic collaborations. Theorizing variation in network composition may facilitate understanding of the circumstances under which transnational diffusion is fluid and better adapted for local use. The lateral form of transnationalism commonly operates at the regional or sub-regional level, although regional settings and south-south networks may themselves be the site of tension (Wood 2010).

Research centers and think tanks

To promote their work, rights-oriented activists in El Salvador established their own network of think tanks, some of which prepared supportive forms of knowledge and bolstered social justice claims. These included CIECOM, which published some of the first reports on the mining sector in El Salvador (Henríquez 2008; Ramos 2009), drawing on financing from the Spanish Fundación Paz y Solidaridad, the Swedish Diakonia, the German Heinrich Böll Foundation, and Oxfam America, among others.

Gold mining in El Salvador was a little-developed sector, and the country's few older mines had closed during the civil war. Activists' limited familiarity with the industry and the absence of a local academic specialization in the field pushed mine resisters to search for outside experts whose work could complement their own. Faced with the task of responding to the environmental impact assessment (EIA) produced in 2005 by the Canadian gold mining corporation Pacific Rim as part of the permit process, ADES, a community organization from the repopulated town of Santa Marta, Cabañas, recruited a US hydrologist and geochemist, Robert Moran, as a consultant. Moran had a track record for evaluating the EIAs of proposed gold mines and exposing the environmental problems that they raised. Having just completed a critical evaluation of the controversial Marlen Mine in Guatemala, Moran took on the task of evaluating the EIA for the El Dorado mine under development in Cabañas.

Moran's (2005) assessment raised questions about the adequacy of the remediation measures to be taken in the event of a cyanide spill, the proposed cyanide detoxification process, the quality of the baseline hydrology report, and the community consultation process. His work, which came at a critical moment in the licensing process, was followed by additional technical contributions from thickly credentialed outside specialists working in collaboration with local activists (Erzinger, González and Ibarra 2008; López, Guzmán and Mira 2008). This collaboration with outside experts invigorated the technical debate, expanding the arsenal of the mine resisters.

Religious networks

The fourth segment of the resistance movement involved a religious link, which consolidated in 2007 when the *Conferencia Episcopal de El Salvador* (CEDES), the ecclesiastical leadership of the Catholic Church, issued a statement opposing the development of a mining industry. Separated by class, institutional roles, and ideology from many of the other actors in El Salvador's anti-mining movement, the Catholic Church leadership provided an expansion of the network into less familiar political territory.

In explaining their position, the bishops concluded that the proposed form of mining "causes irreversible damage to the environment and surrounding communities" (CEDES 2007). According to their analysis, contamination introduced by the proposed gold mines, many of them to be located in the Lempa River watershed, could have devastating human and ecological consequences given the river's central role in the national water supply. The detail behind their decision is undoubtedly complex, but their proclamation highlighted regional learning from a neighboring reference group. They noted the harmful environmental impact of gold mining in neighboring Honduras and Guatemala and the leadership role being played by bishops elsewhere in the region in their call for mine closings.[3]

The Salvadoran bishops' declaration of opposition to gold mining resonated more broadly and in new directions than that of traditional mine resistance groups. Among the major institutions operating in El Salvador, the Catholic Church routinely enjoyed one of the highest trust scores, and Catholicism remained the dominant religion. With the inclusion of Catholic Church leaders in the opposition, conservative sectors, far removed from activist circles, were now linked into the anti-mining message.

The anti-mining coordinator
As the organizational centerpiece of the anti-mining movement, the Mesa helped to coordinate domestic learning about mining problems and facilitated frame alignment around core issues of democratic decision-making and water rights. It played complex brokerage roles as it attempted to coordinate meanings, negotiate common understanding, and represent the movement as it interfaced with the mass public. The Mesa added its own layer of transnational partnership, building ties with a small network of INGOs, some of which also connected with the movement at other levels.

INGOs have played both constructive and constraining roles in relation to popular mobilization in Latin America. Smith and Weist (2012) document the close links between INGOs and the development and persistence of transnational social movement organizations (TSMOs). Drawing on data from the International Yearbook on International Organizations, they find that TSMO longevity increases with denser connections to INGOs. Although northern-based TSMOs on average had more connections with INGOs than the southern-based ones, the number of these connections increased across time for both. For southern TSMOs, the average number of INGO ties in 1953–77 was 1.3; this rose to 4.4 in the post 1988 period (Smith and Weist 2012, p. 66).

INGOs have widely varied relationships with their domestic allies, however, not all of them positive. As was noted in the introductory section, a substantial body of research on transnational activism demonstrates that foreign financial flows can produce new forms of dominance (Petras 1997); deracinate organizations from their local grounding (Edelman 1999; 2008); alter organizational dynamics and mission (Thayer 2010; Lewis 2011; Chalmers et al. 1997); and sow deep

---

3   Bishops across Latin America were voicing similar concerns as the extractive industries expanded rapidly across the region. The 2007 conference of 160 Latin American bishops in Aparecida, Brazil concluded by noting that inadequately regulated resource extraction industries "destroy forests and contaminate waters, and turn the areas exploited into vast deserts" (CELAM 2007, para. 473).

discord among actors as they compete for visibility and scarce resources (Bob 2005). Foreign actors often shift collective action toward delimited forms of project-oriented participation (Chalmers et al. 1997, p. 562). In some cases, local organizations function essentially as franchises of international organizations, subject to highly controlled and centralized direction. INGOs that operate in a top down and inflexible manner, and that attempt to impose an externally dictated agenda on skeptical partners, invite rule evasion, foot dragging, and dissimulation (Hertel 2006) or outright alliance rupture (Andrews 2010).

At the same time, variation in the commitment to partnership, degrees of centralization, funding timelines, staffing practices, and tailoring to local conditions means that domestic and international organizations are likely to intersect in widely differing ways.[4] These include not only top down and centrally controlled connections but also long-term, cooperative relationships sometimes built on principles of solidarity (Stites Mor 2013; Juris and Khasnabish 2013; Olesen 2005).

Solidarity is a complex concept, requiring reflection on the relationship between the individual and the collective, and demanding close examination of the impact of privilege on the quality of connective bonds. Research on solidarity activism identifies many different forms, including strong and weak types, and "altruistic" (one-way) versus "mutual" varieties (Olesen 2005, pp. 107–11). Scholz (2008) defines political solidarity as "a unity of individuals each responding to a particular situation of injustice, oppression, social vulnerability, or tyranny" (Scholz, p. 51), and notes the attendant "positive duty" across the network to take action to address the source of harm. Her analysis distinguishes four types of solidarity: social, civic, political, and "parasitical," the latter representing a rhetorical device that mobilizes the feelings and discourse of solidarity, absent the moral obligations inherent in the term.

This chapter introduces the concept of "domesticating INGOs," a type of INGO that embraces solidaristic principles and supports a relatively high degree of autonomy for local partners, often as part of the organization's mission. People-to-people solidarity organizations, such as the Sister Cities project in El Salvador, tend to embrace this kind of model. This category of INGOs emphasizes long-term, multi-strand relationships with durable partners, and uses staffing and organizational practices that permit deeper rooting in the domestic sphere. Partner autonomy is expressed in terms of mission definition, staffing, and organizational

---

4 Lewis's (2011, 93–99) analysis of the funding networks for Ecuadorian environmental NGOs identifies four subtypes: ecoimperialists (northern organizations that circumvent local partners and establish wholly controlled branch offices); ecodependents (local organizations that depend on foreign sources for more than 50 percent of their budget and are characterized by consequent boom-bust cycles); ecoresisters (locally funded radical organizations aligned with popular movements and south-south networks); and ecoindependents (unaffiliated organizations that are also locally funded, through mechanisms such as voluntary taxes, and that focus on small-scale pragmatic innovations).

style. Although difficult to develop and sustain, this kind of relationship involves co-construction of goals and strategies by local and international actors. Decentralization and flexible identities reduce the distance between internal and external actors in these networks. To attenuate remaining imbalances, local organizations may secure multiple funding sources (which reduce dependence on any one) or negotiate a long-term financial plan with a durable set of partners (ensuring continuity in the resource flow).

This pattern of connections aligns with the concept of "associative networks," which Chalmers et al. (1997, pp. 567–68) found to be gaining ground in Latin America. Emerging as an alternative to the clientelistic and corporatist alliances that historically dominated in the region, associative networks feature flexible linkages with diverse partners and result in less rigid inequalities among participants. Although these networks may link foreign and domestic actors with unequal resources, they typically offer "more chances to escape or shift the ground to avoid a direct test of strength with an unequal competitor" (Ibid., 568). Chalmers et al. saw hints of this development at the end of the 1990s, but their work did little to flesh out the circumstances under which associative networks emerge, the spaces in which they operate, or their engagement with larger political processes. Fuller theorizing about these emerging alliance structures, as initiated in this chapter, may point to new possibilities for domestic and transnational collaboration.

El Salvador had 145 registered INGOs at the time the mining conflict emerged (Holiday 2010). The relationships between these organizations and their Salvadoran partners were highly varied, but several international organizations that aligned with the anti-mining movement, I argue, took the form of domesticating INGOs. Many were solidarity organizations that had entered El Salvador during the 1980s and 1990s, catalyzed by moral outrage over the brutality of the civil war and the role of the United States in the process (Smith 1996; Nepstad 2004; Perla 2008). They included organizations like the Salvadoran Humanitarian Aid, Research and Education Foundation (SHARE), Committee in Solidarity with the People of El Salvador (CISPES), and the Sister Cities project—three US solidarity initiatives with deep roots in the country. These organizations had assisted Salvadoran refugees in Honduras when they demanded the right of return at the end of the 1980s (Todd 2012). Grounding their work in the concept of "accompaniment," these organizations established enduring ties to local communities in resistance. They used their relatively privileged position to echo the demands for local control and alternative development strategies, as embraced by their partners in these communities. As domesticating INGOs, they worked exclusively with El Salvador, developing a nontransferable mission strongly shaped by local frames. As the Mesa consolidated, they supported its advocacy and public outreach efforts, and provided logistical support for international delegations that came seeking inspiration from its struggle.

In addition to the solidarity organizations that arose out of the war, an array of human rights and development organizations headquartered in the US and Europe also developed long-term partnerships with Salvadoran organizations, emerging out of the post-war peace process and repeated reconstruction efforts that followed recurring natural disasters. Less domesticated but with some traits that positioned them fairly well as partners, organizations like Oxfam America supported local organizing for alternative development.

These larger, geocentric organizations operated according to externally derived standards, which can induce intra-coalition tensions. Oxfam's mission-based emphasis on local voice and community control, however, mitigated the rub. Oxfam leaders in El Salvador took pains to reduce competition among their partners, at times funding competitors if both networks endorsed a social justice agenda and enjoyed broad support (Spalding 2007). They also promoted long-term and multi-strand connections, financing their local partners over time and across multiple campaigns. Oxfam contributed to the Mesa's anti-mining work by supporting conferences, research and publications, hosting international experts, participating in direct lobbying, commissioning public opinion polls, and covering basic operating expenses. With financial support from Oxfam, the Mesa opened an office in San Salvador in a building shared with CRIPDES and the Sister Cities project, and launched its domestic campaign.

Political Impacts at the Domestic Scale

Some social theorists and activists regard formal institutional processes and informal non-institutional ones as distinct, even adversarial, fields of action, leaving the connections between social movements and electoral politics under-examined. More comprehensive studies, however, including several chapters in this volume, question the sharp distinction between these forms of civic engagement. My work explores how a domestic movement coalition mobilizes resources, including conceptual and material ones secured through transnational networking, to seek influence at home, including in electoral outcomes and regulatory processes.

In the anti-mining case, the rising tide of organized opposition began to play a role in the political process, particularly as the network extended to unconventional allies such as the Catholic Church leaders. After several years of network expansion, and growing evidence of a leftward shift in public opinion (Azpuru 2010), President Tony Saca (2004–2009) of ARENA, the pro-business political party that governed the country from 1989 to 2009, began to express, in increasingly vocal terms, his personal reservations about the impact of mining on the environment. This turn came in spite of the enthusiastic support for mine development that his party had registered for over a decade. As the FMLN presidential candidate Mauricio Funes gathered momentum in the lead-up to the 2009 election, Saca declared a moratorium on mining permits. With ARENA divided on the issue and the FMLN firmly opposed, Funes became the standard bearer for anti-mining movement. Officially non-partisan, many Mesa activists had long-term ties to the FMLN, but others were drawn to the movement through Catholic Church leadership and environmental concerns. They joined broad networks of engaged citizens to bring the Funes campaign to voters well beyond the FMLN faithful, contributing to his electoral victory in March 2009. His inauguration was followed by months of escalating violence against anti-mining activists in Cabañas (Steiner 2010).

The new government developed a two-prong effort on the mining front. Domestically, it moved to amend national investment legislation and formalize the mining moratorium. Internationally, it mobilized to confront a major legal challenge lodged by the mining companies. Funes began by commissioning a Strategic Environmental Evaluation of the Metallic Mining Sector, funded by the Spanish Agency for International Cooperation and Development, to assess the prospective social and environmental consequences of mining in El Salvador. The resulting Tau Consultora Ambiental (2011) report emphasized the environmental vulnerability of the country and the opposition of organized civil society, citing these as factors that weighed against mine development in El Salvador. It identified the 17 areas in which legal and institutional reforms would be required and 64 actions that would be needed in order to provide an appropriate regulatory infrastructure for mining. These requirements went far beyond the institutional capacity of the Salvadoran state, bolstering the argument for a continued moratorium. Armed with the Tau report, the government moved to adopt a formal moratorium on metals mining.

Government policy fell short of a call for an outright ban on the industry, the position supported by the Mesa, and tensions erupted with the anti-mining coalition. Working with the FMLN leadership in the legislature, Mesa leaders continued to press for a full legal ban, one that would not be easily reversed by a shift in electoral dynamics. Although discrepancies emerged over how best to restrict mining in El Salvador, the anti-mining movement provided forceful support for the government as it was hurtled into international legal proceedings by mining investors.

On the heels of Funes's election, two mining companies filed legal claims against the Salvadoran government with the World Bank's ICSID. Pacific Rim Cayman filed a claim for $77 million, subsequently raised to $315 million in 2013. Commerce Group filed for $100 million in damages, along with the issuance of the extraction permits. Both companies claimed "indirect expropriation" by the government, based on the loss of expected future revenues. They advanced their claims using protections provided in the newly enacted Central American Free Trade Agreement (CAFTA) with the United States and in the national Investment Law, which had been approved by the Salvadoran government in 1999. These filings added a second dimension to the work of the Salvadoran anti-mining coalition, now catapulted to the international scale.

Scale Shift to the International Level: The Deleveraging Hook

Victory at the domestic level would prove pyrrhic if international pressure prevented the realization of clearly articulated public preferences and the campaign commitments of elected officials. Activists now pursued a *deleveraging hook*, attempting to break through external constraints on national decision-making and open policy space for local democratic practices. Deleveraging is designed to disengage and pull back on the constraints imposed by powerful international actors, thereby releasing the state to respond to alternative influences, including those emanating from its citizenry.

As contestation shifts from the domestic loop pattern to that found in the deleveraging hook, movement leaders find it useful to reconfigure their networks, now seeking to add transnational allies who are familiar with the newly relevant institutions and rules. This process introduces "power-node INGOs," such as Mining Watch Canada, which have specialized knowledge of pressure points in international relations and experience in designing communications strategies that target global power centers. Whereas domesticating INGOs focus on building alliances with local partners and integrating themselves into the domestic landscape, power-node INGOs are more clearly outsiders, with their headquarters, staff, and targets concentrated in global cities. Domesticating INGOs labor to build multi-strand and durable connections; power-node INGOs, in contrast, tend to concentrate on a narrower set of issues and connect with shifting local partners through short-term or episodic bonds. Though less robust than the former, the latter provide critical support for scale shifting into new territory.

The deleveraging process may involve lobbying the US congress or Canadian parliament in the effort to weaken the alliances between legislative bodies and multinational corporations and thereby diminish the diplomatic penalty associated with restricting corporate latitude. The new strategy may put direct pressure on the corporations by using negative publicity to raise reputational costs and introducing stockholder resolutions to challenge corporate practices. Deleveraging processes may engage an alternative set of international institutions, such as the Inter-American Human Rights Commission, attempting to counterbalance pressure from an unfavorable arena with affirmation from one better aligned with their goals. Deleveraging may also involve direct confrontation with adversaries in the spaces of inclusion where civil society organizations have gained access to international institutions.

In the Salvadoran case, the deleveraging hook involved confronting the mining companies in an international investment dispute played out in front of a three-person arbitration tribunal in an ICSID conference room in Washington, D.C. ICSID, a little-known facility of the World Bank, became an increasingly prominent international actor in the 2000s due to the rapid rise in the number of bilateral investment treaties, free trade agreements, investment laws, and company-state investment contracts (Fach Gómez 2011; Orellana 2011). Many of these agreements mandated or permitted international arbitration in the event of a dispute between a foreign investor and the state. Using these investor-state provisions, transnational corporations presented a growing number of claims challenging host states for noncompliance, seeking redress and/or compensation for losses. ICSID had registered 459 investment dispute cases at the end of 2013, up from 81 in 2000 (ICSID 2014, p. 7). Latin American countries (minus Mexico) were represented in 34 percent of these cases (11). Twenty-six percent of all ICSID cases involved claims in the oil, gas, and mining sector (12).

Investment disputes have substantial consequences in terms of access to basic human rights, including water and a healthy environment, and condemnatory awards affect future government spending and taxpayer burdens (Fach Gómez 2012). The government of El Salvador was now caught in this complex and expensive area of litigation. It responded by hiring its own Washington-based legal team and filing multiple rejoinders to the company claims, challenging the merit of the accusations and the jurisdictional rights of these corporations to process their demands in this international forum.

As the struggle unfolded at the international scale, the Mesa cultivated a broadening base of international allies and moved to support the Salvadoran government's legal efforts. Collaboration strengthened with two Washington-based INGOs: the Institute for Policy Studies (IPS) and the Center for International Environmental Law (CIEL). IPS, a human rights and economic justice organization, became seriously involved in the Salvadoran conflict in 2009, as Pacific Rim and Commerce Group registered their arbitration demands and the assassination of anti-mining activists in Cabañas began. In the lead up to this involvement, IPS had issued a series of reports criticizing the use of international arbitration to settle investor-state disputes. This kind of process was found to undermine democratic practices by removing debate from the public sphere and locating it in a venue that favored corporate interests (Anderson and Pérez-Rocha 2013). Using its broad network to mobilize support from global justice organizations, IPS circulated an "Open Letter for World Bank Officials" in December 2011, calling for the dismissal of the Pacific Rim case, and quickly tallied 244 signatures (IPS 2011).

The second organization, CIEL, was a US-based environmental law advocacy organization founded in 1989. This group had a legal specialization in the human rights and environmental conflicts, including those that emerged from investment disputes. CIEL focused on improving transparency and public participation in the settlement of environmental conflicts that went into international arbitration. This organization had participated as a community advocate in several arbitration cases before ICSID tribunals, and it had been instrumental in a 2006 ICSID reform that opened space for community participation through the submission of *amicus curiae* briefs.[5]

CIEL staff members were now brought into the Mesa network for capacity-building purposes. They traveled to El Salvador to explain the ICSID process to

---

5   Amicus curiae or "friend of the court" briefs allow groups that are not litigants but whose interests would be affected by the outcome to present their perspective to the court under specific conditions. The 2006 ICSID reform followed two controversial arbitrations: the Aguas del Tunari, S.A. v. Bolivia case arising from the Cochabama "water war" and the Suez/Vivendi case against Argentina, which involved a contract for the distribution of water and sewage services. In both cases, a coalition of community groups requested public access to the documents of the ICSID proceedings and permission to submit an amicus brief, a petition that was denied in the first case and partially accepted in the second. See Orellana 2011, pp. 98–102; Fach Gómez 2012, pp. 537–41.

interested activists and identify the small windows of opportunity for community involvement. In 2011 eight Mesa members collaborated with CIEL to present an *amicus* brief for the Pacific Rim case (CIEL 2011). This document claimed that the Salvadoran government's moratorium on mining permits was the outcome of a democratic process in which local community groups, concerned about community and environmental impacts, used a newly opening political system to press for a policy response. Presenting this conflict as a political dispute between the company and the communities, not a bona fide law case, the brief called for dismissal.

An international support group calling itself "The International Allies against Metallic Mining in El Salvador," which had begun as a small network of solidarity organizations with deep roots in Mesa communities, expanded over time to include 20 organizations in 2013.[6] This network sponsored international delegations and informational tours; protests outside the Canadian embassy, mining company headquarters, and the World Bank; and letter writing campaigns calling international and Salvadoran leaders to endorse the Mesa position in favor of a mining ban. Frequently framing its message in terms of access to water rights, this coalition supported collaboration with anti-mining alliances elsewhere in the region. Growing concern about the cross-border consequences of mining in places like Cerro Blanco, a Guatemalan mine at the headwaters of the Rio Lempa, produced a call for cross-border regulation and the suspension of mining in neighboring countries as well (PDDH 2013).

In June 2012, the ICSID tribunal rejected Pacific Rim's claims to jurisdictional rights under the Central American-United States-Dominican Republic free trade agreement, finding that the Canadian company "did not and does not have substantial activities in the USA" (*Pac Rim Cayman LLC v. Republic of El Salvador* 2012, 4.78).[7] The tribunal did, however, allow the Pacific Rim case to proceed under El Salvador's 1999 Investment Law, which also included international dispute settlement guarantees. As of August 2014, the dispute remains underway. Petitions by international delegations and networks in support of Mesa claims have had little impact on the mining companies, which continue to press their demands at ICSID.[8]

---

6 http://www.stopesmining.org/j25/index.php/who-we-are2, accessed July 26, 2013. The US organizations included the six discussed above (SHARE, CISPES, Sister Cities, Oxfam America, IPS, and CIEL) along with Friends of the Earth, Sierra Club, Maryknoll Office for Global Concerns, the Democracy Center, Voices on the Border, Jobs with Justice, the Washington Office on Latin America, Washington Ethical Society Global Connections Committee, Midwest Coalition Against Lethal Mining, National Lawyers Guild, and Miners and the Environment. The Canadian affiliates were Mining Watch Canada, Council of Canadians, and Canadians against Mining in El Salvador.

7 The 2009 claim by the US mining company Commerce Group was disallowed by the ICSID tribunal because the company had a parallel case underway in Salvadoran domestic court.

8 Pacific Rim was acquired by an Australian mining company OceanaGold in late 2013.

As in Central America, conflicts over mining have erupted in broad parts of the global south. The *Observatorio de Conflictos Mineros de América Latina* (OCMAL) reported 206 mining conflicts in 19 Latin American countries in August 2014, up from 133 in 15 countries in 2010.[9] Peru, Chile, and Mexico registered 36, 35, and 34 conflicts, respectively, in August 2014, with Argentina (26) and Brazil (20) also experiencing numerous clashes. Although a small region geographically, Central America (including Panama) reported 25 mining conflicts in mid-2014. Widespread social mobilization over the opening, expansion, and closing of mines established new territory for transnational networks, operating both domestically and at the international scale. The increasing number of mining conflicts has prompted a growing body of research on this topic in Latin America and beyond (Bebbington and Bury 2013; Thorp et al. 2012; Hogenboom 2012; Rasch 2012; Dougherty 2011; Slack 2009; Bebbington et al. 2008; and Kuecker 2008). Rigorous comparative analysis and theoretical cross-fertilization would strengthen the development of this emerging field of study. Such work would benefit from close analysis of the transnational dimensions of movement organizing and the complex recalibrations associated with political change and scale shift.

Theoretical Implications and Conclusions

This chapter underscores the dynamics of contention (McAdam, Tarrow and Tilly 2001) involved in building movement networks across space, time, and scale. Using a relational approach, which emphasizes process, interaction, adaptation, and sequences, it examines the multilayered intersections between domestic and international actors as movements cross thresholds and reconfigure in new organizational terrain. This work underlines four theoretical observations with broad implications for the development of social movement research.

First, as domestic political opportunities open up but international opportunities do not, movement transnationality and coalition formation play out in two interrelated contexts: at the domestic scale, in the domestic loop process; and at the international scale, in the deleveraging hook process. Each of these processes is simultaneously domestic and transnational, but actors privileged domestic alliances and targets in the first case and international ones in the second. This analysis not only examines each of these complex processes in some detail, it also locates linkages between the two, exploring the mechanisms that trigger a shift across scales and tracing the ways in which coalitions reconfigure when it does.

This study points to the importance of analyzing social movements in a dynamic fashion as they operate over time and across scales, particularly in the context of power relations in the global south. As von Bülow (2013) notes, the study of transnational movements tends to highlight particular campaigns, which

---

9   See http://basedatos.conflictosmineros.net/ocmal_db/, accessed August 14, 2014, and http://www.olca.co/ocmal, accessed August 1, 2010.

are often short lived. Many analyses nicely capture specific pieces of the framing and coalition formation processes, but fail to examine the fuller dynamics of contention, including lulls, reconstitution, disarticulation, and decline. Fewer still trace contention across scales or through various iterations of struggle.[10] Social movement theory suffers as a result.

Second, this chapter locates transnational movements in the concrete political realities emerging in Latin America, both in domestic and international politics. Since 2002, a leftward political shift has been documented in the region in both national electoral outcomes and public opinion (Levitsky and Roberts 2011; Weyland, Madrid and Hunter 2010; Baker and Green 2011). Silva's (2009) work demonstrates the role played by neoliberal resistance movements in advancing this shift. Growing recognition of the connection between social mobilization and political transition calls us to pay close attention to critical junctures, tipping points, and protest cycles that link movements, left-leaning political parties, new government actors, and public policy change. The resulting left-turn governments often fail to satisfy domestic social movements, however, and sometimes perpetuate policies that trigger new rounds of mobilization (Veltmeyer and Petras 2014; Bebbington and Bury 2013; Bebbington et al. 2008; Hochstetler and Keck 2007, pp. 178–82). This vibrant intersection between movement and institutional politics provides an emerging focal point for theory building and conceptual innovation.

Domestic efforts to shift away from neoliberal policy can lead to an intensification of external pressures, including a clash with international institutions that are designed to enforce market discipline. This tension calls us to examine the ways in which domestic political transitions reverberate not only at home but also in the international sphere. The collision between internal demands and external pressures has prompted the leaders of several Latin American countries to look for ways to detach from neoliberal enforcers. Some have repaid IMF loans early, for example, to escape from external supervision, as in the case of Argentina and Brazil, or refrained from signing free trade agreements that include state-investor provisions or onerous intellectual property regimes, which would undercut national development strategies. Others, including Bolivia, Ecuador, and Venezuela, have broken more sharply, nationalizing resources and renouncing membership in ICSID, for example, and rejecting the findings of arbitration tribunals that they see as biased toward investors or impeding the renegotiation of state-investor relations. These experiences point to the challenges that emerge when resistance movement victories in the domestic loop process collide with a closed international system that jeopardizes implementation of the results. These conflicts between democratic outcomes and international rules provide rich territory for social movement theory building in Latin America and beyond.

Third, this chapter draws attention to the little studied phenomenon of lateral transnationalism, a variant of transnationalism that may be particularly critical for

---

10   An emerging body of literature examining movements operating under the NAFTA framework may be the exception. See, for example, Kay (2011).

the analysis of diffusion within sub-regional social movements. Many studies of resistance activism focus on activists in the global north, giving less attention to those in the south. Southern activism, when it does gain center stage, is sometimes approached through the lens of large transnational networks that connect with others at the hemispheric or global level. This top-down approach can leave under-examined the dynamics that emerge from the ground up as dispersed clusters of activists undergo distinctive internationalization processes and adapt frames and strategies borrowed from similar others at the sub-regional level. The latter form of alignment, defined here as lateral transnationalism, often contains a cross-border dimension, reflecting the intensity of borderland histories and the resulting social, economic, and cultural ties. These linkages can be particularly important in promoting the transnational adaptation of frames and strategies that are attuned to local realities. They can also facilitate the construction of joint actions and collaborative demands, an important prerequisite for the development of transborder movements capable of addressing rights violations that spread across a region.

Finally, this analysis calls for new and better thinking about north-south movement alliances. Unlike lateral ties, which have been understudied, north-south ties have received much attention in the transnational network literature. Analysis of their impact, however, has often been over-simplified and under-theorized, leading to summary judgments that are stripped of nuance. My analysis has identified two kinds of northern INGOs that have a stronger capacity to partner with local allies, as interpreted by those allies themselves. Domesticating INGOs, characterized by long-term, multi-strand, and solidaristic commitments, often play a complementary role in resistance movement development and may be able to integrate with relatively few tensions into the domestic loop process. Power-nodes INGOs, characterized by their location in global power centers and their emphasis on change at the level of international institutions, would likely be poor partners in the domestic loop process, given their geocentric focus, weaker local knowledge, and distractibility. They may, however, be very useful partners following scale shift, when new forms of knowledge and tactical skills may be required and the coalition reconfigures.

In neither case are these north-south alliances problem-free. Tensions, clashes, misunderstandings, and suspicions appear repeatedly, exacerbated by inevitable questions about financing and strategic calculations. This analysis pays close attention to the field of power in which coalitions operate, recognizing the challenges associated with constructive alliance formation even under favorable circumstances. But rather than assuming, based on structural imbalances and mutual wariness, that the relationship is foul at the core, this study urges continued research on the range of variation in the forms and quality of north-south network conflict and cooperation.

The transnational dimensions of social movements continue to be a source of strength and a challenge to their development. The passing of the great free trade debates of the early 2000s moved some of these struggles off the top of the news feed, but these complex processes of exchange and collaboration continue to mount, fueled as before by advancing processes of internationalization and economic globalization. Theory building efforts that explore the dynamics of transnational contention will continue to expand our conceptual tools, enrich our debates, and advance our understanding of collective action, that enrich human endeavor through which we attempt to build our social world.

References

Almeida, Paul D., 2010. "El Salvador: elecciones y movimientos sociales." *Revista de ciencia política*, 30(2), pp. 319–34.

———, 2008. *Waves of protest: popular struggle in El Salvador, 1925–2005*. Minneapolis: University of Minnesota Press.

Anderson, Sarah and Manuel Pérez-Rocha, 2013. *Mining for profit in international tribunals*. (Updated edition) Institute for Policy Studies, [online] Available at: <http://www.ips-dc.org/reports/mining_for_profits_update2013> [Accessed 22 July 2013].

Andrews, Abigail, 2010. "Constructing mutuality: the Zapatistas' transformation of transnational activist power dynamics." *Latin American Politics and Society*, 52(1) (Spring), pp. 89–120.

Azpuru, Dinorah, 2010. "The salience of ideology: fifteen years of presidential elections in El Salvador." *Latin American Politics and Society*, 52(2) (Summer), pp. 103–38.

Baker, Andy and Greene, Kenneth F., 2011. "The Latin American left's mandate: free-market policies and issue voting in new democracies." *World Politics*, 63(1) (January), pp. 43–77.

Bebbington, Anthony and Bury, Jeffrey, 2013. *Subterranean struggles: new dynamics of mining, oil, and gas in Latin America*. Austin: University of Texas Press.

Bebbington, Anthony, Hinojosa, Leonith, Bebbington, Denise Humphreys, Burneo, María Luisa and Warnaars, Ximena, 2008. "Contention and ambiguity: mining and the possibilities of development." *Development and Change*, 39(6), pp. 965–92.

Bennett, W. Lance, 2005. "Social movements beyond borders: understanding two eras of transnational activism." In: della Porta, Donatella, and Tarrow, Sidney eds, 2005. *Transnational protest and global activism*. Lanham: Rowman & Littlefield.pp. 203–26.

Bilal, Sanoussi, de Lombaerde, Philippe and Tussie, Diane eds, 2011. *Asymmetric trade negotiations*. Farnham: Ashgate.

Bob, Clifford, 2005. *The marketing of rebellion*. Cambridge: Cambridge University Press.

Cameron, Maxwell A. and Hershberg, Eric eds, 2010. *Latin America's left turns*. Boulder: Lynne Rienner.

Center for International Environmental Law (CIEL), 2011, March 2. "Submission of member organizations of La Mesa as *Amicus Curiae*, Pac Rim Cayman LLC v. Republic of El Salvador, ICSID Case No. ARB/09/12," [online] Available at: <http://www.ciel.org/Publications/P AC_RIM_Amicus_2Mar11_Eng.pdf> [Accessed 29 March 2011].

Chabot, Sean, 2010. "Dialogue matters: beyond the transmission model of transnational diffusion between social movements." In: Rebecca Kolims Givan, Kenneth M. Roberts and Sarah A. Soule, eds. *The diffusion of social movements*. Cambridge: Cambridge University Press, pp. 99–124.

Chalmers, Douglas A., Martin, Scott B. and Piester, Kerianne, 1997. "Associative networks: new structures of representation for the popular sectors?" In: Douglas A. Chalmers, Carlos M. Vilas, Katherine Hite, Scott B. Martin, Kerianne Piester and Monique Segarra, eds. *The new politics of inequality in Latin America*. Oxford: Oxford University Press, pp. 543–82.

Conferencia Episcopal de El Salvador (CEDES), 2007. "Cuidemos la casa de todos: pronunciamiento de la Conferencia Episcopal de El Salvador sobre la explotación de minas de oro y plata," [online] Available at: <http://www. iglesia.org.sv/content/view/226/40/> [Accessed 19 August 2010].

Consejo Episcopal Latinoamericano (CELAM), 2007. "Concluding document." Fifth General Conference of the Latin American and Caribbean Bishops' Conference, May 13–31, Aparecida, Brazil. [online] Available at: <http:// www.celam.org/aparecida/Ingles.pdf> [Accessed 10 January 2013].

Copelovitch, Mark S., 2010. *The international monetary fund in the global economy: banks, bonds and bailouts*. Cambridge: Cambridge University Press.

Cumbers, Andy, Routledge, Paul and Nativel, Corinne, 2008. "The entangled geographies of global justice networks." *Progress in human geography*, 32(2), pp. 183–201.

della Porta, Donatella, Andretta, Massimiliano, Mosca, Lorenzo and Reiter, Herbert, 2006. *Globalization from below: transnational activists and protest networks*. Minneapolis: University of Minnesota Press.

della Porta, Donatella, and Tarrow, Sidney eds, 2005. *Transnational protest and global activism*. Lanham: Rowman & Littlefield.

Dougherty, Michael L., 2011. "The global gold mining industry, junior firms, and civil society resistance in Guatemala." *Bulletin of Latin American Research*, pp. 1–16.

Edelman, Marc, 1999. *Peasants against globalization: rural social movements in Costa Rica*. Stanford: Stanford University Press.

———, 2008. "Transnational organizing in agrarian Central America: histories, challenges, prospects." *Journal of Agrarian Change*, 8(2–3) (April and July), pp. 229–57.

Erzinger, Florian, González, Luis, and Ibarra, Angel M., 2008. *El lado oscuro del oro: Impactos de la minería metálica en El Salvador*. San Salvador: UNES and Cáritas de El Salvador.

Escárcega, Sylvia, 2013. "The global indigenous movement and paradigm wars." In Juris, Jeffrey S. and Khasnabish, Alex eds, 2013. *Insurgent encounters: transnational activism, ethnography and the political.* Durham: Duke University Press, pp. 129–50.

Fach Gómez, Katia, 2012. "Rethinking the role of amicus curiae in international investment arbitration: how to draw the line favorably for the public interest." *Fordham International Law Journal*, (25), pp. 510–64.

———, 2011. "Latin America and ICSID: David Versus Goliath?" *Law and Business Review of the Americas*, 17(2), pp. 501–49.

Fox, Jonathan A. and Brown, L. David, 1998. *The struggle for accountability.* Cambridge: MIT Press.

Fox, Peter, Onorato, William and Strongman, John, 1998. "World bank group assistance for minerals sector development and reform in member countries." *World Bank Technical Paper No. 405.* Washington: World Bank.

Gallagher, Kevin P., 2008. "Trading away the ladder? Trade politics and economic development in the Americas." *New Political Economy*, 13(1) (March), pp. 37–59.

Gass, Vicki, 2002. *Democratizing development: lessons from Hurricane Mitch reconstruction.* Washington: Washington Office on Latin America.

Goldstone, Jack A., 2003. "Introduction: bridging institutionalized and noninstitutionalized politics." In: Jack A. Goldstone, ed. *States, parties and social movements.* Cambridge: Cambridge University Press, pp. 1–24.

Haglund, LaDawn, 2010. *Limiting resource: market-led reform and the transformation of public goods.* University Park: Pennsylvania State University Press.

Henríquez, Katia, 2008. *Perspectiva de la industria minera de oro en El Salvador.* San Salvador: Ediciones CEICOM.

Hertel, Shareen, 2006. *Unexpected power: conflict and change among transnational activists.* Ithaca: Cornell University Press.

Hochstetler, Kathryn and Keck, Margaret E., 2007. *Greening Brazil: environmental activism in state and society.* Durham: Duke University Press.

Hogenboom, Barbara, 2012. "Depoliticized and repoliticized minerals in Latin America." *Journal of Developing Societies*, 28, pp. 133–58.

Holiday, David, 2010. "Country report-El Salvador." *Freedom House, Countries at the Crossroads 2010.* [online] Available at: <http://www.freedomhouse. org/template.cfm?page=140&edition=9&ccrpage=43&ccrcountry=183> [Accessed 4 September 2010].

Huber, Evelyne and Stephens, John D., 2013. *Democracy and the left: social policy and inequality in Latin America.* Chicago: University of Chicago Press.

International Centre for the Settlement of Investment Disputes, 2014. *ICSID caseload-statistics* (Issue 2014-1). [online] Available at: <https://icsid. worldbank.org/ICSID/FrontServlet?requestType=ICSIDDocRH&actionVal= ShowDocument&CaseLoadStatistics=True&language=English51> [Accessed 14 August 2014].

IPS, 2011. "Open letter to world bank officials on Pacific Rim-El Salvador case." December 12. [online] Available at: <http://justinvestment.org/2011/12/open-letter-to-world-bank-officials-on-pacific-rim-el-salvador-case/> [Accessed 4 August 2013].

Juris, Jeffrey S. and Khasnabish, Alex eds, 2013. *Insurgent encounters: transnational activism, ethnography and the political.* Durham: Duke University Press.

Kay, Tamara, 2011. *NAFTA and the politics of labor transnationalism.* Cambridge: Cambridge University Press.

Keck, Margaret E. and Sikkink, Kathryn, 1998. *Activists beyond borders.* Ithaca: Cornell University Press.

Khasnabish, Alex, 2013. "Tracing the Zapatista Rhizome, or, the ethnography of a transnationalized political imagination." In: Juris, Jeffrey S. and Khasnabish, Alex eds, 2013. *Insurgent encounters: transnational activism, ethnography and the political.* Durham: Duke University Press, pp. 66–88.

Kuecker, Glen David, 2008. "Fighting for the forests revisited: grassroots resistance to mining in northern Ecuador." In: Richard Stahler-Sholk, Harry E. Vanden and Glen David Kuecker, eds. *Latin American social movements in the 21st century.* Lanham: Rowman & Littlefield, pp. 97–112.

Levitsky, Steven and Roberts, Kenneth M., 2011. *The resurgence of the Latin American left.* Baltimore: The Johns Hopkins University Press.

Lewis, Tammy L., 2011. "Global civil society and the distribution of environmental goods: funding for environmental NGOs in Ecuador." In: JoAnn Carmin and Julian Agyeman, eds. *Environmental inequalities beyond borders: local perspectives on global injustices.* Cambridge: The MIT Press, pp. 87–104.

López, Dina Lario de, Guzmán, Herbert and Mira, Edgardo, 2008. "Riesgos y posibles impactos de la minería metálica en El Salvador." *Revista ECA*, 63, pp. 711–12 (January–February), pp. 77–91.

Lucero, José Antonio, 2013. "Seeing like an international NGO: encountering development and indigenous politics in the Andes." In: Eduardo Silva, ed., *Transnational activism and national movements in Latin America: bridging the divide.* New York: Routledge.pp. 80–105.

McAdam, Doug, Tarrow, Sidney and Tilly, Charles, 2001. *Dynamics of contention.* Cambridge: Cambridge University Press.

Moran, Robert E., 2005. *Technical review of the El Dorado mine project environmental impact assessment (EIA).* El Salvador, [online] Available at: <http://www.miningwatch.ca/en/technical-review-el-dorado-mine-project-environmental-impact-assessment-eia-el-salvador> [Accessed 4 September 2010].

Nepstad, Sharon Erickson, 2004. *Convictions of the soul: religion, culture, and agency in the central America solidarity movement.* New York: Oxford.

Olesen, Thomas, 2005. *International Zapatismo: the construction of solidarity in the age of globalization.* London: Zed.

Orellana, Marcos A., 2011. "The right of access to information and investment arbitration." *ICSID Review: Foreign Investment Law Journal*, 26(2) (Fall), pp. 59–106.

Pac Rim Cayman LLC v Republic of El Salvador ICSID Case No. ARB/09/12, 2012. Decision on Jurisdiction. [online] Available at: <https://icsid.worldbank.org/ICSID/FrontServlet?requestType=CasesRH&actionVal=viewCase&reqFrom=Home&caseId=C661> [Accessed 1 August 2013].

Park, Susan and Vetterlein, Antje eds, 2010. *Owning development: creating policy norms in the IMF and the World Bank.* Cambridge: Cambridge University Press.

Pearce, Jenny, 2010. "Is social change fundable? NGOs and theories and practices of social change." *Development in Practice*, 20(6) (August), pp. 621–35.

Perla, Hector M., 2008. "Si Nicaragua Venció, El Salvador Vencerá: Central American agency in the creation of the US-Central American peace and solidarity movement." *Latin American Research Review*, 43(2), pp. 136–58.

Petras, James, 1997. "Imperialism and NGOs in Latin America." *Monthly Review*, 49(7), [online] Available at: <http://www.monthlyreview.org/1297petr.htm> [Accessed 1 October 2010].

Procuraduría para la Defensa de los Derechos Humanos (PDDH), 2013. *Informe especial sobre el proyecto minero "Cerro Blanco" y las potenciales vulneraciones a derechos humanos en la población Salvadoreña.* El Salvador: PDDH [online] Available at: <www.ceicom.org.sv/pdf/informecerroblanco/InformeCerroBlanco.pdf> [Accessed 29 July 2013].

Putnam, Robert D., 2000. *Bowling alone: the collapse and revival of American community.* New York: Simon and Schuster.

Ramos, Benjamin, 2009. *El Legado del CAFTA DR: millonaria demanda de Pacific Rim al Estado Savadoreño.* San Salvador, El Salvador: CEICOM.

Rasch, Elisabet Dueholm, 2012. "Transformations in citizenship: local resistance against mining projects in Huehuetenango (Guatemala)." *Journal of Developing Societies*, 28, pp. 159–84.

Risse-Kappen, Thomas ed., 1995. *Bringing transnational relations back in: non-state actors, domestic structures and international institutions.* Cambridge: Cambridge University Press.

Roberts, Kenneth M., 2008. "The mobilization of opposition to economic liberalization." *Annual Review of Political Science*, 11, pp. 327–49.

Rodrigues, Maria Guadalupe Moog, 2004. *Global environmentalism and local politics: transnational advocacy networks in Brazil, Ecuador, and India.* Albany: State University of New York.

Rossi, Federico M., 2013. "Juggling multiple agendas: the struggle of trade unions against national, continental, and international neoliberalism in Argentina." In: Eduardo Silva, ed., *Transnational activism and national movements in Latin America: bridging the divide.* New York: Routledge, pp. 141–60.

Sánchez Albavera, Fernando, Ortiz, Georgina and Moussa, Nicole, 2001. *Mining in Latin America in the late 1990s.* Santiago, Chile: CEPAL, [online] Available at: <http://www.eclac.cl/publicaciones/xml/3/9043/lcl1253PI.pdf> [Accessed 31 July 2013].

Scholte, Jan Aart, 2001. "The IMF and civil society: an interim progress report." In: Michael Edwards and John Gaventa, eds. *Global citizen action*. Boulder: Lynne Rienner, pp. 87–104.

Scholz, Sally J., 2008. *Political solidarity*. University Park: Pennsylvania State University Press.

Shadlen, Kenneth, 2005. "Exchanging development for market access? Deep integration and industrial policy under multilateral and regional-bilateral trade agreements." *Review of International Political Economy*, 12(5), pp. 750–75.

Sikkink, Kathryn, 2005. "Patterns of dynamic multilevel governance and the insider-outsider coalition." In della Porta, Donatella, and Tarrow, Sidney eds, 2005. *Transnational protest and global activism*. Lanham: Rowman & Littlefield.pp. 151–73.

Silva, Eduardo, 2009. *Challenging neoliberalism in Latin America*. Cambridge: Cambridge University Press.

———, ed. 2013. *Transnational activism and national movements in Latin America: bridging the divide*. New York: Routledge.

Slack, Keith, 2009. "Digging out from neoliberalism: responses to environmental (mis)governance of the mining sector in Latin America." In: John Burdick, Philip Oxhorn and Kenneth M. Roberts, eds. *Beyond neoliberalism in Latin America?* New York: Palgrave Macmillan, pp. 117–34.

Smith, Christian, 1996. *Resisting Reagan: the US Central America peace movement*. Chicago: University of Chicago Press.

Smith, Jackie, 2008. *Social movements for global democracy*. Baltimore: Johns Hopkins University Press.

Smith, Jackie and Wiest, Dawn, 2012. *Social movements in the world system*. New York: Russell Sage Foundation.

Spalding, Rose J., 2007. "Civil society engagement in trade negotiations: CAFTA opposition movements in El Salvador." *Latin American Politics and Society*, 49(4), pp. 85–114.

———, 2008. "Neoliberal Regionalism and Resistance in Mesoamerica." In: Richard Stahler-Sholk, Harry E. Vanden and Glen David Kuecker, eds. *Latin American social movements in the 21st century*. Lanham: Rowman & Littlefield, pp. 323–36.

———, 2014. *Contesting trade in Central America: market reform and resistance*. Austin: University of Texas Press.

Steiner, Richard, 2010. "El Salvador—gold, guns, and choice." Report for the International Union for the Conservation of Nature (IUCN) and Commission on Environmental, Economic and Social Policy (CEESP), [online] Available at: <http://www.walkingwithelsalvador.org/Steiner Salvador Mining Report.pdf> [Accessed 1 June 2010].

Stiglitz, Joseph E. and Charlton, Andrew, 2005. *Fair trade for all: how trade can promote development*. Oxford: Oxford University Press.

Stites Mor, Jessica, 2013. *Human rights and transnational solidarity in Cold war Latin America.* Madison: University of Wisconsin Press.

Tarrow, Sidney, 2005. *The new transnational activism.* Cambridge: Cambridge University Press.

Tau Consultora Ambiental, 2011. *Servicios de consultoría para la Evaluación Ambiental Estratégica (EAE) del sector minero metálico de El Salvador: Informe final.* Prepared for the Ministerio de Economía de El Salvador, Unidad de Cooperación Externa. [online] Available at: <http://www.marn.gob.sv/phocadownload/EAE_minero_metalico.pdf> [Accessed 9 August 2012].

Thayer, Millie, 2010. *Making transnational feminisms: rural women, NGO activists and northern donors in Brazil.* New York: Routledge.

Thorp, Rosemary, Battistelli, Stefania, Guichaoua, Yvan, Orihuela, José Carlos and Paredes, Maritza eds, 2012. *The development challenges of mining and oil: lessons from Africa and Latin America.* New York: Palgrave Macmillan.

Todd, Mollie, 2010. *Beyond displacement: campesinos, refugees, and collective action in the Salvadoran civil war.* Madison: University of Wisconsin Press.

Tussie, Diane and Tuozzo, María Fernanda, 2001. "Opportunities and constraints for civil society participation in multilateral lending operations: lessons from Latin America." In Michael Edwards and John Gaventa, eds. *Global citizen action.* Boulder: Lynne Rienner, pp. 105–17.

Veltmeyer, Henry and Petras, James, 2014. *The new extractivism: a post-neoliberal development model or imperialism of the twenty-first century.* London: Zed.

von Bülow, Marisa, 2009. "Networks of trade protest in the Americas? Toward a new labor internationalism?" *Latin American Politics and Society*, 51(2) (Summer), pp. 1–28.

———, 2010. *Building transnational networks: civil society and the politics of trade in the Americas.* Cambridge: Cambridge University Press.

———, 2011. "Brokers in action: transnational coalitions and trade agreements in the Americas." *Mobilization*, 16(2), pp. 165–80.

———, 2013. "The politics of scale shift and coalition building: the case of the Brazilian network for the integration of the peoples." In: Eduardo Silva, ed., *Transnational activism and national movements in Latin America: bridging the divide.* New York: Routledge.pp. 56–79.

Weyland, Kurt, Madrid, Raúl L. and Hunter, Wendy eds, 2010. *Leftist governments in Latin America: successes and shortcomings.* New York: Cambridge University Press.

Wood, Lesley J., 2010. "Horizontalist youth camps and the Bolivarian revolution: a story of blocked diffusion." *Journal of World-System Research*, 16(1), pp. 48–62.

———, 2005. "Bridging the chasms: the case of people's global action." In: Joe Bandy and Jackie Smith. *Coalitions across borders: transnational protest and the neoliberal order.* Lanham: Rowman & Littlefield, pp. 95–120.

CONCLUSION

Chapter 9

Weaving Social Movements Back In

Margaret E. Keck

Introduction

Rio de Janeiro's Carnival took an unexpected turn in 2014. A wildcat strike by the "garis," the city's ubiquitous and socially invisible street cleaners, paralyzed garbage collection during Rio's most iconic cultural event, leaving pavements and beaches littered and malodorous. The garbage workers' union, accustomed to negotiating back room deals with the city government, did not endorse the strike, and the mayor's office complained of having no one with whom to negotiate. Communicating via social media and pitching their struggle to the rhythms of carnival, the "garis" marched in samba time, drumming on orange plastic trash bins, flooding the streets of Rio with their orange uniforms. Even though the strike produced significant disruptions to one of the city's most lucrative tourist events, the strikers captured the imagination of the city's residents and won their support. In the end the city government acceded to most of their demands, including a 37 percent rise in their base pay—taking it to a whopping $466 per month, still well below the cost of a one-night stay at a top Copacabana hotel. They remind us, yet again, both of the giant inequalities in the foundations of the Latin American social landscape, and of how ordinary people, by organizing social movements to insist that their needs (and often their very existence) be recognized, can energize that landscape in new ways.

Social movements are alive in Latin America, but they do not always look the way we expect them to. Over the last three decades, changes in economic, political, and associational landscapes have produced reconfigurations of political space, of political relationships, and of beliefs about what is and is not possible. It has given rise to new forms of contestation—and evolving, sometimes experimental, relationships between social movements and formal institutions. The widespread adoption of democratic political institutions did not, as many expected, push contentious politics off the political stage. It did reorganize the terrain of political struggle, generating at some times more adversarial and at others more collaborative relations between movements and formal institutions.

Although the particular forms these changes take vary between and within countries and regions, they are by no means unique to Latin America. The rapid economic and cultural challenges of the 21st century have severely tested formal political institutions, repatterning flows of information and modes of organization all over the world. At a 2013 American Political Science Association panel on democracy and the state, Claus Offe argued that the question of whether governments have the ability to generate the requisite legitimate authority and state capacity to govern as a central problem for democratic politics in OECD countries. How is that authority constituted—or, as the case may be, re-constituted—if indeed it is? Offe depicted a deinstitutionalization of the political process, pointing to the Greek case as evidence that politics takes place increasingly in the streets or among political parties that do not seek to become governments. When 25 percent of the 15–29-year-old population of Spain is neither employed nor engaged in education or training, he argued, no government can do anything about it. In many countries there is no governing capacity to generate a business plan for governing; instead, governments depend on transfers. The challenge of re-embedding (or simply embedding) capitalism in democracy is evident worldwide.

Scholarship on Latin America has an advantage in this new world: We are accustomed to weak states, and have long been sensitive to the need to weave together the strategies and actions that are enacted (mainly) in formal institutions with those that take place (mainly) outside of them. Studying social movements in Latin America has always required mapping their place in a broader (and often highly mobile) political picture. It has never been possible simply to assume fixed boundaries between inside and outside, formal and informal, routine and contentious. Making sense of this complex landscape has long challenged the creativity of scholars (and of organizers, for that matter), giving rise to a multitude of experiments with different ways of seeing (and doing) contentious action. The articles in this volume illustrate the diversity of those attempts. They also demonstrate why it is important to retain a multiperspectival view of such events, resisting premature closure on our choice of methods at the same time as we continue to map the sometimes surprising configurations of actors, actions, and forms of organization that emerge.

Politics in Latin America has long been a contentious affair, and despite the institutionalization of democratic institutions through much of the region, it has remained so. Through much of the region's history, contention has provoked or responded to elite efforts either to repress or to channel demands for incorporation and justice by excluded groups, demands that have taken different forms depending on the place and the historical period. As in other regions, much of this has been conflict over the distribution of political and economic power, which were often, though not always, closely linked. "The history of the distribution of wealth," writes Thomas Piketty, "has always been deeply political, and it cannot be reduced to purely economic mechanisms" (Piketty 2014, p. 20). Although there have occasionally been periods of growth robust enough to allow broad-based improvements for much of the population without major redistributive measures, the region remains a champion in measures of inequality, matched only by Sub-Saharan Africa (Blofield 2011, pp. 5–9; Hoffman and Centeno 2003). How, and how successfully, people on the low end of the distribution and their allies have organized in the face of persistent inequalities is the stuff of politics in the region. Because persistent inequalities have often been political as well as economic, this has often involved a fight for access to political institutions, as well as for income shares. The outcomes vary both between and within countries. Nonetheless, despite several decades of formal democracy, despite a notable shift to the left and the expansion of redistributive policies in the region, the problem of social and political exclusion remains as serious as it has ever been (Filgueira, Reygadas, Luna and Alegre 2011). In fact, the capacity of movements to make claims and the capacity of political authorities to deliver on their promises are both in disarray. It may be that the robustness of each requires the other.

When we study social movements, we are studying struggles over the distribution and deployment of social power. By trying, as the articles in this volume do, to locate social movements in a relational field, we open a window into a complex of relations and understandings of power—its generation, its location, and deployment—that has undergone significant changes over the last few decades. If we are to figure out where social movements fit in the politics of the region, we must ask not only about where they come from and think they are going, but also about the nature of the arenas in which they are struggling and the capacity of those to whom they address their demands—normally some part of the state—to respond. The answers to those questions affect the ways that activists organize, the way that political leaders lead, and the way that scholars try to study all of these things.

Social movements involve efforts to activate people and other resources they can reach through social networks, and to generate publicity through their actions, in such a way as to gain leverage over the actions of more powerful actors. This may involve direct challenges, through protest or other means, to the policies of states or other power-holders. It may also involve the generation of influence from below, by building what Abers and Keck (2013) call "practical authority" from outside the state, through the creation of new organizations and arenas of action and/or new publics that provide either pressure or expertise.

I am drawing here from Michael Mann's distinction between the despotic and infrastructural power of states. The former refers to what state elites can do without negotiating with anyone, because of prerogatives that states have and others do not. The latter refers to a state's capacity to penetrate territory and implement decisions, acting through (rather than acting on) society. Increasing the state's infrastructural power does not necessarily increase despotic power, and it affords civil society some control over the state, for good or ill (Mann 1993, p. 59). Social power is not simply transferred from one place to another; it can (indeed must) also be generated. Just as Adam Smith saw labor power and innovation combining to produce wealth that did not exist before, political interactions in public arenas may create new kinds of social power. However, neither one is guaranteed to succeed.

When we think of social movements in confrontational mode, we are usually thinking of them as challengers to the state's despotic power. Historically, in Latin America, social movements were understood in this way, and often enough states have behaved despotically in the traditional sense of the word as well. The Latin American left traditionally focused its attention on this kind of power, attempting to devise strategies, revolutionary or not, to seize it and turn it to socially progressive ends, or to protest its abuse. Power in this sense has a location (generally a central one) and a possessor. Targeted mass protest is often directed against what some consider the unjust use of despotic power. Although since the 1980s almost all presidential successions have proceeded according to the constitutional provisions in their countries, a great many presidents have stepped down early. Hochstetler's 2006 study showed that mass protests of some duration figured in all cases where South American presidents were ousted before their time between 1978 and 2003. However, mass demonstrations have also been mobilized to bolster weak governments. In moments of crisis, recent "populist" presidents in Bolivia, Venezuela, Argentina, and Ecuador have called supporters into the streets to defend them against threats to their governments from opposition forces.

Thus the relationship between protest and state power in Latin America has often been complicated. While mass movements have sometimes protested the actions of government, they have equally often protested inaction. Thus they might insist that the state's power be used (positively) to counter the actions of other powerful actors—business, for example, or international financial institutions—or to resolve social problems that were not necessarily caused by the state, but for whose resolution it is deemed responsible. More often, protests target particular state agencies or subnational units. Almeida's chapter in this volume, for example, examines protests directed at threats from both "state-attributed economic problems" and environmental problems. Although the protests he studies are targeted at the state—in the first set of cases at things the state has clearly done (privatized firms, cut benefits, negotiated free trade agreements) and in the second at things the state has done (hydroelectric dams) and not done (prevented cyanide poisoning, protected indigenous peoples), it seems worth distinguishing between instances where the government's position is clearly aligned with the threats and others where governments may claim impotence in the face of forces over which they have little control.

Whether or not the state (or relevant portion thereof) in fact has the resources or capacity to respond to protest is a different question. Sometimes state insiders welcome protests that raise the salience of their agency's agenda and thus help them gain access to budgetary resources. By demanding a response from a public institution, social movements shine a spotlight on that institution's mission. Mapping these different ways of making demands on state power helps to make visible an essential but undertheorized role of social movements, that is, their contribution to the *construction* of political authority. Through the public exercise of (sometimes disruptive) voice, claimants are as often challenging an *absence* of government as they are the *actions* of government. In that sense, they are demanding that governments exercise or develop the capacity to respond effectively to the needs of their citizens.

From Despotic Power to Infrastructural Power

In the 1980s and 1990s, however, there was a notable shift in political attention towards civil society, fostered by important changes in both political and economic spheres. An explosion of civic organizing accompanied the end of authoritarian military regimes in many countries of the region. Instead of expecting political transformation to occur through capture of the state, many intellectuals on the left began to see civil society itself as a site for the construction of alternative forms of democratic governance (Weffort 1989; Avritzer 2002). A different, but also important set of ideas about "civil society" came in the context of economic liberalization and the process of state reform that generally accompanied it. Here, a neo-Tocquevillian vision of vibrant civic community viewed it as a sphere of initiative and autonomy, where citizens would create a great diversity of [private] organizations that should be free of partisan manipulation or co-optation by state agencies.

These different discourses about civil society were in practice hard for most people to disentangle, and to at least some extent, they reinforced each other. Although scholars pointed out contradictions in how organizing initiatives that grew out of politicized struggles ended up collaborating in various civic processes promoted by World Bank projects, a great many people and organizations ended up navigating in that complicated terrain, and developed the skills to do so. The ambiguity of the idea of civil society as a terrain for building new public arenas and as a protected space for autonomous civic action was consistent with rapidly changing societies, where values associated with individual and collective identities competed to shape the cultures of new generations.

In her chapter on Brazilian student organizations, Ann Mische shows how complicated this could sometimes be. Activists associated with political parties learned to highlight or suppress partisanship or other aspects of their identities when that facilitated collaboration in building of particular kinds of publics. These performances were intended not just for distant audiences, but also for co-participants, as they jointly produced the norms and rituals of the new group or setting. This happened when new kinds of student groups emerged in the 1990s, challenging the overtly partisan communicative styles of more politicized student organizations of the transition period. Yet Mische argues that the shared cultural work of building civic unity allows for occasional violations of ritual homogeneity, and shows that suppressed identities can also serve as bridges among publics, at least when those enacting them have developed the communicative skills necessary to move between different styles of interaction at the appropriate moments.

State reforms that accompanied economic liberalization often involved reductions in public sector employment and cutbacks in social programs, and in many instances, assignment of responsibility for implementing them to underequipped municipalities. For some, the solution was development of partnerships with civil society, in which a "third sector" of professional, not-for-profit civic organizations would become service providers. Despite the contradictions this entailed, many feminist and environmental organizations, for example, combined service provision with advocacy, managing in that way to finance their organizational activities in a difficult funding environment. Combinations of different discourses about civil society became available to different kinds of social actors as they constituted new webs of association and strategies for action, and affected the way they positioned themselves.

Women's movements were called upon to traverse a very broad swath of civil society, and in many instances, activists pursued their goals by moving onto the terrain of the state as well. In their chapter for this volume, Abers and Tagatiba show how activists from the women's health movement worked strategically with sympathetic state employees in the Technical Area for Women's Health of the Brazilian Health Ministry (a department whose very existence is the result of past feminist struggles) to affect the formulation of guidelines for treatment of women's reproductive health. At the same time the authors show how the state was a site of struggle for the movement, they also show how hard they worked both to make the movement's expertise and resources effective within the state, and to convince other movement members to accept compromises they deemed necessary for moving policy forward. The performance by movement activists of public roles has been a contentious issue for feminists exacerbated by the fact that with decentralization of many aspects of control over health care delivery, women's organizations took on the role not only of advocates but also of service providers in many instances.

Mapping Movements

Authoritarian governments in most countries of the region undermined labor unions and pre-existing party organizations that had traditionally served as hubs around which other social movements congregated, a format that Collier and Handlin (2010) refer to as the UP-Hub. Even where unions retained important coordinating roles, as for example in contestation of regional free trade agreements (von Bülow 2010), liberalization of the region's economies left them weaker in terms of membership, negotiating capacity with employers, and political leverage. In many countries, unions managed to protect their collective rights (over the right to organize and strike, and over collective bargaining), at the same time as the formal sector of the economy of which they were a part grew smaller (Murillo and Schrank 2005). Nonetheless, within the highly fragmented and diversified spheres of the new "civil societies," unions sometimes looked more like the political establishment, as witnessed in the example of the March 2014 Rio de Janeiro garbage strike described at the beginning of this chapter. How should scholars interested in social movements and collective action try to map—and interpret the associational capabilities of—the great diversity of associational forms that emerged during this period?

The authors in this volume do not have a single answer to this question, nor do I. Most of them, however, approach it from a relational perspective—that is, rather than focusing on particular organizations or types of organizations, they try to unravel the kinds of relationships that develop among them, and the mechanisms that help to turn such relationships into vehicles for collective action. Where we might once have expected these connections to be made through political parties, unions, or churches, we find instead a range of different kinds of linkage (including these, but not restricted to them). Gurza Lavalle and von Bülow, for example, focus on brokerage, especially the development of organizational brokerage. In separate streams of research, they identified new kinds of organizations that had come to play linking roles. Their dissection of the ways that brokerage is accomplished recognizes the different levels of trust that are required for different kinds of collaboration—a discussion that nests well with Mische's discussion of the kinds of adjustments required to create new publics.

New repertoires of organizational aggregation appeared: parallel meetings of civil society organizations were organized on the occasions of national or international conferences; consultative forums were constituted around various public policy initiatives; coalitions formed to protest cutbacks in services or demand new ones; organizations coalesced around ethnic, racial, or gender identities; religious and partisan allegiances continue to shape coalitions and alliances; and so on. With the rare exception of national-level protest movements, the organizational mosaic remains quite fluid. What kind of society, and more specifically, what kinds of social power are being constituted in such a decentralized manner?

Building Social Power

Rose Spalding's study of the development of an anti-mining movement in El Salvador and regionally gives us a careful excavation of how activists from affected communities, specialized organizations, and other allies gradually assembled a coalition capable of challenging powerful mining companies in international arbitration bodies. I discuss it in some detail here, because it provides an unusually clear picture of the possible synergies that can exist between social movement struggles—even very confrontational ones—and the development of the state's capacity to respond.

Although the case study is organized around a campaign, it employs multiple lenses, zooming in for close-ups and zooming out for a wide-angle view. Spalding begins by showing how different actors became aware of and organized around the mining issue, and how by making use of domestic resources and of regional information flows and allies ("lateral transnationalism"), they convinced state officials to change the official stance to one of opposition to mining, closing what Spalding calls the "domestic loop" phase of the process.

At this point we have a significant reconfiguration of the relationship between the state and movement networks. Instead of mobilizing resources in opposition to the state's position, the movement networks must seek leverage to bolster the state's position in international arbitration courts against the charges by mining companies of breach of contract. Spalding refers to this move as a deleveraging hook—a process of assembling the power to counteract the leverage that mining companies' past contracts have over the Salvadorian government. It is in fact a rich example of a case where in a process of social movement struggle, actors from civil society increased the infrastructural power of the state.

Spalding traces out the backwards and forwards linkages of this struggle, locating it in a complex web of organizational networks and processes that developed in the region over decades. The experience of displacement and exile during the civil war in the 1980s had a lasting impact on how communities organized and understood their relations to particular locales. Enduring relationships built in Honduras during that period of displacement opened up channels of information; use of the mining processes being proposed for El Salvador had already proved toxic in the neighboring country. Community organizations were joined by human rights, research, and religious organizations. Inter-organizational networks, some built during the tumultuous 1980s and some during the post-war reconstruction, stretched across the region, facilitating a lateral transnationalism that drew upon common experience and solidarity as well as common goals and targets. Because so many different parts of the coalition participated in and made use of the resources of regional networks, the transnational configuration of the domestic campaign looks quite different from the thinner, strategically activated networks typical of a transnational advocacy campaign. Moreover, the anti-mining campaign was not attempting to gain leverage over Salvadorian government policy by leveraging outside allies, but instead strove to bring it to the center of national politics. This was a thoroughly political campaign at the domestic level, and illustrates the craftwork involved in assembling political coalitions when unions are no longer in a position to serve as conveners and provide organizational infrastructure for such struggles. In the process, there was a notable increase in capacity *both* of social movement organizations to influence outcomes *and* of political leaders and the state to change course at the risk of sanctions from powerful international (and presumably some domestic) interests.

At the point that anti-mining campaigners in El Salvador seek out the assistance of "power node INGOs"—that is, well established international NGOs with expertise and experience in the area of international commercial disputes, they are acting as allies of the Salvadorian government in conflict with mining companies, thus magnifying the state's technical capacities in making the legal argument, and stipulating the legitimacy of the state's position insofar as it is responding to the concerted clamor of Salvadorian society.

Spalding's study focuses on the broad configuration of the anti-mining struggle, identifying a complex of movements and strategies, and recognizing an evolving chain of outcomes. Her "forensic" approach benefits enormously from her more than 30 years of scholarly engagement with the politics and political economy of Central America. This is visible in the rich historical and relational perspective that opens up for us layers of relationships and interactions that we would not easily have been able to see, moving from the micro-politics of Salvadorian communities to the global political economy of mining. This broad view allows us to consider the different kinds of social power being mobilized, deployed, and reconfigured in this struggle.

The Problem of Simplification

This is a more complex view of the place of social movements in politics and society than we generally get from accounts of some of the best-known Latin American social movements. It is worth a brief consideration of why this is the case. There are clearly advantages to a view of social movement studies in which challengers confront the state with their claims, drawing strategically upon allies and other kinds of resources in their environment, and achieve identifiable outcomes. Whether the state appears as direct target or as a potential adjudicator of conflicts with powerful economic actors, it is easier to identify a challenger who is standing obviously outside the seat of power.

Yet the stories told of iconic movements in heroic mode, in which exemplary movements play the role of stand-ins for whole categories, may tell us very little about the state-society relationships into which they fit, their role in associational networks, and their contribution to the accumulation of social power. Inspiring stories do of course help to frame subsequent understandings of what is possible. The Madres de la Plaza de Mayo, the Zapatista National Liberation Army, and the water warriors in Cochabamba in 2000 all inspired millions. But plucked from their contexts, we are hard-pressed to map the pathways of changes to which they may have contributed. Brazil's landless movement (*Movimento dos Trabalhadores Rurais Sem Terra*), famous for defiant resistance to a highly concentrated system of land ownership, itself a transnational broker among movements, has also contributed a great deal to the development of domestic state capacity in land law, agricultural extension, and other areas.

Iconic social movements did not necessarily start out trying to market themselves to large external audiences, though one could argue that the EZLN did exactly that, and very skillfully, from the beginning. They resonated with attentive publics in part because they provided narratives amenable to simplification, and their leaders at some point were willing to collaborate in the simplification process in order to garner support. The stories were eagerly told by sympathetic publics around the world seeking evidence that powerful, seemingly inexorable forces, could be resisted, that "another world is possible." Moreover, they generate expressions of solidarity, whether moral or material, from people far away. They provide excellent examples to use in undergraduate classes, where simplified versions of events capture student attention more readily than do more complex ones. There have always been heroic stories of resistance that have served to inspire contemporaries and future generations of activists, and I hope there always will be. Nonetheless, the process of simplification essential to the widespread dissemination of an iconic story makes them dangerous for analysts and activists alike. As many who attempted to use Regis Debray's *Revolution in the Revolution* as a roadmap for organizing guerrilla *focos* discovered in the late 1960s and early 1970s, the devil is in the details.

How much is this simplification the fault of our scholarship? After all, we are not in the business of providing prescriptions or roadmaps for activists to follow. Yet each one of these stories contains a backstory (or myriad, contending backstories) that belie the simplicity of the narrative. Paying attention to these pushes us to recognize the art and craft of political organization. Consider Federico Rossi's excavation of how the political strategies of numerous political organizations converged in the production of the *piquetero* phenomenon. Here he zooms in on a contentious repertoire whose evolution can be described and perhaps even predicted from a distance, but whose actual production did not grow out of its conditions of possibility. That is, the conditions underlying a repertoire of contention cannot explain its enactment. For that, he claims, we need to trace a process of organization in which committed political activists drew upon the legacies of past struggles and engaged in intense ideological debate over appropriate strategies for action. Out of this multilayered organizational process came a collection of differentiated moves, some of which involved contention and some of which did not.

Rossi's focus on the relationship between the strategies and tactics in the evolution of *piquetero* movements shines a light on how organizers understand the place of confrontational protest and negotiation in their longer-term strategies of political change. These strategies draw upon experiences of and interpretations of experiences in the past, and project towards a desired future. Debates about whether and when to ally with another organization, or to negotiate with state agencies, therefore, reflect not only assessments of the costs and benefits of a particular action in the present, but also beliefs about how the world works and what kind of change is possible. Nonetheless, in the performance of the *piquetero* protests, this kind of differentiation is largely invisible to outsiders.

If Rossi's approach to the *piqueteros* takes a magnifying glass to the strategies of organizers, Tavera Fenollosa's study shows us what we may gain when we examine movements as components of broader events. By viewing the 1985 Movement of Earthquake Victims in Mexico City with an eventful perspective, she is not limited to an evaluation of the movement's organization and strategy or its success in having its demands met. Because she is looking at a larger canvass, she is able to recognize the movement's presence in other emergent political processes, not because the movement had made a strategic choice to be there, but because its actions forced a revision of the arguments that hitherto had justified the absence of home rule in the Federal District. The movement—itself the emergent result of contingency—had upended conventional wisdom about the apathy and civic immaturity of Mexico City's residents. It had also changed their understandings of themselves. This shift in understanding constituted a rupture of the normal unfolding of events—something that would not have been evident from an examination of the movement itself or of its deliberate outcomes.

The Upshot

The chapters in this volume make an important contribution by placing social movements and contention at the center of Latin American politics. For the most part, they do this not by focusing on movements as strategic organizations, but instead by examining reflections and refractions. Movements here are heterogeneous, mobile, and resourceful; they stimulate the body politic. Their actions also respond to political shifts at other points in the polity.

Tavera Fenollosa reminds us that sometimes to see a phenomenon we need to look away—reenvisioning not merely the mechanisms and processes of organization and contestation but also the dynamic properties of time and space. Here, Sewell's "eventful temporality," drawing from the historian's assumption that time is heterogeneous and historical temporality is lumpy and deeply contingent, provides us with an opening (Sewell 2005, pp. 100–2). Attention to events reminds us of the extent to which movements and their supposed context constitute each other, transforming social relations "in ways that could not be fully predicted from the gradual changes that may have made them possible" (Ibid., 227).

Developing an indirect, dynamic, and multi-perspective view of social movements needs a conceptual apparatus that helps us to detect and follow streams of ideas, resources, and relationships across time and space. Mapping networks through, an approach that many of the authors in this volume employ, provides one helpful strategy, especially insofar as we avoid premature closure and recognize the heterogeneity of organizational forms in play. Network approaches run the risk of freezing particular configurations of relationships; finding ways to put these relations in motion in time and space is challenging (Stark and Vedres 2012). Mische (2009, and in this volume) takes on network dynamics by focusing on communicative strategies. Spalding uses process tracing to track their historical evolution; Rossi employs a form of organizational genealogy. Gurza Lavalle and von Bülow focus on the brokerage mechanism to investigate novel forms of organizational linkage.

Psychologists use the term "figure-ground" perception to describe the way that visual systems organize scenes into central or main objects (the figure) and background ones (the ground). One of the classic illustrations of the phenomenon is a picture of a sculptured white vase against a black background. Blink and look back with another part of your brain, and you see a clear picture of two silhouettes in profile, facing each other across a white space in the middle of the image. Look again, and you see that the features of the faces form the curves and crevasses of the vase, and vice versa. I am reminded of this image when I think about efforts to differentiate between action and context, actor and field, in relation to the study of social movements in Latin America.

For as long as I have been studying politics in the region, many of the categorical boundaries that make sense of these things have been stubbornly blurred. Apparent antimonies constitute and mirror each other. Although we can proffer ideal types of formal and informal economies, institutionalized and un-institutionalized political processes, co-optation and inclusion, claims-making and clientelism, all of these boundaries have active frontier zones that are in many cases far more dynamic and interesting than the categories they breach. Figure merges into ground and back into figure again, as the brain strives restlessly to re-imagine the components in a way that stabilizes them; they somehow refuse to settle down.

There is, however, nothing peculiarly Latin American about this kind of boundary-blurring. However, by studying "social movement" activity in parts of the world where political relations and states' capacities are more obviously fluid than they are in the regions where many of our theoretical frameworks originated, the complexity of the processes of which they are part is hard to ignore. The studies reported in this volume take advantage of the dynamic character of their subject matter to generate useable theory. This is a good start in helping us to map creatively a form of social action that is in categorical, as well as social, movement, without imposing premature closure on evolving concepts.

References

Abers, Rebecca Neaera, and Keck, Margaret E., 2013. *Practical authority: agency and institutional change in Brazilian water politics.* New York: Oxford University Press.

Avritzer, Leonardo, 2002. *Democracy and the public space in Latin America.* Princeton: Princeton University Press.

Blofield, Merike, 2011. "Introduction: inequality and politics in Latin America." In: Merike Blofield, ed. *The great gap: inequality and the politics of redistribution in Latin America.* University Park: Pennsylvania State University Press, pp. 1–20.

Collier, Ruth Berins, and Handlin, Samuel eds, 2010. *Reorganizing popular politics: participation and the new interest regime in Latin America.* University Park: Pennsylvania State University Press.

Filgueira, Fernando, Reygadas, Luis, Luna, Juan Pablo and Alegre, Pablo, 2011. "Shallow states, deep inequalities, and the limits of conservative modernization: the politics and policies of incorporation in Latin America." In: Merike Blofield, ed. *The great gap: inequality and the politics of redistribution in Latin America.* University Park: Pennsylvania State University Press, pp. 245–77.

Hochstetler, Kathryn, 2006. "Rethinking presidentialism: challenges and presidential falls in South America," *Comparative Politics*, 38(4), pp. 401–18.

Hoffman, Kelly and Centeno, Miguel Angel, 2003. "The lopsided continent: inequality in Latin America." *Annual Review of Sociology*, 29, pp. 363–90.

Mann, Michael, 1993. *The sources of social power. Volume II: The rise of classes and national states, 1760–1914*. Cambridge: Cambridge University Press.

Mische, Ann, 2009. *Partisan publics: communication and contention across Brazilian youth activist networks*. Princeton: Princeton University Press.

Murillo, M. Victoria and Schrank, Andrew, 2005. "With a little help from my friends: partisan politics, transnational alliances, and labor rights in Latin America." *Comparative Political Studies*, 38(8), pp. 971–99.

Piketty, Thomas, 2014. *Capital in the twenty-first century*. Cambridge: Belknap Press of Harvard University Press.

Sewell, William H., Jr., 2005. *Logics of history: social theory and social transformation*. Chicago: University of Chicago Press.

Stark, David and Vedres, Balázs, 2012. "Social sequence analysis: ownership networks, political ties, and foreign investment in Hungary." In: John F. Padgett and Walter W. Powell, eds. *The emergence of organizations and markets*. Princeton: Princeton University Press, pp. 347–73.

von Bülow, Marisa, 2010. *Building transnational networks: civil society and the politics of trade in the Americas*. New York: Cambridge University Press.

Weffort, Francisco, 1989. "Why Democracy?" In: Alfred Stepan, ed. *Democratizing Brazil: problems of transition and consolidation*. New York: Oxford University Press, pp. 327–50.

Index